Smash a Lightbulb
Poetry for Lowlifes

Jeremy Void

Other books by Jeremy Void

Derelict America

Nefarious Endeavors

Erase Your Face:
The SkullFuck Collection

Just a Kid

Sex Drugs & Violence:
Incomplete Stories for the Incomplete Human

An Art Form:
The Crass Poetry Collection

My Story:
The Short Version

I Need Help:
The SkullFuck Collection

The Lost Letters

---

books are available at

www.chaoswriting.net
www.lulu.com
and
www.amazon.com

CONT.

Chaos Writing

*The TR*TH*

My Psychedelic Suicide

A Crass Philosophy
The SkullFuck Collection

books are available at

www.chaoswriting.net
www.lulu.com
and
www.amazon.com

Smash a Lightbulb

Poetry for Lowlifes

Brutal honesty
meets
narcissistic pleasure
meets
poetic candy
meets
extreme experimentation

punks, junkies &
suburban hardknocks
included

"I admire [Jeremy Void's] ability to portray insanity in the form of art."
— Nick Starinskas

Facebook statuses
& comments;
short sketches;
poetry;
experimental writing;
food for thought;
and SO MUCH MORE

Jeremy Void

Smash a Lightbulb: Poetry for Lowlifes

Copyright © 2016 by Jeremy Void

All Rights Reserved

No part of this book may be reproduced, scanned, or distributed in any print or electronic form without permission. Please do not participate in or encourage piracy of copyrighted materials in violation of the author's rights. Purchase only authorized editions.

ISBN Number:
978-0-578-18166-0

ChaosWriting Press

IT'S A MINDFUCK

www.chaoswriting.net

To all the people I have hurt over the years

To all those who doubted me and thought of me as nothing but a fuckup

To all those who believed in me but were disappointed after every move I made

To all those who stood by me on every step in my journey

And, lastly, to all those who didn't stand by me and ditched me the first chance they got

First Edition
back cover text

Horror, suspense, and humor, mixed with a splash of insanity, and a Punk rock beat traversing the pages and tainting the words with a terminal angst that can only be found deep down inside the madness that lurks inside Jeremy Void's mind. He brings you quick, precise verses that will slice through your skull and fester in the darkest regions of your brain. You will laugh, you will cry, and you might even rip your eyes out of their sockets. You will hate him, and you will love him. So move over, Jim Carroll and Patti Smith and Richard Hell and other well-known Punk rock poets of our time, and make room for this new upstart poet called Jeremy Void. He will rock you, and he will shock you, and halfway through your eyes will be glued to the pages within this book. Jeremy Void brings you Punk rock poetry for a new generation. He tells it like it is, shows you what it isn't, and delivers raucous punch after raucous punch of brutal honesty that is so truthful it seems impossible.

Preface

This book is equivalent to my entire soul, it represents every side of me, spanning every facet of my maladjusted personality. Breaching the realm of experimentation, taking creativity to a whole new dimension, this book is a mishmash of broken puzzle pieces that complete me. In its entirety, in all its shattered glory, it should accurately paint an unorderly picture, rearranged and tossed out the window. The pieces of the puzzle, the paint strokes that tenderly decorate the canvas, the words that run rampant down page after page of madness, to summon a blasphemous mélange of misery and disobedience and an overall indifference that comes surging out like a dropkick to your Adam's apple---all of it comes together to depict a dastardly image of what I was and what I have now become....

Contents

> **:::NOTE:::**
> THESE DAYS it seems I'M NOT AS ANGRY AS I USED TO BE although the anger came can come back from time to time BUT THIS BOOK CONTAINS WRITING THAT SPANS FOUR TO FIVE YEARS WORTH OF MADNESS DEPICTING GROWTH & MATURITY and de-evolution too IT SHOWS ME AT LOW POINTS AT HIGH POINTS IT SHOWS ME CLIMBING THE LADDER INTO ANOTHER WORLD A BETTER WORD and it shows me every now and then missing a rung on my ascent into recovery and CLUNKING MY CHIN ON THE REST OF THE BARS AS I PLUMMET BACK INTO BLACKNESS a sadness I've come to know so damn well IT'S LIKE I'LL NEVER GET BACK UP

Preface IX
Contents XI
Introduction by Sergio Walion XLI
    Telling Stories at 3AM
Introduction XLIII

Part 1 ~~~ 1
Grammar Nazis Must Die

Dear Paper 3

Altruism Isn't a Good Look on You 5
    It Doesn't Compliment Your Ignorance

I Love Words 6

Didn't slip this time 6

American Angst 7

Critique 8

A Bunch of Crazies *8*

Words *9*

Shitty = Shitty *9*

it doesn't fit *9*

The Wrong Place at the Wrong Time *10*

Trainwreck *10*

Don't Bother *11*

An Explosion of the Mind *11*

Hello 9 to 5 ...... *12*

Today's Rebellion / Tomorrow's Trend *12*

Decipher That, You Fuck! *13*

The Art World *14*

{Stark} *15*

The Prompt *16*
    This I know

Midnight Ramblings *16*

The HARDest Decision I've Ever Had to Make *16*

Another Kind of Pretty *17*

GET THAT STRAIGHT!!! *18*

This Is Punk Rock *18*

My Way *19*

28-Years Old *20*

Your Communication Skills *20*

Demolition Dancing *21*

Can't Get It Right *22*

All Screwed Up *22*

Work 23

Ode to Facebook 23

Recovered Poem from 2011 23

The Pledge of Defiance 24

Loud & Fast 24

To Teachers Everywhere 25

A Commercialized Sport 27

Another Year 28

Not Like Ordinary Men 28

SELF-EXPRESSION 28

The Rage 29

Confined to a Box 30

Punk Rock Song 30

Alone 31

Mixed Feelings 31

Another Poem About Nothing 31

If You Don't 32

Untitled 33

Slam-Dancing Queen 33

A Drunk and a Pill Popper 33

Public Opinion 34

Manic 36

For One Brief Moment Social Media Got Smarter 36

Lost & Found 40

At War with the Muse 41

High on Life 41

Labels & Classifications 41

Like I always say 42

Piecing the Past Back Together 42

At the Halloween Dance 42

Loki's Resolution 43

Part 2 ~~~ 47

Fuck the Social Contract: I signed nothing

Pillow Talk 49

For Twenty-Something Days 50

"Hey, Obstacle!" 50

Deadly to Be Trendy 51

WTF? 52

Untitled 52

I CARE———I CARE NOT 53

No Image Available 53

No 54

The VOID of Existence 54

But Who Am I Trying to Impress???? 55

True Story, I Swear 55

Anti-Passion 58

Ode to Facebook, Part 2 58

Back when I was angry, young, and drunk 59

Hate Your Neighbor 61

Fuck Dating *63*

Remember what happened last night? *63*
    Neither do I

An Ideal *64*

Society *64*

I Am Jeremy Void *65*

The New *66*

Face-Time *67*

3AM *67*

Listening to X's "Nausea" *69*

An Artist *69*

Untitled *69*

Coffee Shop Irony *69*

The World Was Mine *70*
    but I stomped on its head

Anarchists for Censorship *70*

No Edge *70*

Paranoid Much? *71*

A Terminal Nobody *71*

Bored Again *71*

The Flame Dance *72*

The Phoenix Bookstore *72*

Bloody sirens Too much Too wild *73*

EVERYONE IS A CUNT *73*

DIS- *73*

Censorship *78*

Ignorant Minds 78

Untitled 78

Notes of an Insomniac 78

Rappers & Their Bling 79

Untitled 80

I just don't care 80

d. a. levy 81

A Misunderstanding 82

Lethal Erection 82
    sung with Lethal Erection

Punk Rock 83

Dark Places 83

Not in Kansas Anymore 84

A Recipe for Disaster 84

Art in the Park 85

My Hell 86

The Muse 86

Disappointed Again 87

Part 3 ~~~ 89
Solution: Piss Everybody Off!

A Poem I Wrote 91

Untitled 91

One of My Earliest Memories 92

I'm a Poser—so what? *92*
    What the hell have you done??

It's the Morning *93*

My Soul *94*

Anti-Fashion *94*

cruising *95*

The Process *95*

I Don't Wanna Die *96*

where am i going ? *97*

Untitled *98*

Sorry *98*

Pandora's Box *99*

Anonymous *99*

No Esteem *102*

Not Just Another Poet *102*

Insomnia As Inspiration *103*

Sex Is Gay *103*

Nihilism Reality *104*

Some Peace & Quiet————Finally!!! *105*

It Drives Me Crazy *105*

Untitled *106*

God, Are You Out There? *106*

Right Now *107*

A Bad Case of the Fuckits! *108*

T'was All My Fault *110*

YOUR LIFE *111*

no more   no less **111**
    I say it how I see it

I'm Back **112**

A Tornado   in Rutland?? **113**

Kill and Let Kill **113**
    sung with ELF

I am perfect **114**

Claimed to Be Smart **114**

The one that got away **115**

Jaded **117**

WAVED **117**

Untitled **118**

At the Brunt of Society **118**

Act Your Age **119**

Conformity—No Thanks! **119**

Thank God I Don't Drink Anymore **120**

No Place **121**

What I think about late at night **121**

2 separate Xtremes = 1 messy outcome **122**

Good vs. Evil **122**

killing time **125**

A poem from my teenage years **125**

Oh Woe Is Me **125**

Untitled **126**

Smarter Than You **126**

Clever Wordplay **126**

A Crude Writing Experiment *127*

Untitled *127*

Pro-Death *127*

Thoughts on Thanksgiving *128*

Trust Me *128*

Claimed to Be Smart, Part 2 ...... *129*
    Confessions of a Walmart Whore

Just for Kicks *129*

Another Piece of the Puzzle, Obtained *130*

Untitled *130*

Crazy, Right? *130*

Untitled Poem *131*

Incomplete Heart *134*

Wed., 11/21/2012 ...... *135*
   — 6:27 PM

Beware! *135*

Kill *136*

Like a Fresh Turd *136*

Rise Above *137*

People That You Hate *137*

The Middle Child Strikes Again *138*

Judgmental Stares *138*

No Respect *139*

selfies are NOT art! *139*

Part 4 ~~~ 141

While you're off living your Hallmark lives....

A Fate Like Cottage Cheese 143

Narcissism Much? 144

Copy Cat Rebels 144

Untitled 145

My Life 146

A Drawing Idea 146

Untitled Love Ballad 147

FIGHT OR FLIGHT 150

Untitled 151

Listen to what I say 151
    but please don't quote me on it

The Way of Things 152

No Wonder 153

Tell me something :::::: 153

A Stranger to Myself 154

Buzzzzzin Bumble Bee Rumble 154

Untitled 155

I wnta anwsers 155

Absurd Nihilism 156

Music 159

A Free-Write/// 159

Do I Haveta? 160

Sick Motherfucker 161

Punks for PC 161

xx

NOW	161
Desperate Times	162
A Toxic Flower … for you!	162
Not Just a Hot Piece of Ass	162
A Crass Philosophy	163
Sitting at the Bar	163
|RUN|	164
Listening to Fang	165
CRACKED!	165
Rhetorical Hypocrisy	165
Scream	166
So Not-Drunk	167
No Offense, but	167
On the Boardwalk	167
The Best Kinds of Minds	168
Locked In	168
Confusion	169
An Emotional Hangover?	169
Trouble	169
Punk Rock Is My Home	170
Up All Night	171
Sometimes	172
Deprivation Much?	172
Afraid of the Truth	172
Fuck You	173
An Education in Punk	175

Putrid Heart Disease 175

Untitled 176

Impersonal America 176

Nihilistic Reasoning 176

Heading to the Rainbow Gathering 177

My Loose Dream 177

Good News 179

A Joke 179

Ghetto Kids 180

Don't ask me! 180

Lost My Mind 181

My Writing 181

A Sea of Gloom 182

Part 5 ~~~ 183

I wanna start an art revolution—Who's with me?

My True Colors 185

Karma's a Real Thing 185

HATE vs. LOVE 186

Two Mental Cases 186

Listening to the Meteors 187

Zen Writing 187

No Exit 188

Altruism *190*
    just sleep sleep sleep and pretend it all goes away

Another Day in Paradise *190*

Untitled *191*

My Luck *191*

And a Monster Is Born *191*

A Mongoloid *193*

Nowhere *193*

Wednesday, November 30, 2011 ...... *193*
    with 11 days sober

In Peace *194*

Hitchhiking—Trainhopping *194*
    A Traveler's Guide to Success

Untitled *194*

The Bleak Shopping Mall *195*

For the Die-Hards *196*

Crazy *199*

Dastardly Deeds *199*

A Dog's Life *200*

The Ramblings of a Madman *200*

A Sensitive Asshole *202*

So Bored of You *202*

On Conformity *203*

Escape *204*

A Freak's Pickup Line *205*

Untitled *206*

Death Defying Stunts *206*

Self-Empowerment 207

Hate, Anger, & Rage 208

No Place Like Home 208

Just Now 212

Untitled 212

A Script in Cahoots with 1,000 Misguided Prompts 213

Some Definition in My Life 215

Audacity 216

The Bars Are All Closed 216

Hey Goth, Fuck Off! 222

Gratitude List 223

Hopelessness In-Action 224

My Demons 224

No Rules 225

God Bless You 225

On Fire 225

To Be an Outcast 226

What You Love! 226

Everything Will Always Work Out One Way or Another 227
   A Text Message to a Friend Who Is Having Trouble Staying Awake Throughout the Day

i am SO stupid 227

The Image 228

My Rights as an Amerikan Citizen 228

True Romance 231

Pissed Off and Loving It 231

Untitled 232

The Old Man *233*

Like a Fly on the Wall *235*

This Is Punk Rock, Part 2 ...... *236*
    Like Sheep in Wolves' Clothing

The Dividing Line *237*

So Sorry *237*

The Bullet *237*

Mrs. Big-Shot NYC Editor, Whatcha Think of This?? *238*

My Mind's a-Racin' *238*

In My Honor *240*

Untitled *240*

Small Town Mentality *241*

A Split Personality *241*

Love Is Timeless *242*
    Forever and Ever

a fucking fuckup *244*

Like an Open Book *245*

Yuck! *247*

Listening to Verbal Abuse *247*

Not Enough *247*

Untitled *248*

On the Red Couch *248*

Untitled *248*

Part 6 ~~~ 249

Oh, the sick thoughts that cross my mind when nobody's around. If only you knew....

Fucking Up, Getting High, and Destroying EVERYthing 251

The Game of Life 251

Raw 252

All the Time 252

On Conspiracy Theories 254

Stalemate 254

Fairy Tales 255

Duality 256

My Wet Nightmare 256

A LIFE?? 257

Editing, a Necessary Evil 257

God / Pure Luck? 257

My Addiction 258

Firework Love 258

A Shot of Junk 259

Note to Self 261

I Don't Care 261

GOODNIGHT, BABYLON!!! 262

ART 263

A Lesson in Trust 265

Western Philosophy 265

NRG 266

Crown of Thorns *266*

Torture *267*

Untitled *267*

Void One *268*

Untitled *268*

Time *269*

Who's the Fag? *269*
    sung with Lethal Erection

My Own Hell *270*

Untitled *271*

Losing Friends in a Day *271*

Thoughts on Christmas *271*

Blind Skull *272*

We're All Sick *273*

Untitled *273*

A Nursery Rhyme *273*

When someone says *274*

Haha, I Found It! *274*

the Ego *274*

An Assbackwards America *275*

Words of Wisdom *278*

Lookalike *279*

Racing Thoughts *279*

Why am I here? *279*

please stop *280*

A Poet 1,000 Years Old & Fat Like a Dead Snake *280*

Burning Bridges 283

why i choose not to argue 283

too soon 284

The Anti-Trendies 285

Filth 285

To Be Shocked 286

Close Encounters 286

Relativity 287

Scatterbrained 287

Everyone Is a Cunt 288

A Sacred Place 288

Verbal War 288

A Common Misconception 289

Life Is Short? 290

The Zipper 291

A Poem for Cyndi 291
    Whoever You Are

Growing Up 292

My Own Wisdom 292

Swearing Loudly 293

Tonight 294

No Shame 296

Social Anxiety 297

A Life-Span of Five Hundred Thousand Light-Years 297

You can't escape your sex 298

Interconnected 298

The Scorpion and the Frog *300*

Nighttime in the City *301*

Someone Said *302*

panic >>> *303*

The Same Old Song *304*

I'm torn *305*

Recovered Poem from 2011 ...... *305*

Two Drunk Punks on Parade *306*
    A Poem for Darby Crash

Life Is Hell *307*

A Text Message to a Friend *308*

Untitled *309*

Not One of Those Days *309*

Hipsters *310*

Such a Bore *310*

GET IT STRAIGHT *311*

Death of an Artist *311*

A Waste of Time & Energy *313*

Mobbed *313*

A Lost Generation *315*

Van Gogh *315*

fuck this shit *316*

Cheaters *316*

Steal This Quote *317*

OMG *317*

A Mass Headache *317*

Having an Opinion 318

Part 7 ~~~ 319

If you're not offended, then I haven't done right by you

a fate you cant escape from 321

Rutland, VT 322
    Home of No Originality

Nothing but a Fuckin Scumcunt 322

9/11 324

A FeW WeEkS AgO 324

Don't You Judge Me 325

The Image Is Fuckkkked 325

Strange Things 325

My Love 326

Silly Spider 326

Inside a Box 326

Prolific? 327

like a fuckin GOD 327

Car Crash 327

Go Away 328

That's what I deal with 328

From 5 Years Ago 329

Fucking Writer's Block 329

!CUNT! 329

I said I was sorry, what's your problem! 330

XXX

Untitled *330*

Not My Friend *330*

Welcome to the 21st Century *332*

Lose Control *332*
    sung with Lethal Erection

Pissing Contests *334*

Growth Spurt *334*

Lies *334*

Brainstorm *335*

Listening to the Grateful Dead—boo! *337*

Tradition *338*

Hipsters "R" Us *338*

To Create Inspiration *338*

Video Games *339*

Band Names *339*
    to name a few

The Poem, the Man, & the Obsession *340*

Stupid Is a Stupid Does *344*

Fuck Facebook *344*

On Addiction *345*
    What else is new?

I know nothing *345*

Destroy All Things Human! *346*

Say NO to Conformity *346*

The End Is Nigh *347*

A Mannequin Nation *347*

The Sun Sets *348*

These Assholes *348*

Applied Knowledge *353*

a polliticaly corect PUNK? *353*

Don't Overthink Things *354*

Love = Cocaine *354*

Something Like a Beast *354*

2-Faced *355*

Self-Induced Mania *355*

A Game of Cat & Mouse *355*

The Beloved Messenger of Destruction *356*

Absurdism At Its Worst (or Best?) *359*

A Forgotten Rebel *360*

Good News *360*

The Story of My Life *360*

People *361*

Quitting Smoking *361*

Suicide *361*

A Midlife Crisis *362*

Mindless *362*

Listening to the Drones *363*

In God We Trust *363*

Work Days *364*

Part 8 ~~~ 367
I can piss farther than you

Too Much Second-Guessing 369

Untitled 370

The Business Show 370

Nighttime in the City 2 370
    The Unrelated Sequel

A Clusterfuck 373

My Last Prayer of Hope 375

Overcoming Your Problem 377
    now what??

Untitled 378

No Fun 378

Untitled 378

On Mindfulness 378

Lost Sick & Fed Up 379

A Thought Disorder 379

My rage won't open the door.... 380

Listening to Johnny Thunders 381

To Me 382

Drink to That 382

wrote this just now 385

Things We Are Not Supposed to See 385

Growing Pains 386

A Fatalist 387

PRETENDERS 387

Fuckin Aggro to the Max! *388*

Getting Better *388*

Trash *389*

Untitled *389*

Punk Rock Love/ The New Church Is Back in Business *389*

Existential Hell *391*

Bored & Frustrated *392*

No Love *392*

Immoral *393*

Reality *393*

A Method to My Madness *394*

Suicidal Plan *394*

Smash a Lightbulb Tonight *398*

No Hope *399*

RULE #1 ...... *399*

On the Edge of Madness *399*

Pogo to Forget *401*

Multiple Choice *402*

Untitled *402*

A Little Piece of My Insanity *403*

MADness Thrivery *403*

Looting for Jesus *404*

THIS IS MY ART *405*

Just Like Me *406*

a CUNT RAWKer *406*
    a more lucid more destructive form of Punk

so Untalented = so Successful *406*

Nothing Matters Anymore *407*

Shite! *407*

Don't Call Me a Bigot *408*

FUN FACT: *410*

A Closet Case *411*
    inspired by the band Closet Space

I can't decide *414*
    so don't make me

Lust *414*

A Six-Word Story *414*

Untitled *415*

Love Love Love *415*

Writing Fiction *416*

A Rally of Skeletons Marching for Equal Rights *416*
    in a rather repressed kingdom—Hold On For Your Dear Life

Shove It *418*

Too Smart for My Own Good *418*

Bad Luck *419*

Why I hate nerds *420*

Gotta Get Outta Here *421*

MadDog 20/20 ...... *422*

Part 9 ~~~ 423
Introspection is a sure way to drive a crazy person insane

so ABSURD 425

Going Down the Pub 426

My Life's Story 427

Unrestricted Self-Expression 428

Untitled Collaboration 428
    with Gabriella Mirollo

Memes 430

For Answers 430

Like Watching Paint Dry 431

Life As a Poet 431
    in RUTland VT

WTF 432

A Joke Is a Joke Is a Joke 432

Hard Times 433

Over 48 Hours 433

To the Girl I Love 434

LIFE 435

Nefarious Things 436

A Tumultuous Magnet 437

My Bestfriend 437

The Hospice Exhibit 440

Nihilism 441
    so what??

Save Me 442

Visceral *442*

Opinionated *444*

THIS IS MY ART, Part 2 ...... *445*
    of the darker variety

In a State of Fear *446*

RUTland VT *447*

THINK ABOUT IT! *448*

Who am I???? *448*

Like a Drone *450*

The Show Tonight *450*
    sung with Lethal Erection

DON'T VOTE *451*

Total Takeover *451*

Smash It Up *452*

Burning Out Is Inevitable *452*

Must Be Said *453*

When's My Turn *454*

Where the Freaks Roam *455*

Months Later *456*

On Picking Sides *457*

A Story About Nothing *457*

Animosity As a Virtue *458*

Not Now *459*

An Outlaw *460*

My Brother *461*

Jaded Eyes *461*

The Punk Scene **462**

A Voice Wrapped in Static **462**

The Greatest Joy in the World **463**

Abuse or Be Abused **464**

An Old-School Punk Rock Number **465**

Keep Your Hands Offa Me **465**

on the outside looking in **466**

Untitled **467**

Reflection **467**
    from Chaos to a Void, and back again

Through the Eyes of a Stranger **468**
    A Self-Portrait

That Fuckin Drunk Retard **469**

Untitled **470**

You & I—Like Looking in the Mirror **470**

Just Think About It **471**

Scum of the Earth **471**

people are morons **472**

A Turkish Cherry Tree **472**

Untitled **474**

One Can Hope, Right? **474**
    My girlfriend the valedictorian brings me to a party in their honor

everything i touch **475**

TOP 5 THINGS **476**
    EVERYBODY DOES BUT NOBODY TALKS ABOUT

Closure **476**

A Drive to Be Antisocial **476**

Yawn!   477

The End

XL

Introduction by Sergio Walion
Telling Stories at 3AM

i don't know jeremy void. i don't think he does either. i spent two hours with him, eight years ago. i found his body around three in the morning. he was drunk and lying face down next to the tracks of a subway station near boston. i didn't have to check for a pulse because i heard him. he was talking to himself. i hauled his body around the corner like a piece of angry luggage, trying to get him to wherever he came from. i never saw him again after that.

the best memories always seem to have a frustrating lack of details. i don't remember how i found him. i don't know why i was out that late. i'm missing the beginning and most of the ending to this story. i only remember him lying face down, and the angry sarcasm in his voice. he was in the middle of an argument with someone i couldn't see, and neither could he.
jeremy doesn't remember any of it.

we lived in the same town and went to the same high school. sometimes i saw him on the subway, but we never had a real conversation. the only reason i recognized him at all was because of how he looked.
jeremy always wore an outfit a character from the movies might wear, sort of like a punk from the 1980's but with dirt on it. i never understood why he did that. i always thought he was trying to tell people that he didn't give a fuck what they thought. but he said it so loudly and so often that i always ended up thinking that, on some level, he may have.

Sergio Walion

it doesn't matter. i've completely forgotten what he looked like. that's how it should be. i don't care what he looked like that night. it's the kind of detail i don't mind losing.

what matters are the stories he told me. he started telling me how he wound up on the tracks that night. like all good stories drawn from memory, it had a frustrating lack of details, and it was missing the beginning and much of the ending. some of the stories were exaggerated. some were plausible. some were pretentious. some sounded like wish fulfilling fantasies, like the kind you find in bad porn or comic books.
but sometimes, he would say some of the most sincere fucking things i've ever heard. without realizing it, he would casually make some observation that was so true that it hurt me. i realized i was watching a person in real danger learning how to describe it.

i almost walked away. but something was different about him this time, i really got a good look at him. not his clothes or his hair or his nasty teeth or his sarcasm or his cursing. those are camouflage.
the whole time i knew him, he seemed to spend covering himself up behind a culture. but something must have happened that night. something had swollen and broken open, and he couldn't hide himself any more than his body could hide the railway beneath it. something was happening on the tracks. jeremy was in the middle of telling a story that was too important to get hit by a train.

Introduction

"From Lethal Erection to beat poet: the Jeremy St. Chaos story."
—some asshole on Facebook

      When I was younger, I wrote a lot of poetry, mostly angry raps about murdering the people I hated, slicing them up into tiny pieces and feeding them to the rabid pigs I kept chained up in my backyard. This was before I discovered Punk rock—or moreover, before Punk rock discovered me; *chose* me. Back then I listened to gangster rap, in which the bass thumped and banged and pounded, and which is rather fast, loud, and angry.

      But that's what the cool kids listened to—or at least the kids who I thought were cool. But they didn't want any part of me, not just because I was white, as most of them were white themselves, having grown up in an upper-middleclass suburbs, acting black—but because I wasn't as good an actor.

      So I discovered Punk rock, which is the epitome of fast, loud, and angry, rap for the broken white kid—the kid like me. I started calling myself Jeremy St. Chaos, charging my hair up like Sid Vicious, and playing in a Punk rock band called Lethal Erection—I fronted the band, with a despicable voice, the attitude of the mentally molested, the morally defected, and wrote all the lyrics. I was a fuckup, through and through, the perfect specimen of Punk rock, as if made in a lab, to act, talk, and *be* Punk.

Jeremy Void

I quit writing raps in my ratty notebook, and started carving song lyrics in my arm with a straight razor.

So that's my history in the craft of writing poetry—I wrote song lyrics.

I explain how I got into writing prose at the beginning of *Derelict America,* so I'll skip over that part.

About a year and a half ago I met a girl who was really into writing poetry, so I started dabbling with it after that. But I never got seriously into it until the aforementioned comment on Facebook, which stirred a volatile pot of anger inside me. But when the pot cooled, I thought, *I've heard people tell me my poetry reminds them a lot of beat poetry;* so maybe there was something within that comment, beyond what the eye can see, a sliver of inspiration, twisted and jagged, spiking through what I thought was an insult at first glance. Maybe it was, maybe it wasn't. All I know is it made me manic, riding the waves of a poetic high—beat poetry, to be exact.

So I went and ordered a slew of books on the genre—my favorite is *The Outlaw Bible of American Poetry,* which is so fucking badass.

And most of all, amid this crazy, sleepless high, I wrote this book. I hope it touches you in a way you've never been touched before, opens your eyes wider than they've ever been opened, and inspires you to write, paint, or draw—or whatever your mode of creativity might be.

This is my wet nightmare.

LET THE

Hahahahahahahahahaha!!!

MINDFUCK

Hahahahahahahahahaha!!!

BEGIN

Welcome to Hell!!! There's no
Welcome to Hell!!! turning back!

Part 1
Grammar Nazis Must Die

Part 1
Grammar Nazis Must Die

Dear Paper

Dear Paper
for weeks I've been
staring at a blank screen
just waiting for
the words to come out of me
        but it's
           no use

I'm stuck
and I have
nothing to say anymore.

Dear Paper
dear paper, won't you
relieve me of
this state of being before I
go apeshit and murder someone....

I'm a writer for pete's sake
and words, they heal me
stitch up the rage that would otherwise

flow right out of me
and swallow some
unsuspecting ASHOLE
whole——
        I could only hope....

Dear Paper
what the hell do you
want from me?
Isn't this enough?
I mean, I
filled up your lines,
with words
now didn't I?

What else do you want?
I fed you
I treated you with
upmost respect
and all I get
is a freaking blank screen
in return ...

and now I'm done
and now it's over
and I'm stuck

Dear Paper
please give me a
sign
give me a prompt
to trigger something
exciting
but nothing exciting

happens here
> ever

Dear Paper
deliver me
> PLEASE

Altruism Isn't a Good Look on You
It Doesn't Compliment Your Ignorance

Relativity's a bitch
when you're sitting there
in class philosophizing, theorizing,
conceptualizing, talking about
different classes, the welfare state,
about others you've never met,
cuz you come from the suburbs.
You come from safety, from riches,
and you've never seen it any other way.
Your college professor talks of
all things progressive, of saving the world,
helping the needy, but has no experience
with such a thing.

So you go out there and give,
cuz you can, cuz it's easy.
You have and they don't.
But that's all you know
about these kinds of things.

I've been to the inner city.
I've gone to a gas station that has

all its products behind bulletproof glass.
I've seen people in rags on the street corner,
with cups of change rattling in their grimy hands,
dressed in dirty, tattered gloves.
I've seen people like you, high and mighty,
self-righteous, with up-turned noses,
walking right past the hungry, past the needy,
not once looking in their desperate, pleading eyes,
sad and gray, with HELP ME written all over.

I Love Words

I love words; I love everything about them—the way they make me feel, the way they make me think. Words are my ecstasy. They flow through me like gas, they make me cum a thousand colors—colors actual and abstract. I love words; love to mold and manipulate them into vivid depictions so visceral I shudder with each syllable, each sound that comes out. I paint with words, I write people and images and creations so magnificent I feel complete and significant. They lift me up and knock me down and spin me round and round, a rollercoaster of alliteration and rhymes—a thrilling downward spiral that twists and loops around and shoots up, before the sudden crashing plunge. So hysterical I am about words that I want the whole world to know. I wanna stand on the edge of tall buildings, the whirring wind buzzing, my clothes fluttering. I'll cup my hands around my mouth and scream—I LOVE WORDS!!!

Didn't slip this time

Jeremy Void: 03
Ice: 542

American Angst

                              I can't think....
                            My head aches....
                     Take me to the shrink....
                            I'm so irate....

*   What do you got?...*
I got nothing....
*   What do you want?...*
I want nothing....

                              I'm so bored....
                      It doesn't make sense....
                       I'm sick to the core....
                 I'm going outta my head....

*   What do you got?...*
I got nothing....
*   What do you want?...*
I want nothing....

                            Your voice sucks....
                          I hate your face....
        Why don't you go and get fucked....
                      That notion's insane....

*   What do you got?...*
I got nothing....
*   What do you want?...*
I want nothing....

                    I wanna take a truck....
                 and drive it off a cliff....

I hate my stupid luck....
It's no way to fuckin live....

What do you got?...
I got nothing....
What do you want?...
I want nothing....

Don't gimme that shit!

Critique

I don't want to shoot down anyone's writing, but at the same time I don't want to be a YES-man all the time. If I see areas that could use improvement I try to point it out, but sometimes I don't point it out in the most effective way. Plus, how do you know whether someone's writing needs improvement or if you're just in a bad mood and as a result their writing doesn't sit well with you in the moment?

A Bunch of Crazies

You work with a bunch of crazies,
expecting everyone to act like a fucking saint....
Not gonna happen!
You work with a bunch of crazies
and get upset when someone acts a little erratic....
What the hell do you think is gonna happen?!

Words

Words are my weapon. If you piss me off, I will murder you. I COULD break it to you nicely, and I would, but if you piss me off, then I won't.

Shitty = Shitty

If you hang out with shitty people, you'll get shitty results.

it doesn't fit

jam the round peg into the square hole,
and jam it hard,
make it fit,
lube it up;
do everything possible to get in.
it's important that we succeed
in making the thing fit.
it's vital that we bash it till it sets.

bang it up,
bash it in,
and keep on smashing that peg.

dings are denting the sides.
cuts and crevices break out like hives.
the peg is starting to look misshapen;
starting to lose its shape.

that only means we've gotta
bash it in harder.

The Wrong Place at the Wrong Time

The wrong place at the wrong time is really the right place at the right time in disguise. Look under the fabric of dirt and grime and you'll find adventure. Things that are crass and gritty have more character than things that are plastic and pretty. I'd rather stand in a pile of shit than go to a famous nightclub with Paris Hilton; I'd rather rob a bank than win the lottery. I'd rather bomb a church than join one.

Trainwreck

My drug of choice: whatever you've got, whatever I can afford, or if not, however I can abuse myself this very moment.

I treated myself as a pincushion, a battering ram, and a guinea pig, in that I shot shit into my veins, I beat my brain as hard as I could, and with whatever means necessary, and I took the unidentified drugs others were too scared to take.

The first thing I did upon entering friends' houses was use their bathrooms and raid their medicine cabinets. I stole, I lied, I cheated and manipulated; I fought and I nearly killed more times than not. I wasn't nice, but the lies I told might have convinced you I was.

Girls liked me, though, and I don't know why. I used them like toilet paper and threw them away.

I was vicious and I was a rat. I hung out in alleys and I hung out on the corner. My dad resented my mom for not having that abortion. Everybody cried when I was around. My sister locked herself in her room for fear of what I might do.

I guess I feel bad; I feel bad that I didn't take more.

I know that I was sick. The hell do you expect? Your society chewed me up and spit me out and left me for dead.

But that's what I was, not who I am. I was a disease, a parasite that would latch onto you and suck out your life. But then, you would bet, I knew nothing else. I was right, you were wrong, and that was the end of that. Love, to me, was a four-letter word, and hate was something that I loved and would do every day.

Don't Bother

You can't please everyone. Sometimes you can't please anyone. But if you're lucky you might please someone. But in any case they really secretly hate you and there's no point in trying anyway cuz they'll never see it your way.

An Explosion of the Mind

Two weeks ago I had a crappy week (although of course there were the good parts too, or else the shit-storm explosive manic fucked-up reactive fatalistic behaviors I exhibited by the end of it all wouldn't have happened, and the week would have resulted in an entirely different outcome). But I have to say I learned a lot from it all and I believe I came out a better person. Sometimes one has to lose their mind to gain a greater understanding which would not have been achieved if one's mind stayed in place, sedated and relentlessly humdrum. I'm not excusing the way I acted, because I was a complete and total dick to everyone who came my way; but I'm just saying that sometimes things get way too tame and complacent and the only way to make any further forward motion is to stir the melting pot round and round and round until it erupts like a volcano; and the fact that I came out the other side with some people gunning after me is only an unfortunate consequence to gaining wisdom. If you've never experienced any form of hysteria, wasting away behind a desk locked inside a cubicle just waiting to die as you pound out red tape after red tape imagining what the barrel of the gun must taste like before you pull the trigger—if that's you, then I don't expect you to understand. Yesterday when I told someone what had happened, read the story I wrote to depict my week at my Creative Writing group on Friday, one woman said she thought I was making growth but then this happened and now she doesn't know. But I *am* making growth; just sometimes things must **EX-PLODE** ...   if one wants to keep on growing.

Hello 9 to 5

Children are smarter than us. They have not been inhibited by standardized education like we have yet. So when a child says something really out there, really creative-sounding, and we wonder how said child thought of something I would never be able to think of myself, it's called being a kid, and kids, by virtue of nature, think outside the box, so far out there it might seem marvelous when they talk. And then they get sent off to school and we can say goodbye imagination, hello 9 to 5.

Today's Rebellion / Tomorrow's Trend

Mr. Media
Mrs. Mainstream
the most devious marriage
they're always popping out offspring
of yesterday's rebellion
who grow up to be today's trend.
It happened to black people
It happened to Punks

Which culture will they vomit on next?
One day they're fighting against
the next day they're fighting with
and then they forget the fight
and instead are fucking right
making more babies
who will grow up and rape
another counterculture.
That's the state we live in.
Goodbye badboy
hello radboy!
Hello mainstream rebellion
who reap Rules & Restrictions
and create just one more fad
to make me wanna kill myself to///
It's just so so so sad that

I don't fucking know anymore.

Decipher That, You Fuck!

The clock face ticks, and tocks, and I wish it would stop. Boredom creeps up on me like a desperate whore, a woman willing to do anything for a bag of crack-cocaine. I envy these women, for they are free. They can do anything they want … or need … to do to get by. I don't really envy them; I mean, why would I? They are enslaved to a plastic bag, which spews lies about life, and I don't know why I ever bothered. Life is a bore, and that I can't ignore.

So I sit here with a book, reading words on a page, but the words are meaningless to me, they don't make sense. My mind races like a couple competing cocks. My brain mocks me and my futile ways, telling me not to bother, for I won't ever be paid.

I recognize this, but still I write, and I will write until the pen dies, and when it dies, the sentence will be severed, alluding to nothing and nowhere.

An endless phrase.

I am

That's where I'll stop, because I'm sick of this story, it's so fucking boring.

But I'm lucky to be alive.

In a way, I guess you could say.

I'm a loner in a crowd, surrounded by millions of milling people. I'm a king who lost his crown. I left it at home. And if my head weren't connected to my neck, I'd probably lose that too.

So, the million-dollar question: Who am I?

Who am I? Who are you? Don't point your finger at me or I'll break it into two. But in the end I know I'll always lose. So why bother?

Decipher that, you fuck!

The Art World

The art world has nothing to do with talent, it has to do with popularity and flowers.

{Stark}

                                                                         SHRINKING

DIGRESSING
                      LOSING MY HEAD

THINGS ARE MOVING
                                          AND THEYVE NEVER MOVED
                  QUITE LIKE THIS BEFORE

I MELT
I MELT
I MELT

MY EYES BULGE OUT
CHILDREN RUN AT THE
SIGHT
                                                                            OF IT
                      THE EARTH HAS
                        FLIPPED
                          around

and Im scaaaaaaared————MUTANTS ARE SWARMING
                                                                                         the streets

                          run away from me

The Prompt
This I know

I don't know anything. I could pretend to know something but that would only end in shame and disappointment. I know nothing, I have no answers, and I prefer to keep it that way. I am just another spec in a universe of shit, I can't possibly begin to imagine the innerworkings of things. I don't preach, I don't like preachers; I don't lecture, I hate lecturers. I try to remain neutral in all things politics. Some would call that apathetic, but I call some shit. I'm a nihilist, I guess I do know that. I do know that I know nothing. I am only a man. I am not a god. People who think they know are full of shit. Sometimes I too think I know, I'll admit, but what I think I know is that I too am full of shit. But I prefer it that way....

Midnight Ramblings

Fuck fuck fuck—— I just saw this crazy cunt sucking a duck, so I said, What the? and went over and punched him in the nuts. He looked at me and grabbed his gun, said, Did you just whack me in the sack? He cocked his gat and put a 22-calliber right in my back.

The HARDest Decision I've Ever Had to Make

I love myself   I love myself not
I love myself   I love myself not
     People are starving
     dying
       getting raped
       and maimed

Yet all I can think about
in this dire day & age
                    is whether or not
                            I love myself.

                                        It's the hardest decision
                                        I've ever had to make!

Another Kind of Pretty

My hair is charged.
My sunglasses shine.
My mind is sharp.
I'm looking so fine.

I stagger
I swagger.
My body sways
as I walk down the street.

I see her there, she looks so neat.
Her colored hair, her torn T-shirt.
Her tight leather and a slew of piercings
that make my heart stop beating.

I don't know if she can see me.
She's another kind of pretty.
I hope she can see me,
cuz I'm another kind of something.

Jeremy Void

GET THAT STRAIGHT!!!

Don't hate me for the words I use. Hate me for the things I do.

This Is Punk Rock

No, he's a queer playing Punk rock. But to me Punk rock was never a game, it was life or death. Not something I could just walk away from when my friends turned on me, when that mixed martial arts coach held me by my throat at the convenient store threatening to murder me & smashed my head again & again on the pavement—I could not just step outta my skin, step outta my spikey leather jacket, step outta my stretch jeans; all those littles symbols & slogans that you & I know so well & which tainted every piece of fabric I ever put over my skin, I could not just leave it all behind—just step into my Punk rock clothing at the Punk rock show where everyone else is going along with it too & dressing up & this Punk rock way of life fits in so perfectly here, so nice & right, but then step out of it right before the cops slam me against the brick wall under the bridge. It was more than just a fashion to me, more than a game, a gimmick, a romantic sensation that seemed appealing from the outside view, it was more than anything I could ever use to describe it. In short, it was my **home.** I went to it when I was angry, I went to it when I was sad. It always knew the right thing to say to make me feel better, to lift my spirits, make me feel like I'm not such a fuckup after all—no, wait, it made me feel like even more of a fuckup than I already felt I was. It told me there's nothing wrong with that, be proud of who I am, cuz if I'm a fuckup I've gotta spend the rest of my life in this skin & I might as well be proud of my defects, my follies, wear my failures like a badge of honor. See, that's what Shane West* lacks. He's a movies star, although I heard he came to California originally to be in a Punk band & ended up as an actor anyway. But even so, that desire to be in a Punk band is what makes him not Punk at all. My

---

* The actor that plays Darby Crash in the movie *What We Do Is Secret*.

theory is, anyone can play Punk, it's not that hard to do. But in the '70s & '80s nobody wanted to play Punk—& I mean *nobody*. So that weeded out all the non-Punks. If you played Punk chances are it wasn't some dream of yours to star in a Punk band; chances are, you just failed at everything else you'd ever done & this was your last hope to do something real with your life. Punk rock was all I had, it was all you had I'm taking it, it was all a lot of us had; but in this day & age, with movies like *SLC Punk* floating around, Punk becomes cool. Punk becomes romantic, a sensation. But I'll tell you this: being Punk is not pretty & it's not romantic. Sure, there were the fun times like surfing a wave of extended hands or busting your knee pretty badly in a mosh pit while the Business played; but then there were the bad times too, like getting beat down, locked up, & kicked around; & for me I had no other choice. I see these Punk kids today who are COOL—& they come from pampered lives & they roll with the jocks & the preps & the metalheads & anyone else who will accept them—which is everybody. I despise the pampered Punks, I'll hate them till I die. And do you know why?—of course you do—it's because they're mocking my lifestyle, they're parading around in the very thing that I hold so dearly to my terminally deformed heart, the very thing that had brought me through year after year of misery & pain; they're fucking my girlfriend & prancing around saying, *Hey Jeremy, I just fucked your girlfriend,* & then going to the next person, *Hey Frank, I just fucked Jeremy's girlfriend,* & so on. It's disrespectful to call yourself Punk but not know a goddamn thing about what that represents. It's just another silly rich kid game, another counterculture for the rich to exploit. These kids got their teeth into everything, & I wanna sink my teeth into them—see how they like it!

My Way

I did it your way
        and failed >>>>

28-Years Old

I'm 28-years old
My moods are always in flux
I have no plans for the future
I have yet to find a place of belonging
I hate authority
I constantly abuse my mind and body
I'm 28-years old
and I just don't know what I want

But I'm doing the best I can!

Your Communication Skills

You really need to work on your communication skills, I thought to myself as the girl kneeled down before me crying and covering her eyes with her hands. I could smell the cow shit from here, that rotten, musty stench radiating from her dirty-blond hair. Behind me a fire alarm roared in the high school, and the students, all soaking wet from the torrential downpour from the ceiling sprinklers which had opened fire on them as soon as the system had picked up its first whiff of smoke—a sudden loss of oxygen and the increase of carbon monoxide—they shuffled out the doors as the teachers attempted to keep them tucked together in a single-file line; only it was no use, they were pouring out the doors screaming and panicking.
And there I was, standing in the playground holding an empty bucket that had used to hold cow manure, and before me this young, blond-haired chick was balling covered in manure. She smelled awful.

You really need to work on your communication skills, I thought to myself, again. And to think, all I wanted was one measly stick of bubble gum; the scent that wafted

briskly from the girl's chewing and sucking mouth was fabulously delightful. It sent me sprawling into euphoria. One whiff and I was gone, off galloping through the greenest grass you'd ever seen, the sun bright and burning in the clear blue sky; and I was skipping and smiling, my tongue hanging loose, through the most gorgeous meadows in the whole wide world—and then came that sharp, reverberating *clack!* of the ruler clapping my desk.
I tore my eyes from the gum-chewing dirty-blond sitting behind me, and there in front of me stood the old hag we called a teacher, glaring at me through a wrinkly, white complexion that reeked of neglect and old age, her nostrils flaring at the bottom of a long, crooked nose.

With a silent huff she retracted the ruler, pivoted and spun, and brought it down on the blackboard with a *crunch!*—the sound made me cringe.

You really need to work on your communication skills, I thought to myself one last time, dropped the bucket in the dirt and grime, and moseyed off into the panic-ridden daytime haze....

Demolition Dancing

Kids from all over meet here ...

>   they swirl and swirl
>   they flail and they twirl
>   elbows and fists
>   kicking and jabbing
>
>   it's demolition dancing

The drummer drums/
The guitarist strums/
The bassist plucks/
While the singer lurches onstage///

Can't Get It Right

I'm trying to fit
learning to lie
I wanna be In
I wanna be them
but every single time
I get knocked back a peg....

All Screwed Up

I apologize if I rant here, because I got so much on my mind. I'm no good at staying sober and I hate myself and my life and everyone in my life and most of all, I hate me, me, me, because I'm fucking crazy and out of my mind, and no one gets me, especially in Rutland, because I like things loud and fast and chaotic and fast, and if things aren't that way, I get even crazier, and that's why the music I listen to is fast; it simply calms me down. And everyone is pushing me to slow down and chill out but that doesn't work for me because now I don't know my ass from my head, and up is down and left is right and I'm so fucking assbackwards all the time because their life isn't for me, and they're trying to squeeze a square peg in a round hole, and the more they smash it to fit, the more it dings and dents and chips apart, and all they're going to end up with is a deformed square that isn't even a shape anymore, but a misshapen block. And that's me and that's how I feel right now, and I don't know anything about getting sober because I can't even seem to get that right. A girl at the AA meeting today cried because she was so depressed and I said to her at least she can cry, because I forgot how to do that a really long time ago, but I'm fucking crying right now. I went to my therapist and showed him this story I wrote because I was really proud of it, getting my shit all out there, and he said it's gonna scare people and they'll think I'm a monster but I am a fucking monster and I don't give a fuck what they think and if it scares people, then fuck em because that's how things were for me and it wasn't pretty, none of it was, and if they're scared, then they will know how it is to be me.

Work

50 miles down the hill   50 miles back up

Ode to Facebook

So many faces/
    So many names/
        So many places/
            I can't keep it straight....

Recovered Poem from 2011

I'm a user, a total loser
I'm a figment, a terminal delinquent
Can't exist without my fists
A demented twit, a little bitch
Can't decide on suicide
I been used & abused
Manipulated, so frustrated
& all this hatred is being wasted
You see me here without a tear
burning up inside, gonna let it loose on the outside
Hatred is all that makes sense to me
Broken bones are in my destiny
Throw a match into the gas
Fuck shit up & have a laugh
My jaded eyes have seen the way
The world's going to hell & I ain't afraid.

The Pledge of Defiance

I pledge defiance to the government of the United States of America and the injustice for which it stands; one nation above God, divisible and quite corruptible, with liberty and justice for some.

Loud & Fast

Living <u>FASTER</u>
Playing <u>LOUDER</u>

My head hurts
    aches
        is falling apart

My brain melts
    stings
        is turning to ashes

My mind bleeds
    opened-wide
        a slapdash of random thoughts
        are racking my insides
        smacking my outsides
        and I run & hide!

you just don't get it, Mr. MAN. you don't get why i need my music fast, why i seek loud, out-of-sync noise, why the beats are smashing, the riffs are thrashing, and the vocals are glass-shattering—no, you do not understand why; but i can assure you there is a method to my madness, a reason I thrive for loud, fast music....

<u>it mends the wounds</u> in my head, <u>it mends the scars</u> crisscrossing my brain, and <u>it mends the madness</u> bleating inside my mind.

                                                                              so   there!

To Teachers Everywhere

I had a teacher who I
met privately with,
and in each session
he would set up a game of Chess
for the two of us to play.

He was good at Chess
and beat me most often.
I won once, I think,
maybe, I don't know.

Another teacher of mine
applauded me for reading
a book called *American Hardcore*.
But then a teacher from the next room
banned that book from the school.
When I asked her why, she said
because in it there's a picture
of a guy carving HATRED IS PURITY
into his arm. Someone could
get triggered if they picked it up.

The teacher who had me
play Chess had me
read a book called
The Basketball Diaries,

a book called *A*
Clockwork Orange.
Only, due to the content of said
books I had to keep it on the
hush-hush, on the down low,
so as not to inform the principal
of such transgressions.
This teacher of mine would
be banished from that school.

I had a teacher who told
a peer of mine to stick a key in an
electrical socket. See what happens,
she told him.

I've had teachers who
have helped me greatly,
who have taught me lessons
I still use today.

But on the other hand, I
have had teachers who
were mean and rotten,
teachers who didn't care
one way or another.

For every class,
there are always two sides:
both *good* and *bad*.

The teacher who had me play
Chess explained that the reason
for this lesson was to teach me to
think ahead.

To teach me to plan out my moves—
something I could never do
right.

                                      It's why I went to five different high schools.

A Commercialized Sport

The fact that nonconformity has become a commercialized sport

is just so

                        so

                                                  so

                    I don't know....

It's a joke
is what it is,

                                              A Joke
  because the moment being truly anti-establishment becomes accepted is the day
                                                  the world explodes....

turns day-glo
                  unfolds and unravels
                                                revealing a fascist
  regime beneath the fabric that conceals our entire established government....

Another Year

My Birthday—
today's my birthday, and
I sit alone in my library.
My brain ticks out regrets like
a printer.　　　　i sit here & wonder

Not Like Ordinary Men

I am not like ordinary men. I think in a way that makes the mass populous shudder. My thoughts and dreams are banned from most libraries, my ideas and schemes forbidden from any text book. I'm just a human being trying to navigate my way through a world crammed tight with let-downs and set-backs. I write because I need to, not because I want to, but there's a magic beneath the pen as it scrawls word for word, as I scribble my internal drama between the lines. It's almost like giving birth, painful to let it out, but boy does it feel good that it will fester inside you no longer, and now you can raise and nourish it. That's a magical thing, isn't it?

SELF-EXPRESSION

IT IS ONLY

SELF-EXPRESSION

DON'T TAKE IT SO
LITERALLY

The Rage

Storm clouds roiling, a blast of lightning forks through. There's thunder, and it rumbles.

I nod my head and say,
Yes, ma'am.

I feel a wave of
kinetic energy intensifying,
my eyes seeing only red, a heat
in my forehead growing, the weight
of it all pressing down.

Walking on the street I imagine
I have powers that could
flip a bus on its side.
I stare at the cars that drive by,
pretending to blast them
with fireballs, knock them out
of orbit.

I wanna kill the passersby,
stab innocent bystanders
in their throats
and watch as blood pours from the holes
I have made.

I smile and say,
Thank you, ma'am.

Behind these eyes, dark clouds
spin tornadoes, they bring fire
and lightning and

acid rain.
I see rage, The Rage, and
it strengthens everyday.

A terrorizing wind to knock down houses and buildings and blow cars right off the road.

One day I will Snap!

Confined to a Box

Most people are confined to a box, and anything outside of said box requires an explanation or else the person doesn't believe it exists.

And I'm sick of explaining.

Punk Rock Song

We stalk the streets in tattered wear.
We sit on rooftops without a care.
Drinking forties and liquor galore,
we sing our songs and scream fuck the world.

We band together in ghoulish suits.
We fight together with fists and boots.
The streets aren't safe, we know this well.
But we stay as one, and as one we'll yell.

Alone

Don't live your life tethered to something or someone that is only trying to tear you down. I'd rather stand alone than be attached at the hip to a nefarious beast. Love and lust, two things that I could do without, two things I mix up way too often, two things that always tear me down. Don't live your life attached to nothing, live free and wild, but don't mistake love for a flame because you'll come to find out that it's really a vicious snake trying to bite your head off. Freedom is lonely but loving someone kills....

Mixed Feelings

I can't decide whether to hate myself or to love myself. Hmm.

Another Poem About Nothing

ive got nothing to say
but if i dont say something soon
i might jus dissolve
        disintegrate
                evaporate....

I am not having a very productive day. The ideas are just not coming rushing out of me like from an automated sprinkler. I'm losing steam, I'm sinking fast, I'm crashing, I'm burning, the car runs outta gas. There will be another day, I'm sure of it, but today is all I see in the here&now.

its cold outside
i stand in the road
i wait for something to change

If You Don't

>>> If you don't
>>> <u>LIKE</u>
>>> MY PAGE

>>> I WILL CUT OFF YOUR BALLS
>>> AND FEED THEM TO MY CAT

>>> If you don't
>>> <u>LIKE</u>
>>> MY PAGE

>>> I WILL CUT OFF YOUR NIPPLES
>>> AND SEW THEM TO THE BACK
>>> OF MY LEATHER JACKET

>>>>>> Kidding, of course.

>>>>>> I'll really just break into your house
>>>>>> murder your children
>>>>>> and hang their heads on my front lawn
>>>>>> for Halloween.

Untitled

Life is not all fun and games!
      Says who????

Slam-Dancing Queen

I'm not really a dancing guy
cuz the way I see it
if bones don't break
if noses don't fracture
if the floor isn't covered in
blood & guts by the end of the night
the only place you'll find me
              is in the corner snoring my face off.

A Drunk and a Pill Popper

I mean, I'm a drunk and a pill-popper, addicted to more and more and more, and I live—no, I thrive for excess; I chase the Pink Dragon like it's my occupation. From one hurdle to the next, I rise higher and grow stronger, and when the Pink Dragon seems to be getting closer to me, it's farther than ever, and I keep after it, picking up speed, swirling my lasso, and hurling it but it always lands just an inch too far to the left or the right, but that's okay, because one of these days I'll catch it and choke it and then I'll feel whole and alive, like I had reached my goals, but my goals are always too far out of reach....

Public Opinion

guy sez to me
you know, you could
better reach the masses
if you didnt cuss so much///

well FUCK THE MASSES
when was the last time
they tried to reach me.

im not trying to please
anybody
who dont try & please
me
its a 2way street

only
the world is
obsessed w/
this Public Opinion

well FUCK THE
PUBLIC OPINION

<u>these are not
my people
& they never
will be</u>....

i read their glares
as they bear into me
these dirty whores
boring me w/

their dirty stares.

theres a reason
i stand here
by myself
a reason i stand alone
w/o you around me

cuz My Life is forbidden
in the popular zone

they try to be friendly
thru their shit-eating grins
they try to gimme sympathy
but where does it end?
their phony hospitality
directed toward the
FREAKS

THESE ARE NOT
MY PEOPLE
and they never will be

you just dont get it
& you never will
see id RATHER stand alone

you just dont get it
& you never will
see theres a reason
i lurk in the shadows
a reason im quiet
a loner a freak & a creep
theres a reason

i dont speak
a reason i just dont give a shit
about the stupid Public Opinion
cuz those goddamn idiots
dont give a fucking shit

about me

im not a people-pleaser
why the hell should i be?
why should i try & please these people
who arent trying to please me!

its a 2way street....

Manic

I think I'm manic right now—just a bit. Who wants to see my nipples?

For One Brief Moment Social Media Got Smarter

I think the point of life is to create. To learn and to create. We start out as babies knowing nothing about what's to come. We have no manuals about how to live our lives, either. We literally start from scratch, with nothing and without a clue. And then we get older and we learn and adapt to our surroundings. That's how the human race started, technology-wise, with nothing, but as life went on, we as human beings learned more and thus created more, and then dynasties were formed, destroyed, and formed again. It's in our nature, engrained in our DNA.

Smash a Lightbulb: Poetry for Lowlifes

D.A.S.: The meaning of life is to give life meaning.

ME: I like that.

ME: But I was thinking if the Bible says that God created us in his own image, and if God Himself is the Great Creator, then wouldn't we be creators too?

D.A.S.: We are!

S.W.: this conversation should be framed and put up somewhere

ME: Everything I say should be framed, because I'm just that great and my ideas and concepts are so amazing they belong in a museum.

D.A.S.: God-complex.

S.W.: http://en.wikipedia.org/wiki/Dunning%E2%80%93-Kruger_effect

S.W.: [basically, the better you are at something, the less praise you give yourself and the more you see that needs improvement, whereas people just starting to convince themselves they're finished too early]

ME: Are you implying I have no talent?

ME: And I disagree with that. I don't think it's that simple. The better I've gotten at writing the more I started to think of myself as a better writer, the more arrogant I've become. But it isn't really arrogance, it's pride.

ME: My whole life I've been arrogant, full of myself (when someone once accused me of acting like my shit don't stink, I told them it doesn't, it smells like flowers—that's arrogance), but the truth is, my whole life I was covering up for the fact that I had no talent—or so I thought. I would take pride in the fact that I had nothing to be proud of, when I was really hurting over this fact, so I acted like it didn't matter to me because it was easier to not care; and overtime I really did not care, honestly feeling like a hotshot because of the fact that I was not.

ME: It's different now. I joke all the time about me being great and better than everyone else, but that's all it is, a joke. I don't think it's the better you are, the less praise you give yourself; I think it's the more confident you are, the less praise you give yourself.

ME: I KNOW I'm a good writer, regardless of what anyone says. But I don't always believe that; I know on an intellectual level, it just hasn't reached my emotions yet. So I always feel the need to prove myself. It's not that I'm a bad writer that makes me always feel the need to prove myself, it's that I don't fully believe I am.

S.W.: no, definitely not! it means that you should never convince yourself of perfection. all the best writers, artists, musicians who are really invested in what they're doing never consider themselves finished. there's an expression that a creative person's favorite or best work of theirs is always "the next one they're going to do."
you probably already see this, when you look back and see you could improve your old work.
it's good to have pride in your work, but reverence is lethal to any art. most recognized and influential artists hated their most famous art. frank kafka, one of the most famous and influential authors, wanted most of his unpublished novels burned after his death. the reason wasn't because he "lacked talent." it was because he had so much of it, and never thought he got what he wrote to sound perfect. he never saw any of it finished or complete.

ME: Of course. In some languages, "perfect" means "death" or "end."

ME: Oh, and I was joking, kinda being sarcastic, when I asked if you think I'm an untalented writer, cuz you've said to me otherwise many times. I just feel really awkward about ending anything I say in LOL. Most everything I say on Facebook that is even somewhat malicious or accusing is a joke and should be taken light-hearted. I haven't truly gotten angry in a long, long time. Depressed, yes. But not angry.

S.W.: oh okay. it's hard to tell when people are joking. i have that insecurity too, but it's good and valuable to have. if it pushes you forward then it's working. i think confidence is good, but i also think so much success comes to people who are also focused on their mistakes and weaknesses.
it's a double edge sword. it isn't helpful to find mistakes or be unnecessarily critical of yourself. but the fact that i hate myself means i can never stop trying to get better.
it's funny, because i usually only post negative or sad things on Facebook, but i think they're great. it means i've got a problem, and i'm admitting that i don't know what the fuck i'm going to do yet. the boring people are the ones who write how awesome their vacation was. there is no fucking way

anyone can be completely happy with anyone, especially in their twenties. everything's in flux, i think.

ME: I was just writing something on my IPad that speaks to that, but then it died, and now I'm on my phone. I was just saying that even though my poetry can at times be very angry, I myself am not angry. I was very angry when I was younger, and at the time my poetry represented that anger. But today it's more that I'm exploring the anger and moreover, I'm exploring the absurdities of life. And also, even though I'm happy most the time, most people wouldn't be able to gather that from my Facebook posts because some of them are quite angry and depressing and even disturbing, but that's what I'm into, and I enjoy that same kind of writing, and plus, it's easier to say I'm hurting because I've been saying that for so long. When I was nineteen, almost ten years ago, I took a neuropsych test at McLeans, and the doctor diagnosed me with: borderline personality disorder with antisocial and psychotic features. One of the tests was that he showed me pictures and I had to tell him what happened before the picture was taken, what is happening in the picture, and what will happen afterwards. In the thick report he wrote up on me, he commented that for every picture there was a crime in progress, some antisocial activity. Which doesn't make me crazy. Look at Stephen King.

ME: It's just what I'm into, and it shows in my writing. You're a very insightful person, so you might have come to this conclusion already, but I bet that you're not as miserable as you say you are on Facebook. You use Facebook as a mode to express yourself, and I know for me I'm not always feeling the emotion I'm expressing while I'm expressing it, I'm just exploring it, trying to shine some light on it, finding out what others think, etc.

S.W.: definitely. and thanks man.
i think it's hard to tell what's a joke or not on fb. i think that puts people like you and me in a weird place, where we can write honestly and sarcastically, and people won't even know the difference or how to respond correctly. which sucks.
so i guess i was taking you at face value and saying, oh yeah, don't forget to hate your writing

ME: Yeah, I know. But I look at it this way: I'm a writer, and as a writer it's my job to convey a message that the reader can understand, which I feel that I do fairly well when writing fiction or even nonfiction essays, but then again, all art is misunderstood by someone. I cover controversial subjects in my writing and there is a lot of depth weaved in, but in order to see the meaning, one must dig through the fat. Most people are too quick to make assumptions, like that comment I wrote attached to Harry's status at which he and that girl were outraged. People who don't know you or me will see something negative by us and immediately assume that person's crazy and want nothing to do with them, and that's fine by me, cuz I don't think they'd like my writing to begin with. Before I published my first book this woman suggested I make my cover more appealing to a wider audience because, she said, it has that potential. My counter argument was that even though certain stories might have the potential to reach a wider audience, the greater part is likely to outrage them. The people who are intrigued by the cover are probably the people who will like what's inside. It's like cutting out the fat, in a way.

G.M.: Just wanted to say to you both that this is the best reading I have enjoyed on Facebook since I reluctantly joined it. For one brief moment social media got smarter. Thank you.

Lost & Found

I wrote a verse
here
and a box opened up
and devoured the words.
I saw each word
dissipate like
magic.
one moment they were
before me, the next
they were beyond me.

At War with the Muse

THINK! I've gotta write something. THINK! What's there left to say? I've said it all already, hashed it out on page after page after page, and now I'm stumped. THINK! I'm thinking but the ideas aren't coming to me as easily as they once were. THINK THINK! C'mon, I've gotta strain my brain; it's a muscle, right? so I've gotta drain it, filter out the wisdom from the nonsense. THINK! Maybe I'm not thinking hard enough cuz I can't come up with new ideas anymore. It's a losing battle. At war with the muse. It's like she left the building, went on strike until I took better care of her. THINK THINK THINK! For Godsake, THINK!!!

High on Life

Life is great, and to all those who think otherwise, which I'm sure there are a lot of you out there, open up your fucking eyes and look around you, and quit your boring ass brooding; it's getting old. Life is good, so you can all go suck a cock!

Labels & Classifications

CAN'T CLASSIFY
IT DON'T WANT YOUR
LABELS DON'T MEAN
NOTHING IS ALL WE KNOW
ABOUT **IT** *IT* IT IS
                ART

Like I always say

If you can't create anything beautiful, then destroy *every*thing beautiful.

Piecing the Past Back Together

I'm piecing the past back together
        that's what I did this morning
sat at my computer looking thru my friends' friends on Facebook
                so many
            familiar faces
who I just cannot place, even after thinking long and hard about it

it's kind of **frightening**
and surreal to know that I know these people
I really do
but I just can't place them....

At the Halloween Dance

Dance music is rotten, it sounds putrid. Like a knife ripping into your ear, cutting through your brain, your mind going blank as the knife finds its way through bits of gushy brain matter, your eyes rolling up into your head, your body jerking about like a spastic, arms flailing, legs kicking, your brain so utterly dull as the blade makes its way through to the other side, and your dance partner, she winces when a line of blood squirts across her face, glistening red and crooked. She stands there, her face screwing up into all sorts of unnatural expressions as the knife flies across the dancehall and lodges itself into the wall like a dart. And everyone stares as you drop to your knees, blood spilling out of both ears. But the music continues, the DJ scr-scr-scratching away on the turntables, the record twirling and his finger stopping, starting, stopping, starting it, unaware of what went down a mere twenty yards away—*the tasteless bastard!*—until a Punk rock kid strolls steadily to the wall, rips out the knife, and hurls it, spinning, at the DJ. The knife finds its mark: the DJ's left eye. An explosion of screams erupts in the dancehall. Now, people are hysterical, running around like idiots, as the woman's rapping breaks out of the sound system as if this had never really happened to begin with, the record turning as people burst through the doors. The Punk rock kid, still in the club, plucks the knife from the DJ's eye, brings it to his mouth and licks the blood and bits and chunks of mashed-up eyeball, and walks away, pocketing the blood-soaked projectile, a bright and steady smiling beaming on his face because of this sick deed he readily volunteered for at his annual anti-dance music meeting, hosted by his older brother Fred, whose girlfriend was mowed down by the car of a raver three years back, and who ever since vowed to assassinate every DJ on the face of the planet. That's how I feel right now.

Loki's Resolution

Loki stood at the altar. Outside of the church, the world was up in flames. The church was the only thing standing secure, the only thing not burning. Loki wondered how that could be, how that could possibly be the case. But it was.

He whipped around with lightning speed, and his cape swooped circularly behind him.

The church was empty, and the bells in the tower were jangling in the forceful waves of wind. Loki looked at the empty benches, at the empty pews …

… and magically he saw people emerge out of nothing, just appear there, the flames thundering outside these walls. He walked up the aisle, and the kneeling ghosts, with pyramided hands, turned their heads toward him as he passed. He felt their stares on him, felt their eyes cutting into his soul—or lack thereof.

The world was up in flames, and it was all his fault, and he knew something had to change—it had to.

He took off in a jog. Then a run. Before long he was shooting down the aisle like a bullet, and his cape caused a whirlpool of wind to surge around him, the ghosts of his destruction vanishing in a puff of thick, gray smoke.

He stepped outside and it felt as if everything just stopped. The flames freezing mid-flicker. He stared out at the city, seeing all the burning skin, all the sizzling bones—all the chaos.

He suddenly dropped to his knees, hitting the stones with an ear-piercing *plop*.

He folded his hands together and, for the first time ever, he prayed.

He prayed to something he knew did not exist. Prayed to change who he was. Prayed to become a better person. Because this madness and disarray was just such a terrible fate. He wanted so bad to just change—to be someone else.

"Please God," Loki said through his tears, staring up at the moon through teary eyes. *"Please God, I don't want to be this man anymore. I want to change. Oh God, I want to change."*

With that last word—*change*—engraved in time, he felt something he had never felt before, something he couldn't imagine feeling, because what he felt was so unreal, so unbelievable, so ... *Godly!* He felt the hand of God; he felt it clamp down on his shoulder. What he was seeing might have just been an illusion, just a blurry field caused by the tears welling in his eyes—what he saw was God Himself.

A transparent, hazy figure, but he knew all too well that it was He—He who makes the wind blow, He who brings the light and He who takes it away.

The blurry figure opened its jowls wide, and a sharp, radiant light sprayed outward, slicing through the night like a laser beam. A whole wrenched open.

Then the jaws of the most holiest of beings, the jaws of God Himself, they clamped shut with such holy might that the clashing impact created a sonic boom which cut right through the city, knocking every burning soul upward and beyond. Around him, a billowing blast rippled and thrashed, and souls were whipped up into the air, the devouring flames suddenly defusing. A coldness swept over everything, and all the falling people landed softly on mounds of snow.

Part 2
Fuck the Social Contract:
I signed nothing

Part 2
Fuck the Social Contract: I signed nothing

Pillow Talk

My life tainted
with broken aspirations that
make me feel less than
and
and
and
my life hopeless
my world broken
my existence floating away on a wisp of smoke
and
and
and
if only I could see her again
be embraced as she kisses me deeply
the girl of my dreams
and
and
and
it's a worthless struggle
step back and give up
as life shimmers past me dissipates and is gone

and
and
and
it's gone

For Twenty-Something Days

I have been sober for twenty-something days, smiling, joking, laughing. And—that's fucking right—I have been living my futile, pointless, null-and-void life—what a redundant way to describe it—soberly, just drifting through an anonymous black hole leading me to the depth of no one, nowhere, and nothing, but I promise you this: I will come out alive and on top.

"Hey, Obstacle!"

"Hey, Obstacle! Go fuck yourself!"

"Why do you say that?" it says. "I'm only trying to help."

"The fuck you are. You stand in my way and try to tear me down, and you call that helping?"

"But, Jeremy Void, I love you. I only want what's best."

I smirk. "What's best, you say. What's best?? You wanna know what's best?" Pause. "Well I'll tell you what's best!" Waving my index finger around like it's a sword. "What's best is for you to go away—tear someone else down, why don't you! See how they like it."

Smash a Lightbulb: Poetry for Lowlifes

My obstacle approaches. Gets in my face. Tears descending its sharp, bony cheeks.

"Go away!" I say, thrusting my index finger straight out in front of me.

Deadly to Be Trendy

Follow the cool kids.
Go to where the action is nonexistent:
the street corner,
the abandoned warehouse,
the deserted avenue,
the ghost town,
around the corner from Hell—
the place where God only comes
in a plastic bag.
Wrapped in tinfoil.
Sell your soul to the Devil
and spit in the eyes of your maker.
Sell yourself.
Pray that God doesn't allow you
in the Land of the Lord.
No cool kids there.
Dive headfirst into the fiery abyss.
Impulses! Don't think.
Act.
Action without thought means fun, fun, fun.
The TV tells us to be dumb.
Dude, don't do that;
do this.
Pop pills.
Stick a spike into your arm

and push down on the plunger and watch
through red eyes your life wash away in hot water.
Make waves, break rules,
break bones, and throw your life down the tubes.
Take a dive.
Disintegrate.
It's what the cool kids do.
Follow the trend.
Say NO to life and YES to death.
Ride the Grim Reaper.
Welcome him into your life and
say goodbye to your friends.
It's the fabulous way of the cool kids.

WTF?

Why are pictures of naked attractive people more likely to get flagged than pictures of naked ugly people? I just saw a picture of two old people jumping naked into a lake, and it showed their bare asses and everything. I'm not gonna flag it cuz I'm not that way. But I feel like if the old people weren't old but very fucking hot, it'd be flagged in an instant.

Untitled

If you catch me sleep-walking, please lead me off a cliff!

I CARE————I CARE NOT

IN MY WRITING I SAY THAT I DON'T CARE ALL THE TIME, BUT THE TRUTH IS, I CARE WAY TOO MUCH—WAY, *WAY* TOO MUCH. I DON'T WANT TO CARE, THAT'S TRUE. I WISH I DIDN'T CARE, THAT'S TRUE. I PREACH NOT CARING, THAT'S TRUE TOO.
BUT—AND HERE'S THE BIGGIE—I KNOW WE SHOULD NOT CARE ABOUT WHAT OTHERS THINK, BUT THAT DOESN'T MEAN THAT I DON'T.

I MEAN I'M ONLY HUMAN!

No Image Available

You look at my pictures
but you don't read my writing.
I've got something to say to you
but it always goes unread.

What am I to do
to make you care about my insides?
Should I put em on display
show myself from the outside in.

Would that make you care?
Seeing me hung up all bloody
my organs sliding out of my gutted stomach
and coiling on the floor beneath me.

At least then you'll see
there's more to me than

just a pretty face.
I got guts and a heart that pumps
and I got intestines and a brain that
races out of control at times.
It's all a part of me, all different sides,
but if you only look at my face
you won't see what I have to say.

No

I am not a whore

I am an artist

The VOID of Existence

Where am I? I'm in a room surrounded by people—but that's all know. Their voices reach my ears but I don't hear them. When I look around me—assess my surroundings—I realize I don't in fact know where I am. Lost in a crowded room, lonely in a bleak and deserted subway train, squandering for truth, a hopeless pondering, wandering the VOID of Existence, just fondling the Angel of Sin's private parts. Rejected again. Destined to desolate planes: Trapped in a spastic plunge. A hole in my head, a wound full of dread. Where am I? you're asking. Never ask the gods Why Me? because the answers you will get are like licking the tainted back of a diseased frog. Dis-ease, deserted and lost.... The world was Mine, but that's just the story of my life—kicked and broken—the world was MINE, but then it just spit acid in my eyes——licked and so very open—vulnerable you know.... Licked!—licked, licked, licking the wounds of poor indecisions; the floor rises straight up and my feet lose their grip on reality as I plunge deeper and deeper into the VOID of Existence, chaotic and destroyed.... It's a hopeless force and I crawl back into my pillow hoping for relieffff

But Who Am I Trying to Impress????

Comb your hair
Brush your teeth
Dress up
Make yourself look neat
              neat
                            neat

But who am I trying to impress????
      not **ME**
             cuz I could care less.

True Story, I Swear

When I was thirteen, the Devil came to me. This is a true story too, I swear. I remember I was walking to the train station, on my way to take the train somewhere, and he came to me—I heard his voice and I thought it was God; that's how the story went. God talked to me and told me of a better way, a way of chaos and destruction, to destroy what I love before it destroyed me. That's what I told everybody at first, that God chose me—Jeremy fucking St. Chaos—he chose me to spread the word of chaos. And I told everyone that story like it made me something, something special, and I even called a Jesus hotline to tell them they were wrong, and I knew they were wrong because God entered my fucking head and told me they were wrong, all those preachers and their love for

Jesus. But you know what, *I* was wrong, *me,* I came to realize later on. It was the Devil Himself, that sneaky bastard, and to think I believed the fucker, every single word he said, about me being the chosen one, about me needing to spread the word of chaos and cause as much confusion and disarray as I could before I died.

But then, I realized I was lied to. That was not God. And when I realized this, I killed myself.

I killed myself; I died. I floated up to those pearly gates in the clouds, those shiny gates that guard the way to Heaven, and I waited there. How long I waited, I have no idea, but it was a while and I talked to some of the oddest dudes up there too, dudes I couldn't imagine meeting; and all around me, Heaven's guardians, with flapping wings and all, swooped past, carrying golden bows and flaming arrows.

When I finally reached the front of the line, that guy standing at the gate, holding a golden clipboard in his hand, said my name was not on the list, and, *poof*—just like that!—another clipboard, this one red and menacing, replaced the golden one and it looked so horrific in his hands, and he browsed down that newer clipboard and said, "Oh, there's your name!"

And he shrugged at me—honest to God, he really *shrugged* at me—and then said, "Sorry, dude, but you're on the other list."

And with those last words—*the other list*—a flaming hole opened up in the clouds where we stood and a serpent's tail whipped out of it, green and slimy with blue and red spots all over, and coiled and licked in my direction, grasping for something—me, probably, when I think back on it—and getting longer as whatever was in that hole fed it up through, until the tail reached me and spun around my torso times & time again, wrapping itself all the way around me, and soon enough I was bound by that *thing* and it tore me away—straight down into the pit—just ripped me screaming—and I'll tell you that was the most scariest part of this tale, the fear of what will happen to me as I plunged into the depths of Hell, the tail holding me in its vice-like grasp, so tight I couldn't even flail my arms and legs as I plunged deeper and deeper. The ground, fiery with rivers of flowing lava swaggering through the hot red surface, was coming closer to me. It grew larger and came closer and I could make out tiny little people getting beaten and whipped and fucked in the asses by smiling demons and then that view of them, as it came closer and closer, faded away because the ground got too big to behold with my eyes any longer and the serpent's tail suddenly released me, and, *boom!,* I hit the ground and bounced back up and came back down one last time and the second time I connected with the red hot surface it hurt so fucking much that I felt like every inch of me would deteriorate under the blaring heat, as if I'd just fallen into a pit of lava.

But I eventually got up and I was naked and barefoot—because all my clothing and my shoes had disintegrated—and I had to tiptoe as if walking on a surface of tiny pebbles, because my bare skin blistered in the heat.

I got up and there was a demon there just sitting on its throne, and these gates were not golden like the ones above, they were red and I assumed they were hot like the ground.

I passed through the gates and I spun around and punched the demon standing there; my fist slammed straight through his back and came out the other side as nothing but bones and muscles, all my flesh having burned away under the raw heat he carried inside him—and I would be lying if I said it didn't hurt. It hurt me so, *so* much, but since I was already dead, my skin grew back rather fast, and that hurt even worse, I kid you not.

I took his gleaming scythe and went right into the bowels of Hell. There I fought many diabolical demons on my journey. I fought and killed them, and when I swung that fucking stolen sickle, a red flame trailed it as it moved through the air, like magic. It was epic, the battle I faced and fought and won, and demons fanned out around me, red and fiery and fierce, and hurled fireballs in my direction, but I ducked and weaved and dodged and stabbed and slashed those fuckers, and demons were falling at the wayside; all around me they were dropping dead. I fought hundreds of them and they just kept coming at me. Soon enough though, the Devil Himself showed up, floating downward on a glistening red fireball, and I fought him too, and I won—boy did I!

Victory was mine: I stole back my soul and left Hell on my own. Once having my soul restored, I floated up up and up and kept going until I was back home....

Anti-Passion

I followed my heart and where did it get me? But fucked up with a needle in my arm. I lived fast, faster than most, but slower than the hardcore Punks that I truly admired. All I wanted was more and you bet I took it I stole it and I cheated to get it and then I just took more. My life felt slippery, like I was tripping and falling flat on my face but the plunge kept getting deeper and deeper and I thought it would be forever before I connected with the ruts and stone awaiting me at the bottom of my plunge, waiting for me to splatter crash and splash all the way back to the nowhere lands. This anger and boredom and jaded sensation wrapped me up in a web of vines and I tried to break out but it only squeezed me tighter in its grasp, gripping me like a vice. This anti-passion was engrained so deeply in my veins, twisting me and driving me insane. Walking through the river against the stream I felt no pain no joy no understanding no ploy just a desire for more.... I ripped and flailed and stabbed and yelled and I fought the devil and he fought back and I was buried alive in a grave brimming with 3-foot-long maggots nibbling on my eyes my skin my toenails and I flipped and flopped and ran and flittered and I dipped and dropped and I was going fuckkkkkkin maaddddd!...!

Ode to Facebook, Part 2

A Dead Culture/
      A Dead-Ended World/
            With These Exploitation Vultures/
                  Whatcha Gonna Do?...

Back when I was angry, young, and drunk

a photo of me from age nineteen or twenty drunk at the Newton Highlands train station at night

W.J.: I've gotten drunk on that saltbox in Newton Highlands many a time....

ME: Yeah, I know, I have a lot of memories there too. I got drunk there for the first time, did drugs there for the first time, I even had sex there for the first time.

ME: Kidding, of course. I don't know why I decided to say that, but it's said.

W.J.: No shame in that. I think all rebellious Newton teens (that I know, anyway) got up to scandalous things at that train stop. I remember taking the train home with you one time and you repeatedly tried to convince me to get off the train with you and I just wanted to go home and sleep and then you fell off the train onto your face on the pavement in front of the saltbox and the T-driver asked me if you were ok and I said you were fine but was too shitfaced to actually check on you. Then again I bet you were too shitfaced to even remember this.

ME: I remember that night. Now I vaguely remember who you are. I remember there were two girls with me the night I fell off the train, I just can't remember their faces or who they were. My face was so fucked up after that. I crawled over to the wall and sat there and fell asleep, and my old crack dealer came by and helped me home. I think. He was a friend long before he started dealing anyway. I had welts and scars covering every inch of my face. Cuz I landed right on my face. But I've done worse damage to myself, like when I tumbled down the staircase, which has happened more than once, and put my face through the wall at the bottom.

ME: We were on our way back from Harvard Sq., right?

ME: I'm kinda surprised I still have a face, after all the damage I'd done to it.

W.J.: Omg now I feel really guilty for not getting off the train and helping you out that night, sorry :(you were also trying to take me home to, as you so eloquently put it, fuck and I wasn't down and just wanted to get home and sleep so I felt like if I got off the train to help you you'd go back to your oh-so-charming convincing me of "You know why I like you? You're not pretty or cute like other girls, and you actually listen to me. Will you come with me to New York on Thursday?"

W.J.: Lmao yes we were on our way back from Harvard Sq., ariana and nick were with us that night but they were sitting away from us flirting or something and got off the train before your and my stop (mine is Waban) came up and when you fell, sorry I didn't check on your face, I feel guilty now that I know you got some serious damage from the tumble. You were also trying to convince me to blow you on the train lmao I passed, sorry. That might have also added to me being hesitant to get off and come to your rescue.

W.J.: Sorry if this isn't ok for a fb status and would have been more appropriate for a message. You can delete it if you want.

ME: Don't feel guilty. I was a jerk, and I wouldn't have helped me if I were you. Shit was crazy back then.

ME: And I actually did go to New York, I think. Andrew and I went to this all day Punk show.

W.J.: I was 15 and too scared to cus I had just met you a few days before lmao. We bought a two gallon jug of Sunny D, poured a bunch out and then poured a handle of vodka into it and you me nick and ariana killed it pretty fast. I lost my shoes that night.

ME: You were only fifteen, shit. I was in my twenties. Wow, I was a prick. It's okay, though, it probably wouldn't have happened if you came home with me anyway. I probably just would have passed out or not been able to get it up or just done something equally or more embarrassing.

W.J.: Lmao it's ok I didn't disclose my age so you're not a creeper don't worry about it I just find it amusing.

W.J.: Seriously don't sweat it these stories were told light heartedly. I'm not trying to rip on you or embarrass you, my behavior was equally... Alcoholic-y.

ME: No, I'm enjoying talking about all this and when I say I was a prick, I'm only saying it light-heartedly too, because if anything, I've gotta look back and laugh. It's like this song by the band Negative Trend: "I Can Laugh About It Now."

W.J.: I can laugh about almost all of it now, too :) except the things I did that ruined people's days/weeks, severe property damage, severe cruelty to people, causing fights while drunk for the fun of it, thievery, etc… Can't laugh about those things. Only repent and dwell.

Hate Your Neighbor

Revel in your
nastiness.
Celebrate your
hate.

If it keeps you occupied
then who am I to say
you should not
feel this way.

Emotions are a
tricky subject,
a very tricky thing.
They give us
meaning, and they
show us the way.

They get us outta binds,
keep us from getting
stuck.
They keep us alive
and for that,

Jeremy Void

you can go and get
fucked.

We need a little
turmoil in
our miserable lives.
We need a little
controversy
to keep us alive.

Art is fueled by misery,
fueled by unhappiness alike.
Artists don't thrive on smiles,
nor do we live off of
kindness.

So I say:

Revel in your
nastiness.
Celebrate your
hate.

Do it for the sake of
everything that is
just a little bit irate.

We hate to live,
live to hate,
and for that
we can all be

grateful.

Fuck Dating

I don't want a girlfriend, I want a trophy.

Remember what happened last night?
Neither do I

Last night I had a dream about soggy hotdogs encrusted with raspberry jelly and I ate the hotdogs, got jelly smeared all around my lips, and with a napkin I wiped the jelly away but ... *poof!* ... the napkin turned into a giant lizard growing larger and larger by the minute. I stepped back in shock as the lizard reached epic heights. It looked me in the eye and said, Jimmy!—some reason in the dream my name was Jimmy—it said, Jimmy Boid, and cocked its head back with striking speed and precision and with that its necked crunched which made me think of thick, hairy strands of confetti; I don't know why, it just did. And out of its eyes came these silver lavish rays that hit the ground and cut straight through. The giant lizard, looming over me with silver laser beams spraying from its eyes, it said, Dance for me, Jimmy. So I danced. I danced nervously; just wobbled and tapped my feet to avoid the menacing sting of those bright silver rays as they zoomed straight toward me, aiming to hit me but my feet were too quick and slippery; or maybe he was just trying to frighten me, I don't know. So I danced and lasers came at me and then stopped suddenly and the lizard cocked its head back again and let out a deep, hollow guffaw that echoed in the mountainside. Did I mention I was in the mountains? Well, I was in the mountains, probably during the days of the Wild West, cuz I noticed I had two six-shooters holstered at each hip and I drew the one on my left with my right hand as fast as lightning, pulled it straight out, cocked the hammer, and with a cataclysmic crack of epic echoing velocity that reverberated through the empty desert and in between the mountains, a bullet ripped through the barrel just spinning and I saw it spin almost in slow motion as it went forward and then immediately curved upward which shocked me completely and then zeroed in on the lizard's giant red eyeball on the right side of its face. With a squishy, sucking sound, like that of a slashed tired being ripped apart as the knife was removed from the tear in the rubber, the bullet jetted through the lizard's eye, and the ground quaked, and the lizard stopped guffawing and turned and stared at me through one working eye and another eye leaking thick purple puss that was just drooping down its face, it looked at me and said, You won, Jimmy, and then exploded and thick, hairy strands of confetti came flying out of it like fireworks, curving through the sky, flittering and squirming, and I smiled cuz I knew all along that the lizard was nothing but confetti. And that was the day the Wild West had won.

An Ideal

I know who I am, but if I told you, you'd think I'd be lying.

Some people think I'm hard.
Some people think I'm soft.
Some people think I'm cold.
Some people think I'm hot.

I know who I am, but if I told you, you'd think I'd be lying.

Society

It would be a lot easier to be myself if I was a likable person, not so detestable, but a bit more sociable, well-versed in manors and social conduct and easy to get along with. But no, I'm a repulsive little rat fink who lurks in the shadows and watches as you get your throat cut by that psychopath who lives around the block, you know the one. I'm sneaky and conniving, a cretin a ghoul a kid with no class who only wants someone to understand him but I cannot achieve social bonding if I only be myself. I'm no good, a social failure, and I know rejection like I know my own little big toe. But anyway, your society is a joke.

I Am Jeremy Void

Why are you so mad at me

What did I   e v e r   do to you

Listen to me   please

Stop talking   and
         listen

For fucks sake   **I**
                              am
                          Jeremy   *Void*

I am not crazy
I am not selfish

I am not lazy
Nor am I   a fucking hellion

                              I
                              am
                          Jeremy   *Void*

Stop yelling at me
Stop your senseless
        ranting & raving

I dont deserve this kind of treatment

I dont deserve this shit

Jeremy Void

STOPPIT
PLEASE, stoppit

Stop　　　　　Stop　　　　　Stop
Stop Stop Stop Stop Stop Stop Stop Stop Stop

and
leave me
alone

                                        if you know whats good for you!

P L E A S E

The New

It's a new day, only <u>new</u> is no longer in my vocabulary. The same old same old, yawn!, boring, old <u>news</u>, blah blah blah. I should hire someone to stick me in the ass with a hot poker everytime I get stagnant. Just a poke, and I'll leap forward and yodel as loud as my lungs can take. It'd keep life interesting, or painful. Interesting, *and* painful.

Face-Time

Your fate is dilapidated, a crumbling, destroyed face that clenches up and kisses the damaged demon, the god of blasphemous actions, death and destruction over yonder, and you're shouting, pounding the steel barricades, screaming till your face disintegrates into steaming-hot mounds of pus just bubbling up and dissipating into cloudy crud that your mother and father eat hungrily for supper, they kiss their plastic plates and hurl them, spinning and crashing, into the blood-stained brick oven that explodes when the door snaps closed and the walls crumble, and soon enough you're running, running for your life, running just to die, your arms flailing as your feet, kicking the defeated stadium beneath you, launch you straight into outer space, to never be seen again———because your fate is dilapidated, the end....

3AM

3AM

    I saw the firetrucks spraying lights,
    red and blue, red and blue, going
    round and round, a fire in the distance
    a fire in the distance   FIRE!

3AM

    The snow falls, sprinkles down,
    like I'm in a snow globe, alone,
    in the dark. I hold out my hands
    and whirl, basking in the snowflakes.
    They surround me, like a tsunami.
    I spin and laugh and frolic. I'm happy.
        alone

Jeremy Void

3AM

    I go to the store, the clerk
    hassles me like I'm a common crook.
    His dastardly smile, like he suspects
    something of me—maybe he's right.
    maybe maybe maybe
    Years ago I robbed the place blind.
    maybe
    They didn't know what hit them.
    maybe

    The store clerk sees me and asks
    if I need help.

    I need help.

3AM

    I buy more fuel at the store.
    A couple Kickstarts and a couple
    packs of cigarettes to last me
    the night.

3AM

    I feel alive, living
    alone
    in a dream, everything's
    surreal because I feel like
    I'm the last man left alive.
    Everyone's sleeping and

    I'm alone.

Listening to X's "Nausea"

Nothing like nodding off in the corner of a dark room while X's "Nausea" plays from somewhere far, far away, but close enough to drift away on a pink cloud held up by their stark lyrics.

An Artist

I don't want to be an artist anymore.

All the pain discomfort
                 and alienation
that comes with creating art

is sometimes too hard to bear.

Untitled

I won't remember you when I'm famous.

Coffee Shop Irony

Just read my poem "The TR*TH" to a couple high school kids outside of the Coffee Exchange. It's funny, my favorite poet d. a. levy got arrested for doing the same. Charged with contributing to the delinquency of minors. Thanks God it's not the '60s anymore.

The World Was Mine
but I stomped on its head

If I told you how I truly felt, well you know how that goes: Now this person hates me. If I told you the truth skewed by own beliefs, well you know how that goes: I lose another friend. If I spelled it out to you in blood and guts and fed it to you on a silver platter, well you know how that goes: I'd have nobody left. In the end all I've got is me, becuz the world hates this man I've become. The world hates the man I can be. The world hates when I live truthfully. I believe that art is the truth, I believe that true art holds no bounds, I believe a lot of things, but when I live true to those beliefs, well you know how that goes: I end up all alone. I'm a sadist. I use self-expression as a way to channel my hateful ways. But in the end it all boils down to one last thing, living in an existence ridden with diseased minds and diseased freaks, and I'm the creep? If I told you how I truly felt, well guess what, I must be insane....

Anarchists for Censorship

This cunt's trying to censor me, saying he'll stomp my face in if I continue to spread this "propaganda"; and then he tells me he's an anarchist.

Anyone see anything wrong with this picture?

No Edge

Most alcoholics/drug addicts live on the edge. My problem was that I didn't have an edge to live on, cuz I'd fallen off it at a very early age. I spent the greater part of my life falling. Falling to my bottom. I kicked and flailed, trying to grab hold of something, but there was nothing I couldn't break.... Everything that came my way and I managed to sink my teeth into snapped like a twig beneath the weight of my plunge. It was hopeless!

Paranoid Much?

Do you ever have those days when everyone is just staring at you?

A Terminal Nobody

     I'm a terminal nobody

              a terminal outcast

a terminal terminal terminal
    loser

I played music
    that nobody listened to

I wrote poetry
    that nobody read

I created art
    that nobody saw

WHAT SHOULD I DO NEXT?

Sometimes sometimes sometimes
    it feels so damn hopeless....

Bored Again

Nothing's interesting. Yawn!

The Flame Dance

The flame dances as death comes nearer.
The electricity coursing through keeps it alive,
and getting dearer.
The other candle, the one representing life—
the life I have, the life that's dying—
it fades out and is forgotten about.
The death flame grows and glowers.
The life inside me ebbs as I suck in
another drag.
Another cup of coffee, another bad habit.
Another wasted day, and the death flame leers.
It dances in laughter, taunting me.
The flame of life is snuffed ... out!

The Phoenix Bookstore

Calling all those in Burlington, VT. As of tonight the Phoenix Bookstore will be carrying four or five of my books.

The Phoenix Bookstore in Rutland will not because it's a "family store," said the old hag who works there.

Bloody sirens Too much Too wild

stop. images flashing. things are moving. stop stop stop, it doesnt stop. im running, im wild, im free. that girl over there is so damn hot & i watch her i wink i see her there & she glares right back: a murderous vision. too many drugs, i cant slow down. im strung out & im falling, but the sky is coming apart. im strutting & i feel good, too good for this pointless verse. there arent enough words in the english drawl to say it all. im rising & im falling, & it feels so good to be a villain, you know.

EVERYONE IS A CUNT

I got thrown out of this feminist Punk show for wearing a jacket that said EVERYONE IS A CUNT.

DIS-

... disable ...
    ... disabuse ...
... disaccustom ...
    ... disadvantage ...
... disaffect ...
    ... disaffirm ...
... disagree ...
    ... disallow ...
... disannul ...
    ... disappear ...
... disappoint ...
    ... disapprobation ...

... disarm ...
        ... disarrange ...
... disarray ...
        ... disaster ...
... disavow ...
        ... disbelief ...
... disburden ...
        ... discard ...
... discern ...
        ... discharge ...
... disclaim ...
        ... discolor ...
... discomfit ...
        ... discomfort ...
... discommend ...
        ... discommode ...
... discompose ...
        ... disconcert ...
... disconnect ...
        ... disconsolate ...
... discontent ...
        ... discontinue ...
... discord ...
        ... discountenance ...
... discourage ...
        ... discourse ...
... discourteous ...
        ... discredit ...
... discreet ...
        ... discrepancy ...
... discrete ...
        ... discriminate ...
... discursive ...
        ... disdain ...

Smash a Lightbulb: Poetry for Lowlifes

… disease …
      … disembarrass …
… disembody …
      … disembogue …
… disembowel …
      … disenchant …
… disencumber …
      … disengage …
… disentail …
      … disentangle …
… disestablish …
      … disesteem …
… disfavor …
      … disfigure …
… disfranchise …
      … disgorge …
… disgrace …
      … dishonest …
… dishonor …
      … disincline …
… disinfect …
      … disingenuous …
… disinherit …
      … disintegrate …
… disinter …
      … disjoin …
… dislike …
      … dislocate …
… dislodge …
      … disloyal …
… dismal …
      … dismantle …
… dismast …
      … dismay …

... dismember ...
      ... dismiss ...
... disobedience ...
      ... disoblige ...
... disorder ...
      ... disorganize ...
... disorient ...
      ... disparate ...
... disparity ...
      ... dispassionate ...
... dispatch ...
      ... dispel ...
... disperse ...
      ... dispirit ...
... displace ...
      ... displease ...
... disport ...
      ... dispose ...
... dispossess ...
      ... dispraise ...
... disproportion ...
      ... disprove ...
... dispute ...
      ... disqualify ...
... disquiet ...
      ... disregard ...
... disrelish ...
      ... disrepair ...
... disreputable ...
      ... disrespect ...
... disrobe ...
      ... disrupt ...
... dissatisfaction ...
      ... disseize ...

Smash a Lightbulb: Poetry for Lowlifes

... dissemble ...
  ... disseminate ...
... dissent ...
  ... dissertation ...
... disserve ...
  ... dissever ...
... dissident ...
  ... dissimilar ...
... dissimulation ...
  ... dissipate ...
... dissociate ...
  ... dissoluble ...
... dissolute ...
  ... dissolve ...
... dissonance ...
  ... dissuade ...
... distaff ...
  ... distain ...
... distance ...
  ... distaste ...
... distemper ...
  ... distend ...
... distill ...
  ... distinct ...
... distinguish ...
  ... distort ...
... distract ...
  ... distrait ...
... distraught ...
  ... distress ...
... distrust ...
  ... disturb ...
... disunion ...
  ... disuse....

Censorship

The Nazis had killed lots and lots of people, but censorship has killed more. My favorite poet, d. a. levy, was shot to death because of his provocative poetry. Not to mention, the Nazi killings were a form of censorship too.

Ignorant Minds

Ignorant minds think alike
        and that is why ...
the world
        as we know it
is going
        straight
                to hell!

Untitled

You say nightmare / I say wet dream....

Notes of an Insomniac

i cant sleep im seeing shit things are talking to me noises are rumbling up & fuck my mind is shut my head is fucked stuck & it sucks & i wonder do you pleasure yourself before you go to bed or first thing in the morning cuz thats what i do i do it all & then some i do everything w/ everyone only theyre too conceded to realize it this is rock & roll this Punk rock this is called yo <u>mama</u> no stopping me no telling me to stop cuz i jus dont fuckin listen to anyone BURN THIS COUNTRY TO THE GROUND!!!!

Rappers & Their Bling

Since when are there raging block parties in the ghetto, where half-naked girls dance atop shiny sports cars and mega surround-sound speakers are mounted up on tall stands and hundreds of people are hanging out drinking fucking million-dollar bottles of champagne? And there's a rapper wearing lots and lots of gold—gold teeth, gold rings, a gold necklace, and a fucking wide-rimmed gold clock dangling over his chest—and the music is extremely loud, and nobody in the neighborhood gets mad and complains, nobody who has to work the following day just to eat one lousy meal is screaming out the window, yelling at these rich morons parading around in their million-dollar outfits and saying this is where they grew up. Nobody is telling them to shut the fuck up, you stinkin' posers; I got work in the morning; I'm really poor and I really got work in the morning so I can earn my keep which you clearly don't have to do, judging from the flashy hubcaps glimmering beneath your lowriders; so please, *please* shut the fuck up and go back to your rich suburban homes and let me sleep in peace. Go back to Malibu, goddammit; back to Beverly Hills, or wherever it is that breeds you stupid fucking posers——and this old woman who has her hair in curls is waving a rolling pin out the window scolding these turds that don't belong here in the first place; she calls them wannabes one last time and slams the window shut with an angry *thump*.
Tell me where this exists! Please! I really wanna know! And if you do, I promise I won't laugh at you and ask if you're on crack. I won't! I promise!

Untitled

I'm a cliché
I'm a poser
Look at me,
I've got a bloody nose.

I just don't care

[No Name], no offense, but I don't care I don't care I don't care. My writing is getting better and better and better, and do you know why?—because I fucking love to write and writing loves me, and I will do it regardless of whether you like it because you're right, it's not about fame and acknowledgement, it's about the craft and I love every fucking bit of the craft. The fact that people enjoy my writing feels good and I can't deny it and I'm happy to know that people are reading it, but that's not why I do it, because IF that was why, I probably wouldn't do it because again, you are right, I am not a celebrity. And what's funny is, you've judged my writing on a very superficial basis because you've only seen the small glimpses of what I've posted here and you haven't delved into the longer stuff, the actual stories I've written that have characters I develop and move and bring to life. I USED to post longer stuff on Facebook but then I stopped because I realized if I want to sell books—which is something I do want, in fact—I have to start with the simple and superficial stuff. So your comments above are superficial too and I don't care I don't care I don't care. I SIMPLY DON'T FUCKING CARE. I love to write and writing loves me and the fact that you don't like it doesn't change a goddamn thing!

d. a. levy

<u>Jeremy Void</u>   who is your favorite poet?

It used to be Richard Hell, you know, the bassist of Television, the original singer of the Heartbreakers (not Tom Petty and the Fartbreakers, no; I'm talking the REAL Heartbreakers, the only Heartbreakers that broke my heart when the singer died of a heroin overdose (R.I.P.)—you know, Johnny Thunders. Richard Hell was the original singer and then he broke loose and started up the Voidoids, which I think are better anyway, and then Johnny Thunders moved in to the Heartbreakers like a greedy pirate and sang such lovely songs as "Born to Lose"; songs as miraculous and devastatingly honest and terribly brilliant as "Pirate Love" and "All by Myself," along with many more classics from his album *LAMF,* which stands for "Like a Mother Fucker."
But back to Richard Hell. He was my favorite poet way back when—keyword, "was," as in past-tense—when I was much less experienced with the underground world of art and literature (but don't get me wrong, I still hold his writing and his music and his everything else that made him RICHARD HELL very close to my heart, for his music was the perfect soundtrack for a drug-fueled existence like my own; and his written work was like an open book depicting the mess in which I exist day in and day out—you know what I'm talking about: that narcissistic wasteland that all great artists find themselves in when they take an honest look at their lives and for the first time ever realize that they are all alone—so alone it's both sad and titillating and so detrimentally marvelous and scary that it gives me a hard-on just to think about it). Anyway, where was I?

Just so you know, I have not slept in over seventy-two hours because I find I'm much more creative when I'm deprived of sleep like I am right now. But this morning the ideas aren't flowing from me like they had before, they're not pouring from my fingertips as my muse bangs out a rhythm on her magical bongo drums to generate ambient wonder and amazement that matches my present state of craziness.

I had an honest vision of where I was going with this, but I'm not feeling it right now—it seems to be going nowhere and now I'm giving up.   Maybe later, who knows?

A Misunderstanding

I'm wondering: Is it my problem if someone misunderstands what I wrote? I am a writer and it's therefore my job to explain my point properly. Or is it the reader's problem, in that maybe they adlibbed a bit or read too far into it or something? Or could it be that we're both equally to blame? I'm sure the last option is possible, but I feel like that's probably rare.

Lethal Erection
sung with Lethal Erection

All drugged up, out in the heat,
ready for a fight, ready for defeat.
Out on the street with an erect mind,
a lethal voice, and a fuck you sign.
I got no time to think things through,
cuz the life I live are the choices I choose.

I'm a fucked-up kid, in a fucked-up world.
An erection hard enough to kill a girl.
Lethal....
I'm a fucked-up man, in a fucked-up town.
The people I see are going down.
....Erection

I don't care if you look at me,
cuz it don't matter what you see.
All that matters is I'm a fuckin screw,
and later tonight I'll be fucking you

I'm a fucked-up kid, in a fucked-up world.
An erection hard enough to kill a girl.
Lethal....
I'm a fucked-up man, in a fucked-up town.
The girls I see are going down.
....Erection

{available on YouTube}

Punk Rock

Before AA I was lying on my couch listening to a CD I made—999, the Clash, the Adverts, Cock Sparrer, the Adicts—and I was thinking, *I still like Punk rock, definitely like it, maybe even love it*—no, just like it—but I can't relate to it as much because I'm not a teenager anymore, however still bored, frustrated, not AS angry, immature, a little wild—not like I was—and crazy, but the music doesn't speak to me like it used to; so I threw my Monster at the wall, making things right: Punk rock.

Dark Places

Most people avoid dark places
       I don't.
It's like they're afraid of
what they'll see

what they'll find
who they'll be
when they come out the other side/

      Me, I embrace the dark
      I welcome dark forces with
           open arms,
      cuz if you look close enough into
      dark places
      you'll find the truth
      glimmering like a ghoulish rumination
      so bright and vivacious
      it makes me feel alive
      like I'll never
         be the same
            again....

Not in Kansas Anymore

It's funny, in Boston all the time I'll meet someone and then never see them again. In Rutland, that never happens. You meet someone and then start seeing them *every*where.

A Recipe for Disaster

Going nowhere for too long.
And Now I Sing the Same Sad Song.
Why me? Why me?
It's a fruitless existence, lower

than low.
Screaming at a wall, chasing my own tail.
Climbing thorns.
The ground drops out from beneath me.
MY WHOLE EXISTENCE is a joke.
My day will never come.
It's a joke, so humorous.
I bet god's having a laugh.
It's All I Can Ask For.
What's the point of going on?
What's the point of surviving?
Why not just die?
Why not jump, jump, jump off a cliff?
Why not start a fight with a chimpanzee?
Why not rob a bank? Why not kick a baby?
So what? Nothing means shit anymore.
Hahahahahahahahahahahahhahhahhhhhahahwdgghdpbgbowge!!!!!!!!!!
KILL YOURSELF now—

Art in the Park

I found out yesterday that the Chaffee Art Center* screens what art they allow in Art in the Park. No wonder all the shit they sell there is so lame.

---

* The one and only art museum in Rutland, VT.

My Hell

Every girl I meet wants to fuck me, every guy I meet wants to fight me. I say things I regret but constantly tell myself I meant it. Stand strong and proud and turn the other cheek on your fellow man is my motto, and yet I'm so quick to help out the victim of persecution which I guess makes me a hypocrite, but a good hypocrite, a hypocrite who pushes negative vibes but acts nicely and kindly to everybody. I hate the nice me and wish to be the mean me but the truth of the matter is I couldn't hurt a fly, unless it bites me and then I will be the first to smash it dead. I'm a typical borderline case: I hate everybody but I'm always lonely and desperate for attention. I'm the first to tell you how much I love you, but deep down inside I hate you and want you dead, only if you died I'd miss you terribly, cuz what's the saying? Distance makes the heart grow stronger and fonder and I end up beating myself up (and off) until you're here and when I get you I toss you out the window hoping you land on your head. Ask Samantha, who I'm sure you know, all about it and she'll tell you she's been the victim of my insanity time and time again, but she loves me anyway and keeps coming back and I keep pulling her my way—except for one time, when she did the pulling for a change—and since she's so quick to forgive me all the time I feel as if she's my perfect girlfriend and I wanna marry her, unless I kill her first in which case I will cry and cry until I meet somebody else and then I forget all about her. A week passes and everybody's gone and I'm alone and beating myself black and blue at how stupid I was for destroying such a good thing. But soon after, I find something else I can stick my dick into, stir it around like it's a pot of stew, pull out, and shoot. That's my life. Welcome to Hell!

The Muse

When the muse is calling ... you've gotta pick up the phone. Because the muse hates being ignored. Or at least mine does....

Disappointed Again

I'm usually more disappointed when I'm right than when I'm wrong. I usually hope I'm wrong but it's rare that I am. Will someone just prove me wrong, please? I have such a pessimistic view of the world and I'm always right and I hate being right because my views **SUCK** and I do not want them to come true; but they always do....

Part 3
Solution:
Piss Everybody Off!

Part 3
Solution: Piss Everybody Off!

A Poem I Wrote

So blank,
like a piece of paper.
My body's numb
in a bathtub, of ice.
My thoughts,
they're depleted.
So bored,
I think I'll eat it.
The time is, I don't know.
I just don't care.
Death is a lumberjack
hacking at a tree trunk.

Untitled

Someday everyone is going to hate me.

One of My Earliest Memories

        I was sick
        my mom fed me some baby Tylenol
                you know, the recommended dose
        and then I asked,
           "Can I have more?"

My mom said no
and when asked she went on to explain:
    "Because then when you need it, it won't work."

And that's how I lived my life:
always needing more of any- and everything that made me feel better than how I was already feeling.

I'm a Poser—so what?
    What the hell have you done??

It's like, everybody's a hypocrite, right? In which case I'd much rather own my hypocrisy than go around believing the lie that I'm better than that. So last night when the girl said she wasn't a poser, I couldn't help but laugh. You see, we're all posers, squandering this universe in search of ourselves, lost and troubled—nobody knows who they are in the end, we're all sick and crazy and so utterly LOST, and nobody is better than this - - than that——nobody is immune to the human disease.... It's called living in a commercialized existence, a world run by corporate giants and these bullshit advertisements on the TV, on the INTERNET, looming over the highway—everywhere you go, there's an ad trying to sell you IPods, McDonald's, a brand-new television set so that you won't miss all the latest advertisements as the corporations beam them into your skull through Blue Tooth technology. It's impossible to not be lost, it's why I avoid TV, I don't watch movies, and I don't follow the news - - - - but still, they're trying to sell you cereal that gives you aids with each mouthful. I'm lost, I'm a poser, I'm hopelessly devoted to destroying myself.... So fuckin what????

It's the Morning

It's the morning, I've gotta slow my brain some, maybe with a stream of words as they pour from my fingertips and rack the keyboard to tap out letter after letter, and it's the morning.

It's the morning, I made it through the night, I'm alive but barely. I'm restless and I'm scattered and my brain is a mishmash of images and I'm lost in an endless torturous fucked-up chain of thought. Get me out of this cage before I take your name down with me on my plunge, grip the wall, grip the ceiling, I'm flailing and kicking and screaming, and it's the morning.

Anyway, where was I? Didn't sleep last night, filled up my mind with retarded things and now I'm here to transcribe it for you. It's the morning and I feel so useless. Anyway, where was I?

That's right it's the morning, I've got nothing to say cuz I said it all already, hashed it out for you on page after page, another futile stream-of-conscious to bore you with, and it's the morning.

One night down, a lifetime of more to go—the morning has a unique smell to it too, like rabid death, like goddammit I can't believe I'm still alive, another whiff sniff and snort of glue and I guess it all gets better, and my life ebbs away … and it's the morning.

It's the morning and I feel so bored. Filled my time with wordless enterprises and now I'm stuck in a relentless turbulence that grips me and spins me and turns me all the way around, and it's the morning and it's the morning, and soon I'll be upside down, and it's the morning. Goddamit it's the morning.

Hurray it's the morning.

Fuck me it's the morning.

I'm so glad the night is over and the morning is here and I can waste my time in the daylight as opposed to the eerie dark of the night and it's the morning it's the morning it's the morning.

Fuck me it's got me again.

My Soul

I'd sell you my soul if you wanted it
but I doubt that you do.

Anti-Fashion

PUNK ROCK

It has nothing to do with
SPIKES
    and
    MOHAWKS

PAINTED LEATHER
    CHAINS
and
    TATTOOS

The fashion is irrelevant.

TAKE IT OFF

cruising

in the car with Bell right now coming back from the show in Rhode Island, gonna crash at his pad for the night because by the time we reach Quincy MA the train will have stopped running, in fact it already has. because it is in fact 2AM and they would have stopped at about 12:30 AM, roughly; and we're just cruising down the highway, got the Lower Class Brats playing on the stereo, and everything is cool, no worries, no cares in the world because life is good like how it should be; I'm heading back Vermont on Cape Air tomorrow afternoon - - fun fun fun!

The Process

Writing, for me, is like vomiting, only everything slows down and I can see the vomit coming out at a snail's pace and before it hits the page I clean it up and dress it nicely so that instead of vomit, <u>ART HITS THE PAGE</u>.

I Don't Wanna Die

When a door is slammed, a window is smashed, and I cut myself on the jagged glass.

I emerge on the battlefield.

Where'd everybody go? I ask as I man my rifle in a gray mist amid all the dead bodies.

The war was fought and has gone away.

With nobody left to fight I raise my rifle and press the muzzle to my—wait, I don't wanna die.

I hold onto my sanity like a crying child, patting its back and saying, *Everything will be okay.*

Spewing lies that dissipate before my eyes, I fall to my knees and cry, praying that God will take away this pain, saying, *Everything will be okay.*

I rest my head on my pillow and pray another day will make me sane—

because the war was fought and has gone away, and I'm too late.

But another day is coming and I'm running to my bed and set my head on my pillow and pray another day will make me sane, because everything will be okay.

Smash a Lightbulb: Poetry for Lowlifes

where am i going ?

where am i going ? i am going somewhere , hopefully , but probly nowhere . i want to go anywhere , be anyone , & do anything ; but chances are , as history has shown time & time again , the floor will rise up fast & smack me in the jaw . im heading that way , way downward , into a downward plunge . the wall wont break my fall this time , ill go crashing straight thru , an eruption of concrete as i continue my descent .

where am i going ? you ask . i thrust my index finger out in front of me & say , NOT THERE ! i know youll be quite perplexed by my response , for i am rather perplexed w/ my reaction . i wanted to say , That Way ! i wanted to say , Im Going That Way , but you know , i never do get what i want .

truth be told , i want success . but what is success ? for me its the absence of a bottle , the lack of chemical stimulants , chemical downers . i only need life to bring me down , thats all . but ill need something to lift me back up , thats for sure .

i want more than what the promises guarantee ; i want a life that doesnt revolve around the removal of something , but a life that obtains anything . i dont want anti-goals , i want real ambitions .

but i have none , so its easier to hope for something not to happen . easier than wishing it wud . but all this wishful thinking will only bring me down , & like i sed , ill need something to lift me back up . something that i cant have . something that is dangerous in my hands .

so im stuck . im stuck fucked & it sucks . i want something , really i do , but the only thing i can think of in this dire time of wanting will make the ground tip sideways & again the wall will break my fall , but it wont .

& so i give up .

& so its no use .

& so i stop wishing & start living for a change . now , theres an idea .

Untitled

People are all the same. We paint ourselves with words—I do it too. I mean I'm a writer after all. We all have images of who we should be, and we tell others as if that's who we are. But in the end we're no different than anyone else. Sick, fucked-up individuals who want to use, manipulate, and destroy. We hate, we divide, and we conquer. The point of life: power. Finding power, destroying power, taking power. We're all the same, everyone's the same. We hate, we fuck, and we kill. That's the name of the game. I'm a very tolerant person, I tolerate everyone, but fuck you anyway!

Sorry

Sorry I don't paint the walls blue with hope,
but splatter bloody bricks through the windows of destructive art.

Sorry I don't make you feel good, like everything is oh so wonderful in life and it's never been better and I'm pushing and pushing through the helpless swamps on my way to be great,
but instead set the swamps on fire and run through the flames naked as Twin Towers everywhere collapse in spurts of smoke and steam and this—this—THIS—is my reason to live.

Sorry I'm not ten-feet tall with a gut full of food and a mind that ruminates relentlessly about the needs of others, and and and—you know—
because I'm selfish and stubborn and yet I'm doing my best to help out others who come my way; but even so your existence doesn't usually cross my mind unless you're right there in front of me.

Sorry my poetry doesn't spin webs of phony prayers of hope and fabricated wonder that brings you joyful tears, but instead it's like a submachine gun as the bullets tear into a condemned man and he's screaming and crying as I pull the trigger....

Trust me, I am good and I'm doing the best I can, and I'm getting better every day I set down one foot after another, and I'm plowing my own way through a shit-filled existence with liars who will cut you down before you step one foot out your door, and I'm living honestly and I give and I give, although you wouldn't know anything about it because I don't vocalize my acts of goodness—wait, I just did.

In short: Sorry I'm not a liar.

Pandora's Box

Once, this girl told me to punch her in the face. So I went and punched her in the face. Then she got mad at me for punching her in the face.

Anonymous

there are jellybeans
in my bag
they snap crack & rattle
everytime
i shift its position.
people might think the clutter
of clacks
is really jellyfish.
but then they dont clack
now do they?

nor do they smack
wobble or break.
people are filing in the door right now.
meek faces
eyes like tombs
hearts that shine,
crumbling ribcages
they find their seats briskly
& snap innocently to attention.
a fat man reads
his stomach made of confetti
i wonder what
it wud look like
if i dug it out with a shovel.
more people come thru the door
more hearts forlorn
more lost souls
minds depleted
succumbing to diseases.
a translucent disco ball
hangs & shines
from somewhere far away
turning on a unique golden string
as a woman sings about
regret
spreads her wings & flies away.
she looks like a butterfly
draped in sin
becoming a caterpillar
wrapped in a dastardly cocoon.
the cocoon breaks & falls
dissolves
   ——& shes gone.
no one sees me tho

Smash a Lightbulb: Poetry for Lowlifes

they cant.
i sit in the back of the room
dreaming about shadows as they
dissolve me in spite.
whered the time go??
my mind is so distraught.
the jellybeans
clicking so silently
they speak to me softly
i know they do
only what they say
is so far beyond my reach
that
my thoughts break
& mutate
& now im hungry for
pig guts & monkey brains.
the shallow masses
reading something gallow
that i cant hear
nor see, it jus is
what it is, but
it isnt, not really;
nothing is....
boy beds girl
girl says ok
but then screams rape
& baffled boy stands there
as sirens wail
& pronounce
evil beyond sin
& they arrive in the blink of a crying eye.
9 messy men
draped like drag queens

each eating 9 M&Ms
pull out 18 9mm guns
as one blasphemous thought
crosses my already baffled head.
boy is shot dead
in the head with one
shiny silver bullet that cuts like
a stick of slimy butter....

No Esteem

Everything I Say Is Wrong, Everything I Do Is Wrong. All I Want Is Wrong. All I Need Is Wrong. My Whole Existence Is Wrong and It's Burning a Hole in My Heart. I Just Want to Be Right, but at What Cost Is Being Right? What's It Worth Because I Know for Me Being Right Means Being Even More Wrong Than Before, so I Take My Heavy Head and I Beat It Against the Wall until I Bleed and then I Look Straight into the Mirror and Ask Myself What Is Wrong with Me, and I Say Through Missing Teeth, Everything.... And Jerk My Head Back and Let a Loogie Fly and Splatter in My Own Fucked-up, Bloody Face.

Not Just Another Poet

I don't seek beauty
I don't seek love
I'm not just another poet
who writes about that kind of stuff

>People are starving
>people are dying
>and all you care about
>is the last guy you fucked

Insomnia As Inspiration

First of all, [No Name], one thing that always helps me get in the swing of things is reading other people's writing. Or you could look at other kinds of art and start with that. Also, about a year ago I started sleeping only every other night and I haven't had writer's block since. I only write the days after not sleeping, but on those days I write so damn much. I mean, I did 5 books in a year's time. I don't recommend not sleeping, though, cuz one of the side effects is for the past year I've been on an emotional roller coaster (which has been driving my writing so much), and before I started this not-sleeping spree, I had mellowed out tremendously.

Sex Is Gay

Sex is gay.
Sex is gay.
I've just got better things to do
than go around town chasing after you.

Sex is gay.
Sex is gay.
The last place you'll find me
is in the wake of a pretty young lady.

I've lost friends.
I've lost acquaintances.
Lost so many more
to this plague of the skin.

Sex is so gay, I don't get it.

Nihilism Reality

It's like, nothing's real; but everything, it all feels like it's there, you know. Like it's right in front of me. I reach my hand out & try to touch it, &—*poof!*—it disappears.   It was never there to begin with.

My reality is only a mere disillusion. It sits there all wonderfully beautiful, but when I will it to go bye-bye, it up & leaves— just like that. Isn't life fun?—I'd say. It's fun but it sucks. It sucks like that whore I picked up in the green-light district, or was that light orange. Either way I'm frequently finding myself quite bored.

I could fly & be happy too, you know—just lift my wings & scoot upward, straight into the sky— but physics can be quite a bitch at times, but only because I believe it to; but without it all things are possible: but but but....

But——nothing!

I knew this girl she hated me. But I changed her mind—boy did I! She fell for me hard & would tell me everyday before she got off the phone that she loved me. I said nothing. She should've still hated me; I know I would've if I were in her shoes; but she was delusional, her reality diluted with butterflies & flowers. She fell for me & landed on her head; I wasn't there to catch her. When we met she had thought I was a scumbag: she told that to my best friend.

When asked I said the reason I never say I LOVE YOU back is because I don't, & just like that I got off the phone>>>>

We broke up because I loved whiskey more than her, is what I had told her before she slapped me five times in the face & then walked off into the night.

Isn't it funny how we perceive reality and how reality tends to deceive us?

Some Peace & Quiet————Finally!!!

The TV is exactly where it ought to be—bashed to pieces and chucked out the window.

Because a busted television set is really a beautiful thing....

It Drives Me Crazy

This drives me crazy. I can't stand when people get a tiny glimpse of me and then think they understand me and my style. No, you haven't even begun to understand me and my style. Like, sometimes people will read a story or a poem by me and think they understand my style, so they throw me a harmless suggestion, like maybe you should practice writing in third-person more so you can get better at that. But I have stories in third-person too. Just because they've only seen one story by me that's in first-person does not mean all my stories are in first-person. It drives me crazy. And vice versa: I show someone a story in third-person and they tell me I should practice writing in first-person more. Like, at the bar last night, this girl who'd seen me read only once was telling me there's a time and place for everything. But I know that. In fact, I know that very well. And every time I perform I try to read the crowd and assess what is best for me to read, I really do. But I can't read minds, and I'm not perfect; and because at the one and only time she'd seen me read I happened to tank it, she assumes I ALWAYS tank, she assumes I don't ever try to read the crowd. She assumes that that tiny glimpse of me says all there is to know. It drives me crazy when people do that.

You see, my mind is like a labyrinth
complete with all sorts of twists and turns, all sorts of dips and rises that wind their way through layer after layer of madness

getting lost is just an unfortunate consequence to having a rather complicated complex
so leave behind your preconceived notions about who you want me to be, and bring a pen and a piece of paper if you wanna take notes, because boy are you in for a surprise....

Untitled

psychosis is in the eye of the beholder

God, Are You Out There?

Why Am I Here?
Why Am I Here?
Why Am I Here?

I've Gotta Get Out
I've Gotta Get Out
I've Gotta Get Out
        of Here Right Now

What's the Point?
I Need to Know
        God, Are You Out There?
        Please Give Me
                the Answers!

                                          If You Don't
                                          If You Can't

Smash a Lightbulb: Poetry for Lowlifes

If You Won't
Tell Me the Answers

Then I Don't Know

Guess This Shotgun Looks Nice
Against my Head

Fits Nice and Firm
Nice and Lovely

and I Bet It Will Blow
Quite a Beautiful Hole
Which Will Bring Me Closer to

the Answers I Seek

God, Please
I'm Begging You to Answer
Me....

GOD
ARE YOU OUT THERE

Right Now

Right now the world is broken, and I fix it with the blunt edge of a sledgehammer. Right now the world is shattered, and I fix it with the crisp point of a pickaxe.

Really, I don't know. Life is happening and I just don't know. I squander this universe in search of some sort of answer, but the only answers I ever get feel like razor blades against my skin—

razors dipped in lemon juice, that is.

Right now the world is fractured, and I fix it with the heel of my boot. The world is damaged, smashed up, trashed, and glimmering with disuse. I stand in the crossfire

I stand in the traffic jam, in the haphazard assortment of nothing. I stand amid the mayhem and I scream

I scream as loud as I can—

This is life. Right now I can honestly say I'm demented, disordered—demented disordered and deranged—and I piece my brain back together with the stammering blade of a jackhammer.

Right now the world is   FUCKED   UP!!!

A Bad Case of the Fuckits!

fuck the rules
fuck the law
fuck the system and everyone
who wants to bring you down
fuck it all
and tear it up
i'm bored and i'm lying
i'm living just to die
what's the point
cuz they'll all just hate you tomorrow
i ain't sold on ideas
ain't a conformist drone

Smash a Lightbulb: Poetry for Lowlifes

ain't a machine the system's tool, a pet
just wanna be me
so fuck the world
and watch it burn
this is our life, our time
let's stand together and set it
bright on fire
i'm unhappy on the fence
i need something more than
what i'm getting
it's the day of judgment
the jury are dead
the judge is suspended
from a cherry tree
the world is ours
so let's live it up
cuz there ain't no laws
that'll catch up with us
i'm bored and i'm a victim
i'm sick of this thing called living
misery is my muse
and i hate everyone
and everything and i will see to it
that it all goes straight to hell
this country is on fire
where are the gas tanks so we can
demolish planet earth in flames
i'm bored and i'm in trouble
i think i'm seeing double
i'm sick and angry this is the day
i take a stand and say
fuck the rules
fuck the law
fuck you because

i'll do it my own way
so fuck off back to
where you belong
and leave me be
and let me have some fucking fun
before my life is done....

cuz it's all done

T'was All My Fault

Have you ever fallen? Have you ever fallen and not stopped? Have you ever fallen and the bottom just keeps getting farther as you plunge into your own destruction....
I know I have. It's the worst, right? When you become like a sponge, sucking dry every life form that crosses your path—it's the worst....

My best friend Andrew—or my old best friend, I should say—was unfortunate enough to cross my path. It's sad. So Sad, it was.
      And I hate myself for it, I hate the way I ruined things, I hate
      the way I extracted energy and used it for my own sick pur-
      poses. It was sick.
           So Sick

He had never done the stuff, he had told me. He had never done cocaine, he had explained, and What Did I Do????——I offered him a free line: Hey, here's one for free. Try this....

Try This!

This was my best friend I'm talking about—our blood strong as diamonds, our bond unbreakable, so fervent it was like it would never tear apart—or so we

thought!———but it did, it broke: I went to Rutland, VT; he stayed in Haverhill, MA, and got married and had kids, and then got divorced and I can't even imagine what happened to the kids after that, probably left in the mother's custody. Probably ... hopefully ... but then again, she's not much more than a trainwreck herself, a drunk a bumb a loser and a mother in the 21st century.
She's just as sick, if not more, and what, 4 kids, 5 kids now, growing up in another American broken home—makes me sad, you know! The state of things.

YOUR LIFE

IF YOUR LIFE IS SO DAMN AWESOME, WHY ARE YOU USING FACEBOOK AND NOT OUT THERE LIVING YOUR AWESOME LIVES????

no more   no less
I say it how I see it

I am a human being
>> no more
>> no less
I feel a multitude of emotions

Some people enjoy the darker stuff because it gives them something to relate to.

While others enjoy the brighter stuff because it pulls them out of the dirty water people typically find themselves knee-deep in when they take an honest look around them.

GET YOUR HEADS OUT OF YOUR ASSES

because this is me
> this is who I am

                                          I am a human being
                                              no more   no less

I'm Back

So glad to be in Boston again. The beautiful city shimmers beneath my feet, I laugh amid the cacophony of noise and lights and cars and high-rise apartments and busybodies working hard and lowlifes not working at all, I stand ten-feet tall looming over the madness that only a place as wonderfully twisted as the big city can hold in its sadistic grasp. I frolic between towering glass buildings, skip gleefully through tunnels, past hobos, homos, junkies, and fairies, running as fast as my feet can carry through crowded roads full of yuppies with brief cases, moms pushing strollers that hold young children, as college boys and girls gather around, passing notes and chatter with one another, laughing their vivacious laughs and posing in their seductive stances, horns blaring cutting through the illuminated passageways, ecstatic traffic jams, bitter old men, crazy old women, loony and talking to imaginary friends, panhandling for their keep.... So glad to be in Boston again.

                                                                      I'm home....

A Tornado   in Rutland??

There's supposed to be a tornado in Rutland tonight. Who wants to go wind surfing with me? ☺

Kill and Let Kill
sung with ELF

Kill and let kill—we want chaos!
Kill and let kill—how can you blame us?
Kill and let kill—total mayhem!
Kill and let kill—it's all that makes sense.

KILL AND LET KILL!!!

Live and let live, is what I plan to do.
I'll let you live whatever life that you choose.
But when you choose to see someone die,
I'll watch you kill through my jaded eyes.

Kill and let kill—we want chaos!
Kill and let kill—how can you blame us?
Kill and let kill—total mayhem!
Kill and let kill—it's all that makes sense.

I hate cops and those by any other name.
Enforcing peace through violence is their stupid game.
Left-wing idealists telling people what to do—
another form of authority, and I hate them too.

Yankee Doodle comes to town, riding on your mother. Stuck a feather in the
        ground, the natives ran for cover—*daaaaahhh!*

KILL AND LET KILL!!!

They say, To one's own.
So when one chooses to kick your ass, shouldn't they be left alone?
Live and let live, so full of shit.
Hypocrites.

DENDROPHILIACS!!!

Kill and let kill—we want chaos!
Kill and let kill—how can you blame us?
Kill and let kill—total mayhem!
Kill and let kill—it's all that makes sense.

                {available on YouTube}

I am perfect

I SING IN A DIFFERENT PITCH
I STRUM A DIFFERENT RIFF
I MOVE TO A DIFFERENT RHYTHM
                     & that's right
I MARCH TO THE BEAT OF A DIFFERENT DRUM
    so what????

THIS IS ME // that is you
                 I am perfect!

Claimed to Be Smart

My dad wanted me to get the flu shot, was pushing me, pressing me, to get it. At the time I had a guy who at first I thought was a friend staying with me, and he was big into conspiracy theories, believed in all sorts of whacky shit. When I told him I was going to get the flu shot that afternoon, he said, No no no, blah blah blah, conspiracy theory, yadda yadda, they will get you, blah blah blah—BLAH!

My dad who I trust for the most part, as I have known him way longer than this guy who at first I thought was a friend, seems to know his shit about these kinds of things, and this guy who at first I thought was a friend was discrediting my dad with his conspiracy babble. Honestly, I took it at first and just let him ramble, but then, when he discredited my dad who I trust for the most part, stepped into the argument. I said, You know, there are two sides to every coin, two sides who flood the media with propaganda that will make you more likely to follow their side. And he said, No. So I said, This country was founded on propaganda, you know. He said, No no. And I said, It's up to the consumer to choose which side to believe in (which I must add is the reason I don't follow politics in the first place). He said, No, not true. There's only one way, this way, and it has to be that or I'll blow my fucking brains out all over the pavement (of course I'm adlibbing here). So I said, Where'd you get this so-called "information" anyway. And he said, There's so many places. I said, Name one. He said, I don't know where to begin. And so on....

And this guy claimed to be smart.
Never trust those who claim to be smart.

The one that got away

Dismissed——
Oh how I miss that girl
the one that got away
sank into my skin
like a spike
A Drooling Tragedy
I'm walking backwards
nearer to
a better day, but now
the days are getting louder
everybody's shouting
I scramble through the crowds

Jeremy Void

all pointing and laughing at me
I cover my head
as the needle punches through
my heart.
worlds apart
Oh how I miss her
oh how life rolls on
and on
and on
and my heart
it jumps ebbs and stops
restarts ... this dreamscape
oh how I long
for escape.
Oh how I need something more
and more
and more
but the answers never come
when I'm awake.
A pinch   a poke
and my head is sinking
my mind is drifting
my eyes are seeping
my conscious slipping fast
as I float away
into an epic oblivion.
Oh how I miss   that   girl ...
beep   beep   beep
           beeeeeeeeeeeeeeep!

Jaded

I'm a pretty boy with corrupted ideals.
My face is dirty but my thoughts are real.
What you see now is all you will see:
just a snot-nosed kid with rotting teeth.

I've dreamed of love, but dreams deceive.
All the love I'm giving you is all you'll receive.
I've got no remorse for shit I've done in the past.
If I've apologized to you, then I'm sorry 'bout that.

I'm not a poor kid and never was.
I can't fight and I'm not too tough.
But I'll say what I want and do as I say.
If you've got a problem with that, then come up to my face.

I've got dreams of ruling the whole human race.
I just wanna kill everyone who stands in my way.
Again, dreams deceive and hope is fake.
If you've got what I want, I will take.

I'm not a bad kid, but I'm not good.
I'm just a stupid kid who's been misunderstood.

WAVED

I wave to just about everyone I see while walking down the street.

I remember once—and I only remember this because I wrote about it in my very first journal about four years ago—two girls were walking by me and they waved. <u>WAVED</u>. Two preppy girls who didn't look like the type that would wave to me. They waved, and I thought it so weird.

Untitled

Say NO to Saying YES   //   Say YES to Saying NO

At the Brunt of Society

I've got a lot of experience with suffering too. I've suffered at the brunt of society countless times. From jocks bashing me till I'm broken and bloody. Teachers harassing me till I'm sick and distraught. Cops slamming me into walls and threatening to break my skull, prodding me with clubs and long, steel flashlights. Parents comparing me to siblings and punishing me because I'll never be good enough. Girl using me till I'm blue and humiliated. The fucking judge racking the mallet against the hardwood bench and sending me off to somewhere just to endure one more fucking year of senseless torment. POs hammering me, doctors badgering me, nurses pointing fingers and orderlies tying me up and sticking needles into my ass. Ever had a catheter shoved into your dick hole when you're completely conscious of it? The most fucking humiliating fucking thing I've ever been through, and nearly the most painful. I know what suffering is, trust me. But I don't fucking care about any of that. Because if anything, I'm glad that it happened to me, it gave me a greater knowledge and understanding which most people seem to lack.

Act Your Age

Grow Up   Act Your Age

Two Phrases I Never Really Cared for When I Was a Kid

All That Time when people barked jeremy when are you gonna grow up I **Was** Acting My Age. Just the Thing Is, They Were All Just in Too Much a Rush to Grow Up Themselves, on the run from their own ages. but you see, for me, I Didn't Care Too Much about What Others Thought or Felt and Feeling That Way Was Quite Disinhibiting, as if i had inhibitions to begin with, which i didn't. i was satisfied with my own immaturity, i was fine with being a Kid for a few more years, because growing up and holding down the same job day in, day out seemed quite the boring life and I Wanted None of It

Conformity—No Thanks!

I will NOT conform
I will NOT wear a uniform
I will not submit
I will not adhere to you
      and the limits you set forth
I will not follow you
worship you
think you're cool
nor do anything to praise you/

I am not you
and I will never be you,
nor will I pretend to.

                                                            I'd rather die>>>

Thank God I Don't Drink Anymore

Last night I got myself in a slight bind. My ride to Burlington turned out to be a total scumbag: 1. he expected to use the money I paid him for the ride to pay for his cable bill even though the deal was I'd pay for ALL the gas, and nothing more, which is what I planned to do; and 2. he wanted me to sign him up for the open-mike—second-to-last, he specified—and then leave and come back in the nick of time to read, missing all the other performers that went on before him———see what I'm dealing with here? And then he had the nerve to say that *I* screwed *him* over, *me!* Dude he screwed himself over. He told *me* he was really angry with me and I told him that's on you dude, not my problem. One of the first things he said to me upon entering his car was, "I'm not in the business of saving you money"—just like how I'm not in the business of giving a shit about his feelings. Why the hell should I be?

Anyway, I'm proud of the way I handled myself. I made it out of there unscathed and I used all the tools available to me at the time. I feel like if I was drinking, even though *he* was the prick threatening *me,* I'd be the one in cuffs. Last night I acted mature and responsible, and if I was still amid the hell of my past, I might have very well acted immature and irresponsible. I mean, I am still <u>Jeremy St. Chaos</u> after all, or at least I was, and today a part of him—like Dr. Jekyll and Mr. Hyde—is still inside me, buried deep down beneath my heart, and if I'm not careful enough, that side will come surging back up—so thank God I don't drink anymore.

No Place

I HAVE NO PLACE
in your phony hell.

I HAVE NO PLACE
in your phony world.

You paint the reality that you live in.

Your world is fabricated by lost dreams, shaped by tormented angels, flapping their fiery wings and spitting balls of hate into the atmosphere.

You live a fake existence....
You are lost, blinded by your own apathy, by your own ambivalence.

<u>just one more MEME to tell you how to think</u>

What I think about late at night

What I think about late at night? I think about a lot of things, too much to dictate in this notebook in a timed slot of 5 minutes. I mean, late at night, my mind usually races; it jumps from one boring, oh so futile notion to the next even more boring (almost humdrum) but equally futile notion. I do my best art late at night and early in the morning cuz my scrambled brain doesn't know when to quit.
It's almost like hypo-mania, per say—a racing, speeding bullet rocketing through my brain, from ear to ear, only when it reaches the other side, it bounces off that wall, almost like a pingpong ball, propelled flung swirling through time as one wave of thought crosses my mind, only to be replaced by the next, and then the next, and then the next, and so on. Like, it's midnight, I've got the Drones'

song "Lookalikes" tearing out of my speakers, I'm smashing the keys of my keyboard quickly, with catlike reflexes and velocity, a poem about rage slung across the computer screen—I'm really feeling the rage, letting the rage feel me, becoming one with it, embracing it—and then, *click,* the song changes, and my mood sinks into an almost depression, becoming melodramatic in my wallowing as I think about her, think about Samantha, about the one that got away, the previous feelings of rage that I had felt flipped around and staring back at me—see, that's how fast I can flip a bitch!

2 separate Xtremes = 1 messy outcome

fight for what you believe in
don't ever stop fighting
but leave room for disagreement
unless you're ready for a third world war

Good vs. Evil

In the sky,
two forces fight,
like a barrage of colors
sparking and flashing with
flittering flames trailing behind.

Tonight is the night that
Good vs. Evil battle it
out to see who is stronger,
who is better, and faster.

Smash a Lightbulb: Poetry for Lowlifes

Good comes clothed in a white gown
with a ring of white glory spun
around His head.
Evil, clad in all black, has a set
of spikey horns traversing up
from His head.

Good, in all His holy might, attacks
first with a spinning kick that carves
a hole in the darkness, like a strike of
lightning.

But Evil swerves away from
the blow, cocks back His scepter,
and serves a howling wind
that whispers far and fiercely
and nips a bit from the scalp
of Good.

Good growls a dark growl and the sky
morphs into redness and with that fireballs
come blasting out of the void,
with a trail of bright yellow following each
flaming projectile as they make their
way toward Evil.

Evil, cunning and nefarious, dips and dodges the balls with all the finesse
He can muster,
like a ninja fighting atop a tightrope,
and takes a blast to His chest
and another to His ribs and
a third to His groin that sends him tumbling
through the sky like a cannonball.

Jeremy Void

Good chuckles, which sounds more like
thunder, and zips and weaves through the clouds
in pursuit of a rolling Evil.

Evil stops gracefully and pushes
the air with His powerful touch, and
below Him a tidal wave rises high up
into the sky, taking out boats and islands
as it rises to the highest point.

Evil smirks with the destruction
He has caused, and kicks the air, sending Himself
barreling toward Good, who steps aside
Evil's fists, grabs His leg, and lifts Him high overhead and brings
Him down and the whole earth shakes.
Now Good is laughing and watching Evil struggle
to His feet.
Evil Himself is not happy, and does something completely
unexpected; He springs up and flips over and lands on His back, then
shoots like a torpedo, across the blue sky, and delivers
a severe blow to Good's midsection.
Good takes the hit and is launched backwards, with Evil continuing to push.
Evil's fists lodged in Good's flesh, He forces His enemy far, far away,
and then releases and kicks back.
Good goes swirling and twirling and tumbling and spinning
and swaying and rolling and wobbling to
His demise.

Bet you didn't expect that to happen.

killing time

I'm bored, bold, and sold. No, I'm bored, old, and cold. No, I'm bored and I think I'm pissing on the lord. Yes.

A poem from my teenage years

i don't got problems
u're the one hu's fucked
i happen 2 be happy
my life does not suck
y do u judge me
w/ your normal fuckin smut

i think it's wrong
2 do as u're told
u think it's rite
2 die wen u're old
society's got standards
that i can't live up to
y shud i even bother
wen i was born 2 lose

Oh Woe Is Me

Nothing's happening. I think for a trivial solution, I'm losing my mind to this thing called life. I'm bored, I need a hobby, I write the pain away—oh woe is me. Slam-dunk anxiety creeping into me—oh woe is me. I'm climbing through filth overtaking me my worrying is endless, I'm cramped—oh woe is me. My mind is stretched, my mental state is broken broken breaking down. I think ... stretched out on the floor, I feel broken, I need something more; I feel troublesome and worried and depleted and ohmygod my reality is slipping I'm going to sleep.

Untitled

If you can't beat them,
<u>KILL THEM!</u>

Smarter Than You

Just realized something that really did wonders to my ego. When I was nineteen or twenty, I got an IQ test done. I scored in the 86 percentile, which means I am borderline genius. But the thing is, when I got that test done, I was heavy into crack. But I'm sober now. Which means I am most likely smarter than you. Ha!

Clever Wordplay

I'm yearning for a yesterday that will never come.
                      I'm dreaming of a tomorrow that is already gone.

A Crude Writing Experiment

> I'm sitting in my library I'm listening to the Saints I'm planning on going to the open-mike tonight at Pub 42 I'm bored out of my skull I'm waiting for something to happen but I don't know what stop looking at me I wonder I ponder I hate hate hate that's all I've got to say right now see you later when the world dissolves in battery acid
> fun times
> right?
> RIGHT!

Untitled

I'm the pimp of prolifia!

Pro-Death

If I had a gun, I'd probably put it in my mouth and blow my brains out. I don't know why I even bother trying in the first place. I've had a really fucking rough upbringing, what with me not fitting in and just getting shit from my peers all the time, and now I'm getting older and you'd think my life would get better or at least even out, because everyone has their day, as they say; but then where's my day? I'm still a social cretin, and things don't get better, they either stay the same or get worse, is what I've always believed my whole life. But then I abandoned that prior notion when I started attending AA cuz I saw other people getting better—but that's great for them. Because for me things either stay the same or get worse, and if I had a gun I'd put it in my mouth and blow my brains out right now.

Thoughts on Thanksgiving

The worst part about the Holidays is that there's never anything original said. It's always, *Happy Thanksgiving this, Happy Thanksgiving that; I'm thankful for this, I'm thankful for that.*

Count me the fuck out.

I'm thankful that YOU weren't sitting at MY table on Thanksgiving.

Can't wait for Christmas. *Have a holly, jolly cock in your mouth!* Maybe that will get you to shut up.

Trust Me

                I suppose I don't know what it's like
                            to be you
                I suppose I never lived a day
                          in your shoes

But not to sound grandiose or anything
        I lived through hell
        and if you only knew the hell that I know
                you might reassess your stance

                        TRUST ME ON THAT

Claimed to Be Smart, Part 2
Confessions of a Walmart Whore

I met a girl who liked to talk a lot and complain even more. First thing she said to me was, I hate the government, they suck. And I listened to her, I really did. You punk kids really have no idea how bad the government actually is, about what they do and stuff. You wouldn't even believe me if I told you. I have insider information. You can't buy this kind of information. I said, But you work at Walmart (she does work at Walmart). And she said, Well I need the money. So I'm thinking, What a freaking whore, letting the government rape her like that, as she claims they RAPE people, for some cash to buy her booze and cigarettes. Doesn't make much sense, you know. Eventually, when I grew tired of her bitching and moaning about the bad bad government, I said, What's so bad about the government? She stopped there and stared at me, probably perturbed that I had challenged her like that. Yeah, I said. What's so bad about the government? And she said, There's so many things bad about it. I said, Name one. She said, I don't know where to begin. And so on....

                                      And this girl claimed to be smart.
                             Never trust those who claim to be smart.

Just for Kicks

        I wear steel toes just for kicks.
        I dress in a way that'll make you sick.
        I go around acting like a total prick.
          And I do it all just for kicks.

Another Piece of the Puzzle, Obtained

Last night I met a guy named Scott. He said he used to work at Panera Bread with me. He knew my name already, he didn't have to ask. I knew his face, but I had to ask for his name.

My past is like a puzzle with all its pieces missing, and one by one the pieces are turning up so I can finally patch it all together, although I know it will never be over, not ever....

... to be continued....

Untitled

I'm soo siiiiick. Can't even think of a good simile/metaphor to show you how sick I am, that's how sick I am....

Crazy, Right?

So weird. I'm sitting in a cab right now and in the backseat is this younger couple. Just as I started reflecting on something I had said to a young guy earlier in the night at the end of the open-mike about how we should embrace are craziness, the guy in the backseat started talking to his girlfriend about craziness and mania. Just as I said crazy in my own head, the guy in the back said crazy out loud. Weird, right?

Untitled Poem

I'm climbing mountains
glaciers of the mind
with pure undulating
roofied cynicism coursing
through my every fiber.

This is the day
we pray to god
to our masters, the puppeteers
in the clouds.
This is the day
we pray on the locals
harvesting their bones
for supper.

The crows are loose.
The chickens gobble and hop
all the way down the dirt road.
It's a bloody Monday
everyone I know is dead
or worse
dying a horrible death.

I stand on top of the highest peak
having crested that thick, spikey
glacier festering in the darkest,
most sensational region
of my scrambled brain.

My body feels heavy
but my head feels light as feathers.
I will sleep never

exploring the demented realm
of the most incessant kind of
paranoia this ruler has ever felt.

My time will dissolve as soon as
the bagel melts into ashes from
the glimmering rays of the sun.

The girl stands in the crowd
this is Punk rock
the band plays loud
and the girl gets knocked about like
a slam pig on Valentine's day.

We are one with each other
she and I are lovers with the same brother
twins sharing the identical unicorns
as we ride the one horned beasts
through the rainbow dripping acidic blood.

This is my time to shout
my time to lift the swirling mountain
out of the golden shafts of bright gleaming
ligatures of miscellaneous limbs.
Some might say I'm sick while the rest
claim I'm a shithead taking a fall.
Others say I'm a god
while the few that I care about
say I'm nothing more than a ghoulish leper
with three separate eyeballs to see with
as the sun explodes and the man on the moon
hiccups in hilarity and dies an
ironic, disasterous death.

Smash a Lightbulb: Poetry for Lowlifes

Nothing from the best
is expected to be less
than the losers who stand tall
in the crossfire as razor-sharp lasers
cut holes in their bowels
and shit-heeled panthers run wild
with black men brandishing skulls
and switchblades.

I learned something last night
I learned that we are no more than mere
systematic pin points of light.
We are simply diseases that have come to destroy
the sky, the moon, and let there be
vengeful waves of sonic rain
coming down like jagged balls of hail
to wreck havoc on the farmers who live
in giant, golden mansions.

Wouldn't it be nice to have such
a high stature as a man with a silver spoon
and a fork made of bones? He carries a shiny
butterfly knife on his back as he hikes
through the line of mad mermaids
who swim as though godsent on a mission
from the devil himself.

I think everything I needed to say
has oozed from my fingertips
and erected cunning words of angry madhatters
skipping along a bombed-out street
where American-made missiles spray like an outbreak
of aids ripping up the earth with its nefarious
agenda.

That's the end of the world as we know it
but we never did get to know it because
how well can anyone know anything and we
are simply ants to the cosmic forces at play.
So I'll say this with my final breath:
My ride home is here and there's always
something to fear, something worse than
anything you could possibly imagine.

Incomplete Heart

But nothing really speaks to me, nothing really stands above anything else. Everything is nothing, nothing is everything; love is hate, hate is love, it's all the same in the end. It's life, it's sex, it's wonderful, it's terrible, I only have nightmares, but some of my nightmares make me wet, if you know what I mean. Although what is a nightmare if you're not crawling through vomit on your knees while demons in loin cloths whip you with spiked cement blocks that coil like a slinky and you're on your knees bleeding and you're screaming although you have a raging erection that's spewing acid and you're wondering, How the hell did I end up in this predicament? It's one of those things where you know nothing will ever   be the same again.

Wed., 11/212012
— 6:27 PM

I have a really hard time around family because I lack skills in acting formal or proper. When I used to live in Boston, before I moved to Vermont, I never learned the act of acting proper, as I seldom needed to act proper. I feel so ill-fit all the time that I just isolate myself. I try to communicate like a "normal" person, but then I just get bored. I hung out with Bell last night and had a fun, sober time. For the first time in a very long time, I could be me, and it's so rare that I even socialize with people in the first place. Sitting or standing around talking proper bores me. That's why when I went to Stowe, VT, for Nana's birthday and to see family, Edwin brilliantly suggested I talk about my writing, promote my stories, in fact bring a story to show around (I ended up bringing "The Haunted Bathroom"). But I just feel so awkward, so out of place, like a stranger in a strange land. There are not too many people in Vermont who think and act like me, either, and even the other Punk rockers around here bore me too. The people who know me, such as other Spring Lake Ranchers, have learned to tolerate me because they've come to find out that I'm not such a dick after all, but rather, just very uncouth. So they let me be me—to an extent, of course—as long as I tone down my crass behavior, which I do—reluctantly. They let me be me as long as I respect their rights to feel safe. That's why I love Samantha so much: I can be me with her—more than anyone else. I can be uncouth with Bell and Andrew and Derrick, but not entirely me. It's 6:42. I'll probably leave in fifteen minutes. I wonder why Samantha hasn't called yet.

Beware!

Fists full of hate!
Eyes full of rage!
A knife in the back
has got me locked in a cage.

Scream to the world.
But nobody cares.
Running in circles,
so you better beware.

Beware of the ghost!
Beware of the hoax!
Beware of the boy
who will stab you in the throat....

Kill

    Kick em in the eyes
    and claw out their balls.

Like a Fresh Turd

I'm as refreshed as a fresh turd right now, it seems, only my eyes keep slipping, my head keeps dipping, and my mind keeps drifting, and my whole world is spinning and I'm sick and dizzy like a yo yo going around the house fast and violently—up is down, left is right—and my head is bloated with indecisions, my mind clogged up with pent-up nonsense, with wasted dreams that are both depressing and real. The whole world feels like a film reel, going round and round, up-chucking tainted image after tainted image, a fabrication that ain't worth a shit.
This is how I feel right now.

Rise Above

They will try and hold
you down!
RISE
ABOVE

You are 　　　　　　　　　　You are
better 　　　　　　　　　　stronger

You are 　　　　　　　　　　You are
faster 　　　　　　　　　　smarter

The world is filled with
CUNTS

RISE
ABOVE

People That You Hate

STAND UP FOR THE PEOPLE THAT YOU HATE! because without opposition we'd be a sick society.

The Middle Child Strikes Again

I grew up in a dog family.
Everyone in my family has a dog.
That includes my immediate family (my mom & dad, my brother, and my
    sister—EVERYONE)
and my extended family too.

                                                                But me, I have a cat.

I grew up in a family of goodie-two-shoeses.
Everyone in my family followed the rules.
Sure, there were the slight bouts of drinking
        the occasional experimentation.
But still—mostly it was
    good grades
    good marks
    good students.

                                                                 But me, I was bad.

Nor does anyone smoke cigarettes.
Nor is anyone diagnosed with symptoms.

I could go on forever.
But the fact of the matter is   I'm just different.
                    CASE CLOSED

Judgmental Stares

I need a Klonopin. Can't shake the feeling that everyone's judging me.

No Respect

I went to this open-mike down at Pub 42 tonight, and the people there just showed me no respect and it really angered me. They have no idea what I've been through. I sold my soul to the Devil and then I stole it back. If those fuckers knew anything about my past, they'd either bow or run away. They'd respect what I had to say because they'd know that this guy is real and he really knows what it's like to be broke and drunk and living only to die. But they won't understand, and they'll only know what they see today: just a sensitive little poet who talks big and thinks he knows about the struggle and the fight, but he really doesn't.

selfies are NOT art!

All that selfies do is feed into the narcissistic slumber in which most Americans will find themselves if they just opened their eyes and realized how stupid they are for believing this crap.

As a result, the entire fabrication of our society is being ripped apart like a prom dress worn by a cheerleader being manhandled by her hot football-playing date.

I think I'm going to click LIKE on the picture in which Sandy is holding and petting her white, fluffy cat while standing in her bedroom surrounded by pictures of her all posted on the wall. This picture is so devoid of intelligence, so thought-revoking, that I might just cum in my pants. This picture not only distracts me from what's important, but it is so cute too. Oooooh!
It's like walking into a funhouse, only instead of mirrors there are millions of distorted versions of Sandy lurking in the hallways waiting to
                                                          kill you and dissect your brain....

That's what's becoming of our sick culture.

Part 4
While you're off living your hallmark lives....

Part 4
While you're off living your Hallmark lives…..

A Fate Like Cottage Cheese

I lash angrily
I caress the demonic beast
of sin
mocking me from deep
down within
I turn a page
I turn two pages
and what's left but
another page to spin.

An anarchist wins for a change
gets what he wants
but then what else is there
to fight for
when the walls of many nations
fall apart?

Feminists in the '60s marching
for women's rights
gay men rallying for the rights
to wed one another

but now the rights have come
and they're kicking down doors
seeking more turmoil to overcome.

It's a holy mess
quit while you're ahead
quit before backs break
quit quit quit or our fate will
come to an end.

You don't seek rights
you seek dominance
you seek injustice
your sisterhood banned together
to reap intolerance on the masses.

Narcissism Much?

The most beautiful thing in the world is the mirror.

Copy Cat Rebels

Today all the bands sound the same. I live in a small town called a city in a small state nobody gives a shit about. It's full of hippies and yo-yos and rednecks and cholos; and kids are shooting dope like it's a sport, unmarried girls are springing babies from their twats like it's a chore—a paid chore cuz the government pays them for it. I go to open-mikes to read my writing and all the performers always play rock and roll covers and there's never anything new—and when I read nobody pays me much mind cuz nobody wants new they want the same old same old. So I hang out with kids who call themselves "Punks," play in bands that have fast chord progression, quick and powerful drumbeats, and vocals that leave you with a detrimental headache what with their vicious screaming that tears holes in speakers. But I was thinking tonight—and this is why I rarely go to the shows around here or simply leave right after I read—I was thinking that I've been there done that, I've heard it all before—times a million. I've heard the sound that your voice makes as you howl into a caustic microphone, I've heard the sonic riffraff your guitar makes as you pound out power chord after power chord, the bass wobbling and wailing and the drums rumbling in a series of face-paced thumps and crashes. I've heard it all before, and frankly I'm rather bored. It's like … it's like they're singing the same exact songs about the bad bad government, about child rapists and lying politicians, about capitalists and the big business takeovers—white-collar criminals running down mom and pop stores with their corporate bulldozers that dawn their logos on the large rolling wheels as they tumble and plow through the places of small-town business. I know this is going on, you know this is going on, so singing about this going on doesn't change a goddam thing if you ask me, it only prolongs the problem. It doesn't bring about change, especially not when a kid dressed in rags and patches and pins and studs screams about it incoherently into a broken microphone through dented speakers when only more kids who dress in rags and patches and pins and studs can hear it—kids who will listen and then start their own bands and go and bitch and moan about it too. All it does is create more copycat bands, more mimics of rebellion, more washed-up burnt-out thick and tuneless nuisances that think rebellion means complaining to people who feel the same exact way and wanna complain about it too.

Untitled

> HIDE
> in the closet
> & don't come out
> until
> the coast is clear.

My Life

I watch my life pass me by.
It moves as quick and fluid as a snake.
It slithers and its tongue trills
as it cranes its neck to take one last look.
Its eyes are black as led, and its lips,
curving around its face as it smiles, are red
as the slash running across my wrist.
Its stare, the stare of life, cuts through me
like razor blades dipped in lemon juice.
My eyes start to leak, my eyelids droop.
My whole world is spinning and jiving.
My legs wobble and I drop down, straight down.
I let the tentacles of death embrace me.
I let them tear up my clothes, rip holes in my skin,
inject drugs into my bloodstream.
My life, your life, our life, it's gone, gone, gone.
It passed us, the two of us, by....

A Drawing Idea

Who wants to draw me a picture of a liberal and a conservative pissing side by side and in the middle is a guy dressed like a referee pointing a revolver at the sky? And they've gotta be pissing on the American flag.

— *painted by Josh PANDA*

Untitled Love Ballad

I'm awkward and alone
a freak a cretin....
People glare at me
and they think—
        I don't know what they think
        but I can speculate for sure
and I speculate so much
that these wayward assumptions
spin around my head
and I'm dizzy
and I'm sick

and I bend over and vomit
into the kitchen sink—so gross———
these putrid mix of false assessments
they make me cry;

and I'm socially mixed up
I hate you but I love you
and it never seems enough.
See these tears spurting out of me????
wanking myself senseless in the
solitude of my own misery

I'm running from you
you only want a hug
and I'm running
run-run-running and you'll
never catch up to me.

It seems I'm sick again
another toke to make things right
I'm a living joke, a hoax a phony
but this world doesn't know me even though
they think—
       I don't know what they think
       but I can speculate for sure
and these derelict speculations make me
angry and I'm swinging after you
punching and kicking for you to love me too.

Babe, I just want a kiss, and I'll kill you
if you don't deliver it soon.
Watch me as I stick this loaded gun in my mouth
and I'm pulling the trigger just for you, babe.

Smash a Lightbulb: Poetry for Lowlifes

Just for a little spec of attention
just for … I don't know what it's for
just for just for
just so you can see me here
and you know
I'm disclosing my sacred love for you
and I tell you I mean it it's true

but I find myself alone again
sitting at home again
touching myself in those forbidden places
that your mother warned you of
but it just feels so good
ratcheting myself senseless
    all the way around the clock,
jacking myself deeply
    and quite sincerely
working up the courage to eventually

talk to you
to tell you just one thing….

But the words don't come out right …
they catch in my throat and I choke em down
I take a toke and the whole world undulates beneath my feet
I feel slippery and demonic and I say to you, babe
I whisper softly in your ear
the tainted secret released
I coo so innocently against your skin
that I hate you
but I need you
and I'll kill you
if I don't get you
and watch as you bleed out

on my bedroom floor.

That's what love is
 for me.

FIGHT OR FLIGHT

I heard—so dont quote me on it—that Webster Dictionary changed the definition of the word literal to mean metaphorical, like "I could literally eat a horse"—a metaphor. But—and heres the biggie—if literal means metaphor, then the metaphor is no longer a metaphor.

THIS is our world
THIS is the society that we live in

Last night I watched a stand-up comedian tell jokes on Netflix Instant in front of a lie audience. Except for maybe one or two clever statements, the jokes were rather lame—just spraying obscenities out of his mouth as much and as quickly as possible. But—and heres the biggie—the crowd before him was eating it up. Like, at the mention of his uncle sucking a tiny dick, everyone broke out laughing like it was a virus of some kind.

TRUST NO ONE
NEGLECT RESPONSIBILITIES
 RUN AWAY HIDE INSIDE
Be a closet case   before it's too late/

Untitled

I've been on Facebook way too much these past few days; I'm becoming normal. What is happening to my life?!

Listen to what I say
but don't quote me on it

I'm sitting in a crowd, of a few old men, they talk but I don't hear what they say. Their minds like eyes, their eyes like spies, their voices cold as ice and sharp as a knife. I sit here in this great world and wonder things that only the drunken cloaked woman lurking in the dark and dank shadows can understand, comprehend, and she scoffs and scowls in that bleak tone that sounds like a revving motorcycle as the angry rider kicks the pedal and cranks the handles.

This is my life, coming to terms with nothing, trying to understand something, learning anything my small mind can comprehend with its midget legs and arms of a giant that reach and reach and reach but the legs are too stubby and they get stuck in cement and the arms keep reaching and reaching but my brain feels heavy and I give up and go to sleep instead.

This foreign world seems so ordinary to me, like been there done that, and yet it feels so different and I find myself on an indifferent playing field, wanting something more but something seems to bore me and I find my mind slipping as my eyes seize up and I fall asleep in the shower as the plummeting spray bounces off the edge of my skull and the tub is closing in on me fast, getting tighter, and the lights are brightening and opening holes in my head, so as to spray me with this relentless kind of knowledge that seems almost insufferable and I pray to no one asking for relief. But then the relief comes to me unexpectedly and I look up at the clouds—the churning, shifting, and spurning webs of fluffy fog that puff out and fold over—and I marvel at the magical undulations of the spacious skies and

for once this life makes a little more sense to me and that something that lurks up there comes into focus and I find satisfaction in such a bleak world and I walk away with my head upright
only to get shot down around the corner by a jagged spike of lightning that came from below and that seems to be the story of my life.

So I'm sitting in a crowd of a few old men, listening to their chatter come like waves of sonic might and I hear their voices which sound like churning rice and I watch and observe, basking in the wisdom of a thousand years of abuse, absorbing the worldly trinkets of information that seem quite foreign but still so ordinary and I think to myself, This is life, this is good, and for once I understand what it means to be bad and I understand the crashing collision of stumbling over a bed of rocks and stones and ruts and that precious bite as the rocks rip into your skin and for once in my horrible existence I see the glorifying truth and I'm falling and I'm wondering plummeting and crashing into stacks of romantic bliss and I'm not looking back. And I'm having a blast. And I'm running from the law with my one-eyed widowed girlfriend who holds a knife to my back. It's over I know.

It's over and my whole life has only just begun....

The Way of Things

Things fall apart. Things get rebuilt. Things fall apart. Things get rebuilt. Things fall apart. Things get left abandoned. Things rot and grow mold. Things stay abandoned. Things become infested with maggots. Things stay abandoned. Things get found by mischievous teenagers. Things get covered in spray-paint. Things stay abandoned.

No Wonder

No wonder you hate me, you didn't believe me when I said proceed with caution. Believe everything, trust nothing.

Tell me something ::::::

       Why do you hate me??
       Did I do something wrong?
       Did I step on your toes?
              or something

C'mon,
I need to know!

       I'm not a bad person.
             I'm really not

             I swear to GOD!

             I'm only human

             and
             I've made my mistakes.

YES   it's true.
       But so **FUCK**ing what?

A Stranger to Myself

It's in my experience that people who claim to be smart are usually not, people who claim to be mature are usually fairly immature, people who claim to know who they are are usually the farthest away from an understanding of self. I'm not smart, I'm definitely not mature, and I definitely do not know myself like I wish to. I am an impulsive hypocrite, I talk shit and put people down, I spit, I swear, I eat with my mouth open, sometimes I'm scared of my own shadow, I'm quite the idiot at times, but there are other times, although rare, that I can be quite sincere, but in those time of me being honest and real for a change I'm honesty thinking about how to evade you for the rest of my life because you are a lazy bore and you mean nothing to me.... I'm a loser, a scoundrel, I cash checks that I surely cannot catch. I have a bone to pick with the world because the world has turned against me and the world has turned against me because I turned against it and I turned against it because I was bored of waiting for the light to turn green, see what I mean. I'm lazy and ignorant, I talk big and move slow, I run with wolves who despise me and I despise them because we're one big family of spiteful cretins looking out for numeral uno, stashing knives behind our backs as we wait for the precise moment to stab our brothers and sisters in the back. I am not smart, I am immature, and I, me, this man typing this rant on this filthy laptop at this very minute, am a stranger to myself..........

Buzzzzzin Bumble Bee Rumble

A little while ago I hear this epic buzzing sound in my apartment, louder than the music I had on. And so I'm thinking to myself, Please don't be a bee. Please don't be a bee. I turn off the music and listen for where it's coming from. I listen closely and notice it's coming from behind my bookshelf. So I stand up and ease closer to the shelves to investigate. Please don't be a bee. Please don't be a bee. I creep closer to the shelves. Please don't be a bee. And closer. Please don't be a bee. The buzzing gets louder as I get closer, and closer. Then I ease my head slowly to peer past the shelves. Please don't be a bee. Please don't be a bee. My eyes breach the edge of the shelves and I'm sure to be as stealth as possible as I go about this. Please don't be a bee.

I turn the corner, and HOLY FUCK! a massive brown-and-yellow, oblong dot is ascending and descending the screen, ascending and descending the screen, and being deflected as it tries to push its way through. I jump when I see it. Please be on the outside of the screen, I'm thinking cringing and stiff while one eye searches for something to swat the yellow beast with and the other eye is fixated on it as it climbs the screen and drops back down, buzzing all the time, the sound increasing with each and every collision with the screen.

HOLY SHIT, I'm thinking. Please be on the outside of the screen. I keep a steady eye on that thing as I search for something to swat it with, when I realize finally that the thing is in fact on the other side. Thank God, I say to myself while still watching and hoping my eyes are seeing correctly by deciding the thing is on the other side after all. I keep watching and then the bee cuts right and disappear sbehind the wall and you wouldn't believe how grateful I feet at that moment, sighing with unbearable gratitude.

Untitled

Looking for inspiration on Facebook—*what a joke!*

I wnta anwsers

You cant ask a liar if hes a liar, the answers you get will always come out slanted. So where does one go when they want to know the truth? not to friends & family becuz they dont wanna make you mad, not to those who hate you becuz they do wanna make you mad.

You cant trust noone becuz their opinions are always skewed by years of learned behaviors, acquired biases——— The truth is always distorted by users trying to get one over on you. The facts are always slanted by those who walk on eggshells, trying so so hard to please you. You cant trust yourself becuz your head is the number-1 offender, always spinning fabricated realities so mixed up & lost & in a world of your own.

So Where Do You Go When You Just Need to Know?

Absurd Nihilism

I had a thought
but I lost it
      it's gone
and now I'm here
on the train
heading straight into
      the void of existence

Fake people amid
a tumultuous drinking bender
I snort the fumes of endeavor
wrap a damp rag all the way around
my beaming face
the world never felt clearer
and I'm here
in a devilish wet dream

I'm screaming
      for it to cease
an orgasm worth
      five thousand stolen tears

Smash a Lightbulb: Poetry for Lowlifes

I dread the explosion
I'm crying can't you see
the beaten erosion
of spurts of gasoline
spraying like from a canyon
auto-erotic-afixiated
I'm fainting
        fast
I won't look back

Let me off this
runaway freight train
that barrels like a rocket
speeding like a bullet
that punches
        twenty-two holes
in the poisonous spider
cuming spurts of venom

and I'm sick
and I take the sexual vile
lather it on the American flag
wrap it all the way around my face
take in an extraordinary breath
with an epic but delightful inhale
my feet rise my mind shuts off
my body's flying
and the whole world evaporates
like sin-induced flesh
touched by the hand of death
tied to a tether and beaten
like a ball that swirls
like a flushed toilet

and I'm riding the sandy waves
another pointless day I'm made to serve
chaotic and symbolic wisdom
that coils through my mind
        my head
just coils and turns
raping me with a diseased rod
laced with spikes and studs
a scud rocket
shuttling through the void
stuttering it's delightfully twisted
I ride the waves of rape
surf the mass murdering sea
of life
of death——it's all the same
                in the end

I'm dying
but nobody knows me
I might be flying
but nobody cares
another tainted façade
another wasted day
another lowlife loser
another mournful boozer
another another another
        and I'm cruising
through
the
streets of
        nothing
the endless roads
        of waste
the filthy avenues

the tainted lane
a hole
      from which I emerged
and I'm going straight back there
      without a hope
      or a care///

I'm going nowhere
      FAST

Music

Have you ever been listening to music and then a song comes on and the lyrics match the state of your life so perfectly that you could cry?

A Free-Write///

It's a free-write in my Thursday writing group. It's only me & Brian here, Steve didn't show; he's up on the hill, said Chris Cone. So we're here writing. I read Brian a few pieces from *Smash a Lightbulb: Poetry for Lowlifes* with the hope to pull some topics of discussion out of his twisted mind. First I thought pleasure— pleasure drives me insane ('This orgasm is too much to take at this present moment,' was the prompt I came up with))). Second I thought obsession (I'm obsessed with pleasure / obsession is pleasurable— —it climbs into my brain and fucks me senseless from the outside-in—the inside-out—upside-down and all around me a static pressure surges lifting me straight up into outer space))). *C'mon Brian, think of a topic,* I pressed. *Anything, Brian. You're good at that.* Me, my topics are always dirty—crude, rude, & lewd;—but not today: he has nothing, no idea no concept no head on his shoulders which produces thought-provoking (or thought-REvoking, depending on which way you look at it), evocative concepts that rattle my chain,,, whip me till I'm blue and confused,,, hold me down and hock loogies in my face. (The other day, in Boston I was at my friend Brandon's place and I told him and Fink the story of when the kid had told me not to spit on him; comes up to me rather rudely and says, "I hear you've got a reputation for spitting on people while your band plays" [I was the singer], and adds: "Don't spit on me!" So during our set I called him up to me and hocked a loogy in his face. When I told this to Brandon and Fink they both said he was asking for it. When I told this same story to a crowd of four or five at the show in Providence RI a few days later, one guy said he would have socked me in the face; another guy concurred; at the table a guy and a girl laughed as these two big guys joked about how if someone had hawked a loogy in one of their faces, unless accidentally discharged while coughing, they'd both deck him, right off the bat, no questions asked. I chimed in: "I'd hump his leg<<<")

So it's a free-write, Brian had declared....

Do I Haveta?

Who am I?
What am I?
Do I really haveta be someone??
Do I really haveta be something??

Cuz all I really wanna be is me!

Sick Motherfucker

Where you see strange
      I see normal....
Where you see pain
      I see enjoyment....
Where you see hate
      I see love....
Where you see love
      I see lust....
            You sick motherfucker!

Punks for PC

I'm making so many enemies in this "Punk rock community" group on Facebook this morning. If I can't speak my mind and say what I feel, then it's not Punk rock. Sorry, but it had to be said.
As Johnny Thunders once said, "Fuck em if they can't take a joke."

NOW

I feel like complete fucking shit today. **NOW,** how do I exploit that feeling?

Desperate Times

Desperate times calls for desperate measures. So let's all go and get desperate together.

A Toxic Flower ... for you!

A flower dipped in toxic waste
is a beautiful thing,
because the beauty of it
comes from the lack of knowledge
of what it will become.

A flower that grows straight
and maybe tips one way or another
seems boring
to me.

A flower that's unpredictable
intrigues me
so much more.

Not Just a Hot Piece of Ass

See, I'm not just a hot piece of ass.

                I know my shit................

A Crass Philosophy

Sometimes to really enjoy art one has to let go of form and what they know about the craft, they have to leave their preconceived notions about what it SHOULD be like at the door in order to truly grasp what the artist is trying to do. Art is not about following rules, or at least it isn't for me. The reason for the level of crassness is because these are all very deep thoughts and ideas but I'm showing them in a crude setting, kind of as an ironic statement. Like, scholars dress in suits and ties and carry around briefcases, but me, I carry my luggage in a ratty old backpack, wearing filthy clothes, with fucked-up teeth and tattooed skin—but still, I can think about stuff on a deep level too. I don't need the makeup and the plastic to think; all I need is a mind that doesn't seem to ever quit. If that makes sense. So I remove formalities such as grammar and show it at its rawest level.

Sitting at the Bar

I'm sitting at the bar   I'm sober   at the bar   sitting here   sober & writing about how I'm   at the bar   sober   & I'm writing about it. Okay, where was I? I'm bored I guess. The music playing is wretched and I wanna go   someplace else   someplace not here. Okay, where was I? Okay, this is the nature of the beast. This is only human nature   only natural to be bored   while this crap is being played   by two drunken old guys & one   sober young guy about my age. I know his name   his name is okay, maybe I don't. Okay, where was I? That's right, I'm here   I'm at the bar. Last I checked I was sipping a Red Bull   &   writing this crap   in this notebook   at the bar. Okay, where was I? I think I was just leaving.

/RUN/

The Land of the Free
    is not free   at all

The Home of the Brave
    is mostly populated by
<u>P U S S I E S</u>

The world that we know and love
    will most likely be nuked by
    terrorists.

^{HATE} flourishes, whereas _{LOVE} has died
        many, many years ago.

We think we're safe.
        But we're not.
                Nobody is
                    SAFE

The terrorists have won.
Our fate belongs to them.
    The terrorists have won.
    Get it through your head.

Now all we have left to do is ………………… **|RUN|**

Listening to Fang

Listening to Fang before the world wakes up makes me feel giddy with hate, and I might just punch my cat in the face.

CRACKED!

Everything is broken.
Everything's a joke.
The caustic mirror
looks back at me

and I hate the faces
that it makes....

Rhetorical Hypocrisy

I am such a hypocrite and I feel this strong, overbearing urge to justify my ignorance by saying, *Hey, everyone's a hypocrite, we're all the same in the end, just useless vessels living in a delusional state, and at least I have the guts to own my own hypocrisy,* right? I mean, the <u>bad</u> hypocrites (since we're all hypocrites in the end, as I have said, there must be degrees of hypocrisy so that I'm not so bad after all, not so full of shit, not as much of a sanctimonious bastard as the rest of America's wasted inhabitants) the bad hypocrites are the ones who won't fess up to their bullshit, you know the kind. Noses angled upward, always ready to point out your flaws at any given moment, almost as if they carry around a list of defects and description and if anyone so much as acts out any of the follies on their list, an extended index finger drops like the judge's mallet, racking an invisible podium as they point out what's wrong with you—those are the worst: so self-righteous, so anal-retentive, so snobby and vindictive—those are definitely the worst breed of humans to ever inhabit planet earth. And I sure ain't that bad, am I? Like, I mean, sometimes I find myself preaching on a subject that I know nothing about, preaching like my word is gospel, with an unyielding desire to show other like-minded individuals what I wrote, as opposed to standing out like a Muslim in Texas, a sore thumb as you will, like a wretched case of herpes that had spread beyond the boundaries of my mouth, having dominated my entire face in a grotesque mask of bubbly puss and bloody zit-like bumps that radiate and pop. See, I admire anyone who has the guts to stand against the mob. Every recognizable revolutionary to have stepped foot on this planet stood against the mass majority in some way or another, and I think that's great, and I promote such action in my writing, telling others to step forth on angry feet with a righteous clenched fist reaching for the sky (as long as you recognize that your newfound feeling of rectitude is founded in bullshit you'll be okay) and I think all should stand for something; but what do I stand for but nothing? I write politically driven poems and share em with like-minded folk, and what does that do in the way of revolution? This one time, years ago, I sat on the curb eating pizza out of a box and when I had eaten every last bit of it I tossed the box on the ground and this guy pulled up in his car and asked me who's gonna pick that up?—and I just looked at him and shrugged saying, Um, not me, and walked away. So I guess we're all hypocrites, huh? only some of us are sicker than others and the sickest are the ones who stand for causes so righteously that everyone who opposes them is wrong—so glad I'm not one of those!

Scream

I scream at the sky to explode the sun. I scream at my mind to explode my head. I scream at the mirror so that my face will shatter. I scream at the ocean to defuse the volcanoes. I'm screaming at someone, possibly you, to dissolve in acid, maybe if you want me to.

So Not-Drunk

On my way to Pub 42 to get so not-drunk.

No Offense, but

How many times have I been browsing down my Facebook newsfeed and I stumbled upon these great words (lyrics/poetry) and I comment THAT'S AWESOME DUDE, DID YOU WRITE THAT? and in response they go: NO, IT'S A SONG.

Like a slashed tire I then feel quite deflated because I liked those words, they were inspiring to me, but the perpetrator claimed they were only a quote.

        Only A Quote.   A QUOTE!!!

<u>Happens every time</u>....

On the Boardwalk

I'm walking along the pier. To my sides, waves of red water splash at the planks holding up the boardwalk. Some of it sprays me. The sky is green, and thin black clouds drift in front of the pink, shiny moon, creating a glow like no other. It is really a rather beautiful sight. I walk, smoking a cigarette, and the smoke streams out of my mouth in a yellow haze. The colors are mesmerizing. It's almost as if this is a dream. A gray sea serpent pokes its head out of the red water and watches me. Farther out, another gray sea serpent sprinkled with green dots surges straight up and loops through the air and dives vertically into the water so perfectly that it doesn't even stir the water when it breeches it on its way back down. Now a purple sea serpent with specks of gray only dotting its tail exits the ocean and rounds the green sky so smoothly and without having fully left the water plummets, while its flimsy tail, which is forked like a snake's tongue, kicks out and follows its descent, flicking from side to side as it fades into the sea...

The Best Kinds of Minds

Think with your head, not with your dick. But the best kinds of minds think with both.

Locked In

The chains rattle as I yank my arms away, but their hold pulls me back and keeps me bound to this wall. I would try and run, but the shackles clasped to my ankles would make me fall and shatter my skull on the floor. How'd I get here? How could I have done it again? Again and again I keep making the same mistakes. I know this cell and the writing on the walls better than I know myself, and of that I'm quite ashamed. Yet I brag about my faults, about my downfalls and my defects, because perfection as you know it is a fairy tale that my mom and dad told me when I was a wee little kid. And I believed the stories, thought riches and fortunes were in my future, and yet here I am, chained to myself and I hate myself.

Confusion

Flashbacks
I read between the lies
finding myself
I'm about to take a dive.
Worrisome figures
surrounded me as I climb
the ladder into
your thighs—forever lost in lust

An Emotional Hangover?

They call it an "Emotional Hangover." I don't think that's the right term. It should be called an "Emotional Depletion." An "Emotional Void." "Emotions Go Bye Bye." "Emotions No More." A "Jaded Sensational Fucking Cunt Whacker of a Loaded Gun Holding Up the Emotional Convenient Store."

Trouble

I don't look for trouble,
trouble looks for me:
      I only welcome it....

Punk Rock Is My Home

Punk rock is not a fashion.
It's more than an attitude.   ((much more))
It partially revolves around a type of music.   ((partially))
The values us kids carry always seem to vary   from kid to kid.
It's not a trend

                              not a cult

                                              not a flavor of the week
                                                        of the month
                                                           of the year.

It's not a political party.   It was never meant to get political.
Did I say it's not a fashion?

                              a trend?

It might be a lifestyle,
                                    but to me it's much much more
                                                                than that.

(<u>If that studded jacket makes you Punk, then a FUBU sweatshirt makes a white kid black.</u>)

Punk Rock
is
My Home

                                                       It's where I go to get away
                                                  from your sick sick society.

It's where I go
when I need to escape …
      <u>the family</u>   <u>the job</u>   <u>my high school</u>

I bet that the closest some of these Punk rockers on the scene today know about being a misfit is from the band the Misfits.

Where's the danger?
Where's the rush?
Where's the rebellion?
Where's the drugs?

                                                More importantly,
                                                where's the fun?

The scene today is watered-down by kids who will never know what it is like to be a true loser, a freak, an outcast to society. Exiled from everywhere you go.

Shunned by all your fucking peers.

Up All Night

Chances are I'll be up all night editing and doing other random tasks that involve wasting time and procrastinating and waiting for the world to end, etc. etc., and if you're looking for me, look in the mirror, you might find me there. Just say Jeremy Void three times backwards, or forward, I don't think it matters....

Sometimes

I'll be walking down the street and then see somebody whose face I wanna punch, or who I have the sudden urge to push out in front of a truck.

These
thoughts   I can't always control them, you know.

Some people
might call me evil.   A bad person.

But then,
Who the Hell Are You????
What the Hell Have You Done??   Huh!

Deprivation Much?

Sleeping is a waste of time, and eating makes me hungry. That's why I don't like either of the two acts.

Afraid of the Truth

I think people are afraid of the truth. Face it, we were born to die. Everything we do while alive is to prepare ourselves for our inevitable demise, to protect ourselves, to prolong life as much as we possibly can. But what for?—the great existential question. Why bother trying when death sits bitterly on the other side of the rainbow, waiting to take you to hell? Why do anything? We might as well just sit around and wait to die, right? Curl up into a ball and let death take us.

Why even wait for death, then? Why not just do it ourselves? Death is taking too long; I don't hear him knocking—and I have this noose that could do just fine.

Right?

Wrong.

I guess that's the part that's open for interpretation, the part where you can feel free to adlib all you want, cuz I'm not writing this story, you are! I'm only giving you the outline, supplying you with a prompt to jumpstart your career as a writer—metaphorically, of course. I can't give your life meaning, other than point out the obvious, which is you are going to die, pain and misery waiting for you in your future. Pointedness is subjective, and relying on the ideas some fuckup brings to the table, even though that is the foundation of our society, the masses absolutely dependent on the decisions of others, is foolish, downright stupid; for fuck's sake, think for yourself, and not only because I tell you to because that would be quite paradoxical—and I know nobody is reading this anyway, those who do happen to give it a second glance having tuned out by now.

That is why the world is brimming with cunts, overflowing with them—and trust me, I am no exception.

Fuck You

Fuck politically-correctness.
Fuck overly sensitive left-wing commies,
 telling me what is and what isn't politically correct.
Fuck right-wing religious fanatics.
Most of them are too old to be believing in imaginary friends.
Fuck missionaries,
annoying preachers preaching about how much they love Jesus.

Jeremy Void

Don't they know Jesus hates faggots.
If there is a God, fuck him too.
Fuck the government.
Fuck Obama,
just another thieving nigger destroying our country,
robbing us of our freedom.
Fuck all forms of politics:
social, economical, etc.
They cause more problems than they'll ever fix.
Fuck the lies told to us as kids.
Fuck the lies taught to us in school.
Fuck the land of the free because I haven't found it yet.
Our founding fathers were gun-toting drunken assholes who loved whores.
Fuck society for taking those values away.
Fuck society for taking everything away.
Fuck cops, fuck cops, fuck cops,
enforcing unjust laws.
Fuck the rest of the world for hating this country and thinking they're better.
You don't see foreigners risking their lives to live in your country.
And fuck foreigners who risk their lives to be in this country
and *still* think their country is better.
Fuck racism.
Fuck reverse racism.
Get over it!
Fuck white liberal guilt.
I never owned a slave.
I'm a kike.
My people were slaves before there was such a word as slavery.
Fuck me,
and most all of all, fuck you!

An Education in Punk

In high school when our teachers snapped the whip and cracked the ruler against the white board, I was skipping classes and picking up an education from bands like Crass.

Putrid Heart Disease

WAKE UP AMERICA! I'M BORED AND CRAZY, MORE OR LESS; I'M BOLD AND SOMETIMES QUITE BRAVE BUT MOSTLY I SUFFER FROM A LAZY AILMENT KNOWN AS PUTRID HEART DISEASE. IT MEANS MY HEART HAS DEVELOPED CRISP CUTS ALL THROUGH ITS INNERS AND THAT HAD LEFT ME A BITTER TEENAGER ALWAYS WANTING TO BREAK EVERYTHING AND EVERYONE THAT GOT IN MY WAY. TOSS BRICKS AT WINDOWS, I DID THAT. KICK BYSTANDERS IN THE HEAD WITH MY STEEL TOES, I DID THAT TOO. I WAS MAD AND DISORDERED, BUT TODAY, AFTER FIXING MYSELF TO A MULTITUDE OF DIFFERENT FORMULAS TO EXTINGUISH THIS DISEASE, I FOUND A SOLUTION———WHICH IS KNOWN AS ART AND ARTISTIC CREATION. I'M STILL A HATEFUL MUTANT BUT TODAY I'VE DIRECTED MY RAGE AT A PIECE OF PAPER. INSTEAD OF THROWING BRICKS AT PASSING CARS I THROW DOWN CHUNKS OF PAINT ACROSS A LARGE CANVAS WITH JAGGED EDGES AND INSTEAD OF FIGHTING FOR MY KICKS I WRITE AND THINK AND PRODUCE AND THINK AND BECOME SOMETHING BETTER STRONGER AND FASTER THAT MIGHT WANNA KICK YOUR ASS AT TIMES; BUT IT'S ONLY AS A RESULT OF THIS PUTRID HEART DISEASE. BUT WHAT I REALLY NEED TO DO IS DESTROY A PIECE OF PAPER WITH CRISP PEN STROKES AND MAKE SOMETHING OUT OF NOTHING AND TODAY I CAN FLY IF I SET MY MIND TO IT———SEE WHAT I DID THERE?

Untitled

Run, run, run—just don't run me over.

Impersonal America

How can anyone feel a part of anything when this society has adapted such an impersonal form of communication? Tell us how you feel but not to our faces, and we'll tell you how we feel but only if we don't have to look you directly in the eye.
No wonder I'm so lonely all the time.

Nihilistic Reasoning

Existential thinking turns into nihilistic conclusions. It starts with: Why am I here? what do I want? or even, Who am I? But then my hopeless outlook on life, my defeatus, fatalistic points of view, my self-depracating brain & mind that likes to hang me up in a web of pointlessness, kicks in & the answers roll right off my fingertips: Who am I? No one/// What do I want? Nothing/// Why am I here? I'm really not when I think about it. I come from the land of nowhere—isn't it grand to have such a futile outlook on life. Isn't it wonderful? No, it's nothing. It's nothing, nowhere, & I'm no one—such fun. Today's one of those days when nothing gets done.

Heading to the Rainbow Gathering

So I get a ride up to Rainbow Gathering, but I say first I gotta stop home and grab some stuff. The guys drives me to my place and then I run in and grab my stuff and then I come out and he's gone. Well, I'm partly grateful for that because he could have ditched me god knows where and I was smart enough to not leave anything in the car, too; but I'm also partly bitter because it's just my luck to end up with an asshole like that whereas my friend staying with me right now has been going back and forth from there to Rutland all week with complete ease.

My Loose Dream

The loose dream
I'm peeing energy
through my spine
I'll drop on a dime.
When the storm comes round
the only place you'll find me
is in the sky wind-surfing
the tumultuous spirals of time/
The dream is loose I'm breaking
through my own mind, I'm kicking
down every door in my path.
We're all losers squandering
the many colors of the broken rainbow
that dawns from the retarded donkey's ass.

My mother's never smoked crack
in her entire useless life
except for when she was pregnant
and I sat suspended

in the pit of her melting heart
waiting to be hatched through her bloodshot eyes - -
it was a nine-month stint, you see.
I went in she started
I came out she stopped.
Explains a lot, doesn't it?
Where the hell do you think I get my ideas from?
I just reach my withering, hairy arm
into my torturous pre-birth
and come out glimmering a gap-toothed grin
my eyes twisted and jagged
thinking about the loose dream
as I plummet into that happy blackhole
you know the one....

which shows me chaotic sins and joyful shits
a loser's wet dream
a loser like me
a loser I am
and a loser I'll be///
The loose dream is vivid and bright
frighteningly visceral like a real-life
kick to the balls
plugged in and vicious I plunge
into a whole other world
a world only my loose dreams reveals
and if you see me here
I might very well be sleeping
cuz I'm pissing energy
into the timeless toilet
flushing tumultuous spirals
down the virgin's wet drain.
What goes in must come out - -
in and out, in and out————

and life is simply thrusted
in my face
my brain starts to bleed
a thick, hairy puss that leaks
through my microscopic eyes
I'm falling to my knees
surfing on a wave that
only my loose dream can provide....

Good News

You can snap your fingers for this one—— Guy comes up to me and says he likes the stuff I read. Says he and his wife are opening an underground record store right here in Rutland and my writing is the kind of stuff they're looking for. He wants to carry my books, he says. And he'll let me do readings right in the store too.

A Joke

Anyone who says "Hey dude, you can't joke about that. Anything but that" is a HYPOCRITE.

| You're making jokes about rape, and then you're saying, "Hey, you can't joke about suicide. That's not cool." | While the next person is making jokes about suicide and saying, "Hey dude. Don't joke about rape. Not cool, dude; not cool at all." |

SEE WHAT I MEAN?

Deeming one subject unsuitable to joke about is like sending a ball of snow down a long, steep ski slope.

It keeps rolling
and rolling
and rolling   until it gets too big to contain.

And then you end up with a dead Mickey Mouse on your hands.

DO YOU GET ME NOW?

Ghetto Kid

Big asses & sideways hats—You Make Me *SICK!!*

Don't ask me!

When in doubt read a poem by someone you hate. Read a poem by someone you admire. Write a poem about someone you hate. Admire no one. Be yourself. Emulate and copy but don't obsess and become.

When in doubt do nothing. Do everything. Be no one. Be everyone. Go outside and punch the first sucker you see in the face. Punch yourself in the face.

When in doubt suck back a loogie and let it loose on the mirror. Go outside and scream at the top of your lungs.

When in doubt read a poem by someone you love. Write a poem about someone you love.

When in doubt kill yourself, give birth, rob a bank, give to charity.

When in doubt do everything cuz if you don't the system wins.

When in doubt stand on your head and sing like you're at the opera. Sing like it's opposite day, turn words upside down and hash them out backwards.

When in doubt … don't ask me I have no answers. I'm just a bum I'm just a king I can't sing and I can't love.

When in doubt fuck off.

Lost My Mind

It took 5 days to lose my mind.

I'm guessing it will take another 5
to gain it back.

When will the ground stop moving?

My Writing

I wish my writing would incite a riot!

A Sea of Gloom

It's February
the air is warm,
the sky is blue,
& i find myself
surfing a sea of gloom.
I want to be happy
really i do, but
all i see in the forseen future
is a dim star
shining its shades of gray
all across the land
ebbing
& going black.

It's hopeless
i traipse the vaccuum
going back & forth
wondering
WHAT FOR?

I kick a stone
innertia pulls it
across the road
it hits the curb & stops,
& then it occurs to me
in my diminishing skull
that fate
has got no place for me....

Part 5
I wanna start an art revolution
—Who's with me?

Part 5
I wanna start an art revolution—Who's with me?

My True Colors

Don't hate me when I finally show you my true colors/

Be grateful that I'm comfortable enough around you to do so.

Karma's a Real Thing

Karma's a real thing. You read "My Story: The Short Version," didn't you? In it, as you may or may not remember, some asshole forces himself on my girlfriend and I take the liberty of jamming a steak knife through the fat fucker's neck. Well, that asshole is dead now. Years later he was stabbed to death for forcing himself on the wrong dude's girlfriend. Karma's a real thing, I'm telling you; although it's not exactly the way the Buddhists say it is. Basically, you'll eventually piss off the wrong person, and I don't need to be the wrong person, cuz someone else will.

> At the time I FELT like there were no other options; and I felt like I was trapped, but I wasn't, I know now. I didn't have to resort to his level. I'm not sorry for the way I acted, and I do think it's hysterical that he got murdered in the same fashion I almost murdered him myself all those years ago,

and I do think he deserved what he got for ruining other people's relationships like that, the scumbag he was. BUT there are always other options, I've learned in these past few years.

And I think that's a very powerful statement, it says a lot. When a person feels desperate, when they feel like they're trapped, they tend to act desperately. You can't expect anything more from a person in that state. But—mark my words—we are never trapped, this is AMERICA, and in America, we are never trapped. Just sometimes it feels like we are.

So remember that, next time you feel the need to act out just to prove that you are free!

HATE vs. LOVE

It all starts with HATE
the greatest of motivators.
It all ends with LOVE
the ultimate pacifier.

Two Mental Cases

Like
two mental cases should never
get together
unless the end result is to
        DESTROY
           destroy everything cherished
           & cherishable

Like
the end result of two mental
cases joined together in a
love(hate)-filled affair it
        SELF-DESTRUCTION

Like
I'm incapable of loving but I love you all
the same, and for that let's go WILD

       it's a mistake we all make

Listening to the Meteors

Walking in the rain listening to the Meteors. Things just don't get better than that.

Zen Writing

I don't love a whole lot. I might have loved you way back when but that has passed and now I'm here, today is not yesterday, nor is it tomorrow. Today is today, and yesterday I soared in the clouds with vicious bats. Tomorrow I might climb a mountain, but today this muse is shoutin for me to create something worth viewing—something higher than might but smaller than that which bites. Words are the love of my life, the thing that keeps me going when all is down and the bets are rattling at me telling me to quit.

I fall asleep as streams of words pour from my mind, I walk through a matrix of words as they buzz past my sight. I listen to the words; they speak to me, they glow and fluctuate in the night. They stand above everything and when I die, these words will whisk me up to heaven

                                                    so I can say goodbye.

No Exit

I look at the painting
on the wall
the EXIT sign glows,
reflected into my head.
I've come to the city
yesterday afternoon
just to sit
in an empty room
all by myself
thumbing through
my mental glossaries
       in search
          in desperate need of
             for I want
something
to satisfy
me—my desire to create
a world beyond
what I'm used to;
but there's no exit
from this surreal playground
and those four
glowing red
letters that spell out
EXIT
painted across the painting

Smash a Lightbulb: Poetry for Lowlifes

bright and clear and beautiful
they mock me.
For I came
to the city
and now I'm sitting alone
in an empty room
as the dawn sprouts big hairy legs
and crests the mountainside
the time—five AM
the place—an empty room
in a crowded cabin
hidden deep in the depths of
an almost deserted wilderness.
    No stars
    no moon
    no sounds
    no movement
just me in an empty room
listening for the slight whisper
of the wind passing through
and the haunting murmur
the ominous gurgle
of sleeping bodies sleeping
but here I hear nothing
but my own steady breathing
and the cackle of flickering flames in the fireplace
and the crisp sound that my pen makes
as I form words on the page....

Altruism
just sleep sleep sleep and pretend it all goes away

I'm doing everything I can to make the world a better place. More than most people, at least. It's not that people are lazy or blind or just asleep, it's that people simply don't care one way or another, and no one is going to make them care. And not to mention that people are lazy and blind and sleeping while the whole world goes to hell around them. The common consensus of most Americans seems to be: *The walls are burning down around us. Where's the gas tank? Let's make this building REALLY burn to the ground!*

Another Day in Paradise

I don't know you too well (I wish I got the chance to know you better but I don't see that happening anytime soon), and so I can't say whether or not you're good enough. But I can say this: you're as good as you let yourself be. If you measure yourself by how well someone touches you, you're neglecting other factors such as this person may very well not be good enough for you and as a result their touch wasn't satisfactory. But you have the right to feel angry, I understand that; I get angry all the time, and anger is a great thing because anger is a result of something not being right in your life, and when things are not right you've either gotta fix it or accept it. I always tell people that anger is a great thing. Personally I consider it a virtue, and sometimes I would consider love a vice because we hide behind love and happy feelings almost like it's a cop-out, just another way to escape; and when you're feeling angry, it means the truth is starting to sink in and you've gotta do something about it. Anger is a motivator; love is a pacifier. Our government wants us to love each other; our whole modern day society is built on love, because if we love we'll never want anything more. Sorry, I'm in kind of a philosophical mood right now, so I apologize about the rant here. But either way, let yourself feel whatever you're feeling and don't fight it, just let it run its course, embrace it while it's here.

Untitled

I will only be your whore if you pay me. No exceptions.

My Luck

When one door closes
        another one opens....
only I run thru too fast
slip on the black ice on the other side
crack my head on the pavement

        What's worse....
a dog moseys up to me
stops and cocks one hind leg
and fires a line of piss in my mouth

And a Monster Is Born

Baby grows older ...
        Baby becomes a monster ...

You spoonfeed him,
and then send her off to school.
You take him to church
and teach her to pray.

And you're asking yourself why.
What's gotten into your baby?
She is a monster, and

he will destroy.

Your baby threw a book at his teacher, and the projectile gave her a black eye—

why, why, why!

She's hanging out with an older crowd who all smoke dope—

oh no!

And to think,
you're actually
asking
                            yourself
                                                            why

Just because he
ate your food doesn't
change the fact that
      your baby hates you.

Just because you took
her shopping and bought
her all the clothes that you want
doesn't change this fact.

Sorry, Mom
Sorry, Dad
      but your baby hates you!

A Mongoloid

I'm a mongoloid
> if that's what you want to believe.

I'm a mongoloid
> if that's what you want me to be.

Nowhere

I DON'T BELONG ANYWHERE

At Least I'm Doing Something Right

Wednesday, November 30, 2011
with 11 days sober

It's really fucking cold in here. I want to get high right now. I found out about a new drug on the market. I want to try it, just once. What could possibly go wrong? Everything, [my sponsor] thinks. For fuck's sake, it's legal, and it doesn't show up in piss-tests. I'm one-hundred percent positive nothing could go wrong, but I think I'll listen to someone else for a change. Every part of my being wants to get high. I was at an NA meeting earlier today, and I was one-hundred percent honest when I said I don't want to get high. Now, I'm one-hundred percent positive I do want to get high, but, like I said, I'm usually wrong. I'm not always wrong, but for the most part, I am; so I'll listen to someone else for a change.

In Peace

I don't fucking care anymore. Let me lose my mind in peace!

Hitchhiking—Trainhopping
A Traveler's Guide to Success

No need to test the water
no dip-dip with your biggest toe.
Whether it's cold or hot
you'll find out soon enough.
Just dive on in
splash-splash-splash
and see where the clash might take you.
You could end up in Japan
or maybe even Jerusalem.
Just keep on taking risks
as you navigate your way through existence
and then just keep on pushing buttons
twisting levers until
you end up back at home
safe&sound in a bed of your own………………………

Untitled

I'm FUCKKKKKIN scared!!!

The Bleak Shopping Mall

Sitting outside the bleak shopping mall at night watching the stars twinkle in the distance as the daytime lights up the streets like wildfire & cars a riffraff of death & destruction in arms.

There was something special about the aloneness,
but now I find myself towering over townhall from a sharp, stony peak—the sunlight like gunfire, a green yard glowing, voices penetrating the nothingness that is
here
now
I'm alone
I'm dead
I'm alive
but overfed
zeroing in on the NOTHING

A bleak reality
meek existing
dripping pen ink
down the unicorn's back—
see what I mean?

The bleak shopping mall at war with the junky's sunken eyeball, the world overrun & deserted....

The bleak shopping mall stands tall above everything else, so derelict & desolate, & I sit there watching as life spreads like a virus. It spreads & devours, the sun murders the beautiful dark heavens.

For the Die-Hards

I'm just a lazy sod
I sit at shows and write poetry
while the band goes on….
I don't dance, but
instead leave that for the die-hard
fans
I used to dance way back when
as the band pounded and thrashed
I used to jump and swing and flail
I used to be a die-hard myself
I was so hard and raw
my life so fast that I died hard
HARD
like a ton of bricks tumbling into
a wasted, stagnant riverbed
I splashed and drowned.
Others they crash and burn
but me I plummeted straight down
down
down
a rolling, dilapidated, wasted soul
down
down
down
and into the shallow stream
cracking my head on ruts and stones
the stagnant wake absorbing my
fallen soul
eating me like
a raven eats death.

So today I don't die-hard anymore

Smash a Lightbulb: Poetry for Lowlifes

cuz I already died hard once
and once was already way too much for me.
I died hard twice, thinking
in my ripe, rebellious age, Let's fucking
do it again.
I died hard thrice, three time's
a charm as they say on this
ungodly plain.
But it didn't work out for me like that
cuz
three times is just me getting started
and I died hard again and again
and again
my red, puffy face slapping the green grass
outside of my parents' place.
My belligerent body,
swirling and twirling, seeing
ghosts as they
float up to the heavens and evaporate,
getting tossed head-long
into a brick wall by
3 policemen brandishing
clubs and badges.
Plummeting plunging delving deeper into a river
that goes way over my head,
falling feet first, but turning
rolling
swerving
shifting
my pale, naked skin
clapping against the cold, wet surface
as if meeting steaming-hot pavement instead.

That's how I died hard—

Jeremy Void

I died hard and got sent straight to hell
the devil bound me in chains
and whipped me senseless
with a giant snake,
almost like a python
with big, gnarly spikes
protruding out from its
scaly skin.
Only the devil couldn't hold me there much longer
no, he could not—
cuz I broke out
stole a menacing fork from hell's
luxurious mess hall and went and
jammed it in the fucker's eye.

I got out just to live again
just to die again.

So I've come to realize
that dying hard is just not
the life I want for me.
I'm a retired die-hard, guess you could say
and now I leave the dying hard
to the younger ones
who have yet to learn that
dying hard just does not pay.

Crazy

I'm fucking crazy. I mean, ca-ca-ca-cuckoo. I do shit that might seem to others as obscene, a little out there. Well, so fucking what! I don't need friends who are going to judge me. I don't judge you. I let people be, but that doesn't mean you can come around and judge *ME*. I make mistakes, but I'm working on my shit, and that's what counts. I admit I have problems, I'll be the first to admit it. I don't need you to point it out to me, cuz I have eyes too, I see myself when I look in the mirror, I really do. But for a friend to put me under the microscope, to analyze me, diagnose me, and then abandon me cuz they don't like what they see—fine! I don't need you anyway. I bet I could just as easily put YOU under the microscope, and I bet I'll find many things about YOU that I myself will not like; but here's the thing: I DON'T! A good way to learn to hate someone is by putting them under the microscope. And if the looking-glass is broken, cracked—*damaged!*—well, what the hell does that tell you? The blind leading the blind—a whackjob analyzing a nutcase. What the hell do you think you're gonna find, anyway? Just think about it! We're all good, we're all equal, but we're all sick, it's a guarantee. So save your judgments, cuz I don't need it anyway!

Dastardly Deeds

I AM MY OWN GREATEST CREATION, BUT THE POWER I HOLD IN MY HANDS IS MADDENING AND I SNUFF IT OUT WITH DASTARDLY DEEDS. I SELF-DESTRUCT AS A FORM OF PACIFICATION. THE MIND IS A FRAGILE TOOL, AND MY MIND IS LIKE A DELICATE LEVER—THE SMALLEST AMOUNT OF PRESSURE IS ENOUGH TO SET IT OFF, AND NO ONE CAN SAFELY PREDICT THE OUTCOME, IT RUNS RAMPANT, RACING THROUGH TIME, SLINGING THOUGHTS LIKE A FUCKING GATLING GUN. IT'S UNSTOPPABLE, AND I SNUFF IT OUT WITH DASTARDLY DEEDS.

the end

A Dog's Life

You know that dog
that's always chasing cars?
Well I am that dog
and he is me, forever
chasing cars and one day I
will get hit and die and the last thing
I see before the dark nothingness washes
over me will be a surge of
rising bubbles that pop and
clatter with a burst of smoke
and steam.... That
is all that this life
(or whatever you wanna call it)
has in store for me————

The Ramblings of a Madman

Mentality dissipates at
night, after the sleeplessness
catches up. It's maddening
when hippies sing about love
and hope and you stand there,
in the dark, sweating crazed
thoughts in hysteria, relieved
the dark all of it burns bright
the ambient noise is like
a frying pan banging off a kitchen
counter your ears burn and you
pray to fall asleep .... soon.

Smash a Lightbulb: Poetry for Lowlifes

Dread fills you builds you up
with fear worse than the skunks
tittering in the brush and a crack
like a gunshot smashes off
somewhere in the dark, your
skin ceases up and you realize
you're alone alone so alone
the place you came from has
disappeared and a radiating ring
pulsates like a snake on flames
in the distance another crack
and you're off running through the
        woods.

Branches scratch and claw
ripping into the fabric soaked
in sweat your sweat my sweat
our sweat trees howling above
you as the breeze whispers
telling you a horror story about
the kid lost eaten by bears
left to the scavenging chipmunks
and this only validates the
fear you feel of being
alone and in the dark
and the woods and then
you wake up and a midget
with a flesh-colored patch
over his left eye is gnawing
on your right thigh and
maggots squirm on my
skin tittering and biting
and nipping deeper and
deeper into me and you

realize I can't move you're
stuck fucked your life
sucks and I swear I'm dying................
       and the paper runs out.

A Sensitive Asshole

When you're feeing down
      I'll lift you up.

When you're feeling up
      I'll knock you down.

                                I'm just that kind of nice.

So Bored You

Idle conversation, directionless talking, chatting and flirting, relating for the sake of relating, looking for validation, for laughs, chuckles, teeth clacking, tongues clucking, eyes wandering, rolling back into the back of my head; I'm falling asleep, slipping away into a nothingness that only comes about from sheer boredom.
I look at the clock, ticking and tocking relentlessly, staring at me from its perch on the wall—*mocking me!* The sound it makes is incessant, like ambient diarrhea; so irritating I wanna smash it with a rock. It moves too slowly. My mind dying, my head sinking, I'm nodding and I don't care who sees. Being here is useless; there is no gain, nobody left to save.
All I see are blank faces; everybody is so blank, so utterly numb, so dumb it becomes retarded. I'm better off slapping my own chest, trying to bite off my own

ear. Like a dog chases its own tail, I chase a dream, a hope, hoping things will change, be different for a change.

Insanity—doing the same thing again and again but expecting different results. I know the results, but I do it anyway. I do it because life is hopeless. I know things will never change, be the same until I die. I know the world is doomed, so coming to this place is no different than anywhere else—a pit of despair, of rot, worthless human interaction that I could do without.

On Conformity

YESTERDAY
    I went to this big gathering
              of people.

EVERYONE wore suits and ties.
        ME I dressed casual
        with big holes in my jeans.

SOMEONE SAYS TO ME
        at least I'm not afraid to
        be myself.

                Am I?

Escape

Why do I do this to
myself?
Deprive myself of the necessities
that one must endure if one wants
to live right
& happy——I'm so unhappy.
Another sleepless night
another racked and aching head.
I stare up at the moon as a shiverous
tremor seizes me, holds me tight.

I'm beating myself raw.
I'm screaming for help, but
nobody can hear me over the
ghouls that stream from my
bloodshot eyes.
I'm seeking pleasure, searching every drawer,
throwing clothes across the floor
knocking books off the shelves,
setting fire to my entire home——the fire

blazes bright and alive....
It ripples and thrashes, and the moon
the dark sky
the stars scattered up there so bright and vivid
make me feel oh so scared and alone.

A waking fit, I'm kicking holes in the ceiling.
I'm throwing plates and bowls
across the kitchen floor
they crunch and crack and scatter
and the sound of breaking and smashing

makes me feel like something
   like something
but I know I'm nothing—tap-tap-tapping my vein.

I lean back and let myself float away
drift upward and the whole world never felt the same.
Why must I
fight reality so often?
You know, reality is kicking my ass all the time.
You know, no I don't, and I thrive on escape
I live for internal mayhem
I need escape, and I'm taking it any way
that I can.

Because it's the only way
out of this place....

A Freak's Pickup Line

Open-mindedness is good and I'm said to have an open mind myself; it's so open that if you look deep enough into it you can see outer space. Only there are no stars up there, just a big black hole (a void). Sorry, I've had a bad day/night (a bad life, more like it), and while I was screaming at a white wall because the whiteness was so bright it was hurting my eyes but it was way too scary to go outside and face the darkness alone, I thought maybe I could go online and find a mate who could step out into the darkness with me and it wouldn't seem so bad anymore; we'd marvel at the starry beauty, the sacred emptiness that surrounds this planet. So what do you say?

You wanna go for a walk with me?

Untitled

If I hate you, you're probably gay, retarded, or crippled.

That, or I'm gay, retarded, or crippled.

Death Defying Stunts

1. I drove into a tree head-on and at full speed
2. Climbed out of a pickup truck window into the bed and back in through the window, while doing roughly 80 miles per hour on the highway
3. Taunted a car full of black girls in the ghetto
4. Wore a jacket with a homemade back patch that said EVERYONE IS A CUNT to a feminist Punk show
5. Lit my hair on fire numerous times
6. Shouted back at the cops who had us pinned against the wall beneath a bridge in Haverhill, MA
7. Challenged an anonymous woman threatening me with her shotgun
8. Fell of the train
9. Fell down the stairs and put my face through the wall at the bottom
10. Attempted to steal the entire PA I had found in the church basement while above me a hardcore show was underway
11. Etcetera, etcetera, etcetera

And today I was afraid of a chainsaw....

Self-Empowerment

I will not be victimized
I will not suffer the brunt
of your conformity
I live for one soul, one being
and it's all I need in this world.
One living creature, an overseer,
someone watching my back
looking out for number one.
I live for me and I follow
my own rules
I write my own laws
I'm the untamed cat that walks steady
on the edge of the roof with no concern///
I will only fall if it seems appropriate at the time.
Walking on the edge—not thinking but
lunging headfirst into the icy waters
is how I go about things.
I paint my own world
the colors I choose to see.
I fill my life with the necessities
that I deem fit for someone like me.
So take your rotten conformity
take your rhetorical nonsense
take your colors and your slogans
take your mythical teachers
and take your rules & restrictions too
and shove em in your mouth
and swallow down your pride

cuz me
I'm still fucking alive/

Hate, Anger, & Rage

Hate, anger, & rage are all agents of change. Without discomfort nothing would get done. We'd stay stagnant, which in my opinion is worse. That's what this world has devolved into: animals so obsessed with love and thinking love is awesome and we need nothing else, but look where it's got our society—apathetic, hopeless, & in love. I love you, I think you're perfect, and I never want you to change. Or I hate you, you're terrible, and I see your flaws. I get you gotta accept others for who they are, cuz they might not want to change and that you gotta accept. But as a whole, this world needs more anger, hate, & rage. It's what makes the world go around, it makes us learn and grow and become better people.

No Place Like Home

I sit on the side of the parking lot, watching
social interactions, people communicating.
I watch them get a little rowdy—
the cool kids talking in their cool-kid slang.
They don't even notice me there, in
my dirty, outdated clothing, skipping
stones across the concrete.
Maybe the girls look at me, but they
only sneer, roll their eyes, and avert their glares,
giving their attention back to the cool kids at play.

Some of the girls dress like hot cheerleaders,
all pom-poms and miniskirts, with little frilly edges.
Some of the boys wear baggy gear, pants sagging,
with thick headphones pressing their ears flat to their heads.
Some boys wear their sport's uniforms,

Smash a Lightbulb: Poetry for Lowlifes

supporting their team, whereas some girls
dress in tight spandex, hips and tits showing like
a few bulbous lumps.

I watch them interact, feeling
like such an outcast, a loser,
unaccepted by my peers, when I hear
from behind me a ruckus, shouts,
loud noises.

I crane my neck and jump back when I see the rowdy bunch running in circles,
bouncing off one another, smashing about, slamming and crashing, heads bowed
and charging, feet scurrying, arms swinging, legs leaping and kicking and stomp-
ing—

what a sight!

Hair stands on end, as if electrified,
dyed a variety of vibrant colors.
There's loads of black leather,
jackets patched and studded,
girls clad in fishnet tights,
some heads shaved.

Amid the strange dancing/bonding
I see a kid about my age, half his head
bright-pink, the other half jet-black.

He is beckoning me with his hand.

His black jeans are tight, with
a white patch sewn over his crotch.
More patches are cluttered down his legs.
He has PUNX tattooed on the knuckles of

Jeremy Void

his waving hand.

I point to myself and mouth the word, *Me?*

He nods quickly, excitedly, still beckoning me along.

I stand up cautiously, the cool kids
still horsing around in the lot.
They don't even notice me as I turn to fully
face this kid, and then something light
hits me in the head.
I look at my feet and see a
red plastic cup rolling to a stop on the ground.

"Loser!" one of the cool kids shouts,
which is followed by a volley of laughter.
I sneer at them, but it goes unnoticed.

The kid is now standing beside me, grasping
my hand and tugging me along, pulling me
toward the roiling pit of human destruction,
getting more violent the closer I get.

Then I'm there, standing on the sidelines,
when something shoves me straight into the pit,
too quick for me to react, for me to stop myself,
before I get swept up in the bodily tornado.
I get shoved, knocked around, pushed forward
and back and I can't think, I see a circle of
others surrounding me, and it hits me all of a sudden.

I'm one of them.
Them!
Part of their group. They accept me, let me play their game.

Smash a Lightbulb: Poetry for Lowlifes

Which I find amusing—enjoyable.

Swirling and twirling, a bombardment of banging bodies,
spinning with and against the flow, their arms
whipping up a frenzy and their feet kicking, bodies going
batshit crazy, spasmodic, apeshit, out of their
skulls and high on pure adrenaline.
I've never felt higher myself. The ebb
is simple enough that I catch on immediately.
I waltz wildly as they do, my legs flying high overhead.
I swirl and deliver a backhanded whack to
some guy beside me, and he stumbles,
tumbling down as I watch guiltily, thinking,
Oh my! What have I done!
But he's smiling as the bystanders hoist him back up
and give him a shove back in.

Spinning around, I notice my clothes ripping,
slashes appearing all on their own, with no
help from anyone, like from a ghost.
My white pleated pants fade to black
and tighten around my legs.
I feel the hairs on my head rising,
stiffening and hardening, as I scan the scene
around me, loaded with kids dressed unusual,
all smiling, laughing, having a blast.

I too am dancing dancing dancing like a fuckin maniac.
I'm having a fuckin blast.
The fuckin noise continues to blare from somewhere;
it's beginning to make sense to me, the metal-grinding sound
starting to sound like a guitar; that headache-inducing thump
is the bass, and the twin machinegun-sounding, irregular
rolling rumble that comes out pounding, like an anxious heart,

is only the fuckin drums, and this *music* sounds great,
like an orgasm in my ears,
fast and energetic, loud and vibrant, a visceral
feeling, putting me in a trance—a flailing and kicking
trance. It makes me feel alive.
I forget all about those fuckin "cool" cunts while I spin

around, tossed about by others who I suddenly trust!

Just Now

Just now a woman told me the first time I met her I walked in to a crowded room full of people dressed fairly "normal," only my own style of dress was a bit out there—a torn T-shirt with a litter of safety pins holding it together, tight black jeans, and black, spikey hair. She said I just walked in there without a care in the world, seemingly with no concern (or regard) for what anybody thought of me. I just walked in nonchalantly and lay down on the floor in front of everyone and spread out and made myself at home.

I don't remember that specifically myself, but it does sound like something I might have done.

Untitled

Spit on things you don't like.

A Script in Cahoots with 1,000 Misguided Prompts

#12
Who am I? Well, Lets see! Getting to the root of my problems with a razor-sharp hammer drilling through my exoskeleton, one thwacking crash at a time. What do I want youre asking? I want to break my skull with that hammer, dip razorblades in acid & carve thick, singeing crevices into my skin. Itll burn at first, Im sure of it, but then I/ll be walking on clouds with demonic clowns carrying children that they had stolen out of the grasps of cannibalistic serial killers. That is the goal, I guess: subliminal release, a couple of stilts to hoist me up into the bluest of skies & then I/ll be leaping over the moon in no time. Its an easy fete to accomplish when theres no gravity to keep me grounded, souring through the swirling vacuum with many black panthers who Im rather weary of at first glance, but somehow they complete me, make me feel whole again. I think thats where I am today, anyway.

#66
I have learned almost nothing thru & through, spiraling downward into tumbling caves that rumble & rip apart as I continue my rippling plummet in between boulders that roll & rumble rapidly & the green swampy water comes at me fast & Im instantly splashing through the smoke screen as the radical space shuttle spins & whips & wobbles & it makes me sick as shit, just tipping & twirling round&round, & immediately I curl over to vomit but instead clomp my heavy head on the side of the toilet bowl—aint that a bitch! Wait a minute, what was the prompt again?—I think I forgot.

#142
Growing up I learned crap, shit, fuck all—nothing worth a fucking damn. Peer pressure sucks, bullies beat you up, putting your hand on the kitchen stove incites burning flesh, etcetera etcetera. I dont trust people who smile too much, because behind the smile is a knife & trust is like letting them plunge it deep into my spinal column. Experiences create biases, we/ve all got them. Humans are

pack animals, & our brain capacity can only cope with a certain amount of people seen as individuals; whereas the rest are smothered in thick, prejudiced blankets. Now, if you yourself find that you are held tight by the blanket my experiences had weaved together through many years of fright, then be reassured that your existence is only a mere number to me, that you are reduced to a uniformed drone, not the least bit different than your predecessors, the ones who made you who you are & the ones who can break you with a single breath that billows out of their gorge-like throats, you know how it goes—I mean its only human nature to hate; its human nature to love a select few individuals & deem the rest a category of 1,000 men, like terrorists for example. But then again, these biases are pertinent to the survival of our entire race, in that we must judge to survive, to protect us from the most vicious of predators who pray on the flesh of the naïve ones. You see, without biases we all might die, perish in a cacophony of thieves & pirates, you know. Its sociology 101.

(But then, she says, "I dont remember learning that in sociology," grinning meanly through snotty lips—the fat, arrogant bitch that she is—with a snobby undertone weaved within. My response was only: "Well...." I know shes thinking that none of this real, none of what I say, but its in fact too real, so real it become surreal & that explains it all. The pedantic cunt with arms crossed, brows slanted, nose up, & a smirk that seems oddly planted on her fatty fatty lips of the most grotesque—Im thinking, How the hell should I know? I dropped out after the first class.*))))*

Anyway, moving on....

#1,000
        last but not least, whatever the hell that means
My biggest fear is to melt. I know its inevitable, for a body to decay, ripped apart by hungry, nibbling, squirming maggots. My soul melts while my body decays; or is it the other way around, my tormented soul might float away & never come back, & my body will remain a hollow vessel with no hope of prospering when life offers me a couple tainted limes for my troubles. Thats how I/ll end up I know, but then again Im already quite empty. Years ago my withering soul picked up its bags & left me here all alone. And the older I get it seems the more jaded my algebraic matrix seems to become, until my life fades

away completely & I find myself even more alone than before, with no hope to speak of, except for a six-foot-deep hole dug in some lifeless cemetery. Is that what anyone wants, really?? In forty to fifty years, everyone I know will be dead....

The end!

Some Definition in My Life

I love Punk rock, this is true. I love it more than anything, because it made me, it gave me definition, and definition was always something I lacked growing up in Newton, MA.
THEY had definition, I didn't.
They were football players, I wasn't.
They were baseball players or lacrosse players
they had popularity and girls and money and cars
and I had my rag-tag T-shirt and a FUCK OFF attitude that couldn't be bought, but it was not enough....
it was never enough until I found Punk rock!

Punk rock spoke to me in ways no girl ever could, it whispered softly in my ear, it spoke to me and promised things ....
it promised something more! something more than what I was getting.... Which was absolutely **nooooothing.**

Audacity

Two girls just had the audacity to tell me my clothes don't match. I'm pretty sure that, on my list of things to care about, whether my clothes match falls far at the bottom.

The Bars Are All Closed

Aaaaaaaah!!!——the world is turning red, images quickly flashing in my face, unstoppable, relentless, they come at me in shallow bursts, spurts of colors and shapes and everything flickering and it doesn't ever seem to quit.
Only one phrase streams through my head, on repeat, a nasty rumination that keeps me completely insane:

The bars are all closed....

What does that even mean????

It's nighttime, I'm cold, it's dark, and the full moon above me leaves its imprint in the stark night sky. My head stays pointed down, my eyes fixed on my feet.

I feel like I'm boxed in. Concealed. *Like the bars are all closed*—there it goes again. Nothing makes sense, nothing's connected, nothing seems relevant anymore.

The streets are dark, illuminated by a hazy gray light that has settled in places but is drifting in others. I hear noises. Laughter. From somewhere far, far away. The sound like a jolt of electricity running down my spine; I cringe—I know they're laughing at me.

Smash a Lightbulb: Poetry for Lowlifes

I don't even wanna be out here in the first place, not now—not ever. I'm only out here because I can't sleep and at home I started seeing bugs crawling on all the furniture, everywhere there were bugs, and even though I knew they were only a figment of my sleep-deprived imagination I couldn't take it. Leaving immediately was the only thing I could do that doesn't involve me ripping out my own eyes, just to stop me from seeing
just to make the mad images go away.

I don't look up, I don't look straight ahead, nor do I veer my focus to my left or right, I just keep my eyes aimed at my feet and my head angled downward.

I cross the street. Far away headlights flicker, flash, and beam—translucent and eerie—creating an ominous feeling that reminds me of the decrepit wasteland my world has become. I'm so sad.

The bars are all closed....

I'm in a vacuum. Vast emptiness. I kick a stone and trace its path as it slides across the smooth, oily road. It hits the curb with an ear-piercing clack, stops there, as though waiting for me to give it another kick, so it can continue moving along because nobody ever wants to sit still. Not even a silly stone wants that. Right then and there I feel closer to that stone than I have ever felt to anyone else in my entire life.

But then, it's hopeless. I step past it, over the curb, and onto the sidewalk.

My eyes still trained on my feet, I don't see the beaming full moon above me, but I sense it. I can feel its sharp, buoyant glow as it highlights parts of me that I wish to stay hidden.

The bars are all closed....

I hear the buzz of tires, can feel the rumble, the quake, the rattle, as a car plows past me, its ferocious headlights cutting through me to show my insides. I don't want that.

I look up to see the minivan's left turn signal start flashing as it stops at a red light.

I stop too.

The bars are all closed....

I'm afraid to go any farther, for this person, this driver, whoever, has seen too much of me, and now I'm too embarrassed to move. So I wait.

The bars are all closed....

The light turns green.

The bars are closed....

What the hell does it mean?

The bars are closed....

The minivan turns left.

The bars are all closed....

I wait, watch, and then proceed again as the minivan disappears down the road.

I pass a lone sign. Look at it.

        THE BARS ARE ALL CLOSED

I do a double-take.

Smash a Lightbulb: Poetry for Lowlifes

CHILDREN AT PLAY

I'm sinking, I can feel my body plunging deeper, my mind slipping farther and farther, deeper and deeper
into oblivion///

The ground drops out from beneath me and I'm falling, I don't know where I'm heading, guess it's wherever gravity takes me as I plummet deeper and deeper into darkness.
I blink blink blink, rub my eyes, and see the sign still standing there, just a few feet away from me. I crane my neck, checking my surroundings, and everything seems to be in check.

I look up at the sign again:

CHILDREN AT PLAY

I hate children, there's no joy in having them, they ruin your life, the way I see it. It happened to my parents, their lives ruined, and now all I can do is cry about it at night as I try to fall asleep, only to wake up in an even more horrid nightmare than this thing I call a life. I can't take back what I had done, I can't change the past, or at least that's what they teach me in AA, and I'm the fool for believing them, I guess. For having faith that there's a better path to follow, a road less-traveled but which carries even more benefits than the road I had to sludge through every fucking day of my useless life.

I'm alive & healthy, but what good is that when your mental state is in a state of distress? I'M NOT FUCKIN HEALTHY, I'm a fucking mess.

I stop in place then.

A few paces ahead of me is a bright and radiant block of light that immerses everything it touches——but not me, I would not let it soil me like that.

Jeremy Void

I reach one hand into the rays that open up a hole which floats in the darkness like a small island in the middle of the ocean; my hand crosses the threshold, entering the spotlight, but right away I reel it back as if it has been badly burned by the translucent beam.

What the hell is wrong with me? It's only light.

"The bars are all closed...."

I whirl.

This time I didn't think it, I *heard* it—a slight whisper carried by the wind, as if someone had suddenly pinched my butt, and I whip toward the man or woman who had done it—I whip toward him/her hard—my whole body twirling as my head spins and I glare in the other direction from the way I'd been walking, only there's no one behind me, no one in sight, except for a homeless man pushing a shopping cart down the sidewalk, him and the cart looking almost silhouetted in the distance, under the full moon's glow, just a shadow drifting down the road and minding its own business, generating a faint jingle when the tin cans and glass bottles in the cart rattle.

I think I'm losing it.

I stand at the edge of the light, not even daring to take my chances and go through. I finally decide to tread around the edge and I'm careful not to cross through as I step sideways, one foot after another, sliding circularly around the bright, beaming rays that radiate sharply against the sidewalk.

I think I'm losing it.

I reach the other side of the light. *Phew!*

The bars are all closed....

Smash a Lightbulb: Poetry for Lowlifes

I ignore the thought this time, the nefarious rumination that won't leave me alone. My eyes start to sag and I feel almost dreamlike, everything around me becoming liquid, wobbling and undulating like thick, gooey Jello, the world overlapped by a shade of purple that blankets everything I see.

I'm scared.

My eyes sag.

Maybe I could just sit down somewhere and rest my head.

There's a bench on the corner up ahead, just past the upcoming intersection, and I can surely sit on it as I rest my eyes for a moment.
I walk slowly, my balance slipping quickly, everything unclear and bleak, fazing in and out of focus. *C'mon, you can do it,* I tell myself. *Just a little bit more to go. You can make it.*
I get to the intersection and my right leg crosses my left and knocks me off balance; I stumble hard, but catch myself on the steel pole holding up the WALK signal, and my head slams into it and bounces right off, and my vision fades out as my legs give, and I blink blink blink as I try to keep myself up.
I plop on my knees and fall flat on my elbows in the street, and scrape them slightly. I push myself up.

The bars are all closed....

I rise to my feet and struggle to stay up; I stagger across the street as quickly as possible, blinking rapidly to keep my eyes stimulated. *I'm not gonna make it, no way am I gonna make it,* I think—and then gravity kicks in and pulls me straight down and I crash into the ground just as my lights ebb and then fade and then shut off...................

... darkness ...

I open my eyes, and I'm in bed. I hear multiple people snoring. I rub my aching head, feeling like I've gotta puke all of a sudden. I don't hold back, I just bend over and vomit right beside the bed.

Then I sit up. I stand. At first I have a hard time staying grounded on my feet but in the end I do manage.

I head over to the light shining through the window. It's dim and as I get closer it doesn't seem to bother me anymore.
When I'm standing directly in front of the window, basking in the brightening dim light, I notice the bars, vertically planted to obstruct my view of the outside world.
I look at the bars and the only thought that enters my head is:

The bars are all closed………………………………………

Hey Goth, Fuck Off!

I would be Goth too if my mom killed herself and my dad beats me cuz he said it's all my fault. If my girlfriend chained me up and forced me to watch while she fucks some other guy. Or if I had no balls and liked to bitch and moan and complain about everyone being mean and nobody liking me and boo hoo my life sucks so I'm gonna go and dress in black and tell everyone how bad it is because they just have no idea what it's like to be me—boo hoo!

Gratitude List

I'm grateful for a lotta things.
For starters, there's AA.
Thank you, God,
Bill and Bob. Thank you all
for joining together to create
a place where I can go,
a program I can work,
a set of traditions to model my life
after.
Then there are my parents.
Thank you, Mom and Dad.
Thanks for all the help,
the support, for not
kicking me to the curb.
I can walk, I'm healthy,
although my teeth are rotting out of my face.
A pen and paper—two things
I could not live without.
The computer, sure, but the craft of writing?
I might as well drop dead where
I stand.
There's sunshine and music,
darkness and silence.
Misery, of course.
I'm fucking miserable.
Thank you, God, for that especially.
Thanks for the depression.
Thanks for the sickness.
Thanks for the emotional malady.
I guess that's what makes me an artist—
looking at things under a
different light.

A different light?

Yeah, right!

Hopelessness In-Action

What's with this common belief that we have to be someone or something? Why can't we just exist? Accept the nothingness or worry endlessly that our purpose has yet to be fulfilled? Which is easier to do?

My Demons

I'm mentally twisted, morally sadistic, but I got a touch as soft as sand, as gentle as a dandelion as the breeze brushes through and knocks the pedals loose and they explode like dust. My thoughts are corrupt and rotten, my insides are bitter and mean, but I'm telling you my skin is delicately sound, and as my inner voice screams for you to leave, my outer voice chides for you to come in, to come here, to join me in the sandbox to build this castle....

My demons are rattling my cage, racking chains against the thick steel bars holding them in, but I keep them at bay, neatly tucked away inside a prison of my own making, and they don't seem to bother me there....

Except when I fall asleep at night and terrifying nightmares ratchet the insides of my brain,
but then I wake up and forget it all as I go about my day...............

No Rules

You were born into a world in which people, everyone you meet, would stop at nothing to change you, to make you just like them. Condition you to think, act, and feel in sync with the mass majority. The quote-unquote "normal" folk who get along with others easily, like it's their vocation to, like they were born with a second brain—a brain that feeds them knowledge, awareness, an understanding which you don't seem to have, my friend. They mingle with ease, and you struggle with such a thing, and they want you to cooperate, which, unfortunately for them, is not engrained in your DNA. You will not, CANnot, cooperate. It's not hardwired in your blood.

This is your time to rise above the social construct and shout that you will not fucking take it anymore; you will not be the system's puppet!

God Bless You

Would you believe me if I said I love you?
Would you hate me if I said I didn't?
Do you care enough to see the difference?
Or are you just dreaming that I would leave you alone?

On Fire

Just lit my hair on fire again—for the umpteenth time. Never set it aflame with hair this long though, and the flame kept burning and now I smell like ass—no, worse than ass!

To Be an Outcast

It's easy to take the side of everyone else in the room. Too easy. And that's all I see: a bunch of sheep. Just because you wear black clothes doesn't mean you're not a sheep, doesn't mean you're not just like everybody else. Darby Crash dyed his hair blue to see what it would be like to be the only nigger in an all white school. Richard Hell walked around New York City wearing a shirt that said PLEASE KILL ME. When I wrote my poem "Fuck You" and showed it to an influential member of the Rutland Punk scene, whose name will remain anonymous, he called me a Nazi. A Nazi? What, because I used the word nigger? I called Obama a thieving nigger. Would calling him a thieving African American be any fucking better? Or is it the fact that I even mentioned race that makes me this alleged Nazi? Sorry I'm not a good little white boy pretending race does not exist.

And just so nobody gets the wrong idea, I'm Jewish.

Tonight I read my poem "To the Girl I Love" at the Alley, and the guy from Ham Job shunned me for it, but fuck those stupid cunts.

In the '70s Punks wore bright colors—colors like pink. Crass said they all dressed like peacocks, and they didn't want to dress like peacocks, so they started wearing black.

Today everybody wears black.

What You Love!

Destroy what you love before it destroys you!

Everything Will Always Work Out One Way or Another
A Text Message to a Friend Who Is Having Trouble Staying Awake Throughout the Day

I was just thinking that this issue where you can't stay awake won't be an issue 10 years from now. I think it was Einstein who said that everything with a beginning has to have an ending. And if it still is an issue, you'll have found a way to cope with it. You've been presented with a dilemma and you're going to do what all humans do when presented with a dilemma: you'll learn to adapt. Like, I get vertigo. It started when I started taking [a certain medication]. Excessive movement causes vertigo, going up and down stairs causes vertigo. If you think not being able to stay awake is rough, try getting spells of vertigo. It's scary as shit. So as a result I didn't go anywhere, I barely left my apartment cuz I was afraid of getting vertigo in public and every time I went out in public I got vertigo. That was about 3 to 4 years ago. Today I still get vertigo from time to time, but I've adapted to it. I've figured out coping mechanisms to put in place when it happens, which is very rare cuz I've also figured out ways to prevent it from happening in the first place. I was presented with a dilemma and I adapted. It took some time but that's only natural. I wanted a quick-fix to solve the problem but my psychiatrist said the problem was physical and my doctor said the problem was mental. Each doctor pushed the problem onto the other. It was really frustrating but over time it just worked out.

i am SO stupid

      have you ever noticed it's only stupid people who say they are smart?

      everything is relative, so in the eyes of a moron, one might seem pretty damn smart.   i used to believe I was stupid.

      i believed it with all my heart.

today i KNOW i am smart.
do you know how i know?

because i am so stupid....

The Image

Chapter 1:
    The image is dented

Chapter 2:
    The image is cracked

Chapter 3:
    The image falls apart

My Rights as an Amerikan Citizen

The state has created: an enemy
out of me;
the state has decided: who I am
to be;
the state has saturated: the last of
the full-blooded American Indians
in dreams;
the state has divided: we parted into
two separate wings....

The hippies sing their songs of love
while the new business men

Smash a Lightbulb: Poetry for Lowlifes

of Amerikan industry
move in and take us
up the butts.
There's this new thing coming:
pick a side or die
the gangs are at war fighting
for territory and money and drugs that
the CIA floods into the city streets.

We are at the whims of every rich man
on the face of the planet
we are pulled apart like puppets
scrabble and run across the sunset
we are mixed up and lost
as we press the keys on the keyboard
sign on to Facebook and check out
the latest gossip of a nation on fire.

The flag sails at half-mast
as another star blinks out of existence
the country is overrun by warhounds
pretending to be mobsters
as they play make-believe on Facebook
as they dial into God and check out
the recent gossip of a country that is dying.

This is life we need a new distraction
something to take the focus away
from the real enemy that keeps us at bay
keeps us fighting and killing and keeps us
locked in dismay.
Fight eachother so the focus isn't on
the white-collar thieves who layoff another
hardworking man, who send the goonsquad

out prowling to maim and abuse
another honest soul that gets by by telling the truth.

We dial into a system, we offer up our necks
for comfort and safety, for a state of disbelief
———but where does it end?———————
for the privilege of surfing the web and finding out
about what clubs the famous rockstars had frequented.
This is our right as an Amerikan citizen: to be
kept updated about the last guy
Paris Hilton had fucked, the last trash heap who
had been caught at dawn fondling a hooker
beneath the bright and vibrant stars of
Hollywood Avenue;
this is our right as an Amerikan citizen:
to be kept blind about the real problems going on
in this world that is burning.

This is my right as an Amerikan citizen: the freedom
to be distracted—the freedom to choose
one of two sides that had been deemed acceptable
by men that I don't even know;
this is my right as an Amerikan citizen:
the privilege to eat as much bullshit as I want
to diverge and digress and read up
on all the latest tabloids and see who is fucking who
who visited which club at what time
and who died of a heavily expensive drug overdose
in the night.   It's my right …

True Romance

Lost in your glare
your smile is the only reason
that I'm here
the glint of your shiny white teeth
and your hair that waves majestic
lines through the air.

I'm lost and I'm alone and the only thing
that could make this moment better

is if you noticed me too....

So I kiss the mystery on the lips
and drift away on that sullen fantasy
of what could be
of me and you

if only you would notice me too.

Pissed Off and Loving It

Sometimes you get angry and your situations are always testing your patience it seems, but sometimes when you feel you should be angry, you actually feel satisfied because the very thing that should piss you off you can instead use to your own advantage. You can use it to justify your actions, and while part of you is ticked, another part, a more slick and sneaky version of yourself, is scheming and planning and using that anger to your own benefit.
Well, I guess that's the nature of the beast. The epitome of anger. The realization that although you're rather pissed, you can take that vindictive feeling as a

motivation to create something new, or I guess you could also justify your pacing your apartment with a butterfly knife being discharged and flung up and down and around and out and then folded back into the blade just to be let loose on the world again. You could utilize that irate sensation as a rational to slugging a hole in a wall, to punching straight through a pane glass window, or to take a sludge hammer to a cinder block or even chuck a brick at your neighbor's house. There are so many different avenues one can choose to go down when that angry sensation touches the mind, when that rageful wonder hits you in the heart, when you fall to your knees and scream as that pinch of pissed-off adrenaline comes railing through your head.

I don't know, I guess anger is as normal to anyone as masturbation is to a hormonal teenager coming into his own. As natural as that spontaneous hard-on that young men try to conceal when they're in school or at work or talking to that busty cheerleader-type as they wait for the bus to come take them home. It's normal, and it's wonderful, and it generates a high of its own. It's important that we don't run from it, it's important that we don't hide. Like any natural tendency it is important that we embrace it and cherish it but still we must not perish because of it,
but learn to grow and prosper as a result.

Untitled

No disrespect, but
YOU SUCK

The Old Man

I woke up.
My head hurt.
My dreams were so surreal
in the night.
I remembered lots of things
that happened, things
magically woven, like
a sweater crumpled
and burned to ashes.
My mind was on fire.
A chain of flames
swung like whiplash
and crashing into a pool of blood.
The old man sat on his blue stump.
He held a cane that looked like
a snake, the head of which
twitched and jerked in his hand.
His eyes were firm, his stare
sharp like shards of glass.
He sat there and stared numbly
up at me, like he was watching
the TV.
I looked away, trying hard
not to meet his gaze.
This man there, he stared like
he had beef with me.
Then he stood up,
cane in hand, and walked away.
The back of his head was
a mirror,
and when I looked in it,
I could not

see
myself.
What I saw was
an ominous black hole
swirling and shifting in shady
arrays, roiling violently,
with thunderous flashes showing
an ever-present skull.
I gasped when I saw it.
Gasped and jumped back.
The mirror shattered.
An explosion of glass.
The shards trickled on the ground
as the man kept walking
away from me,
fading
into
the
black.
Then he whirled,
and I woke up,
with his horrifying expression
burning my soul.
It was all I could think of
as I got dressed
and went to
work.

Like a Fly on the Wall

It's like
I write shit on Facebook
but nobody notices.
I say shit in real life
but nobody cares.
Like a fly on the wall
I'm taken for granted
just a piece of a-æthetic wonder
subliminal and silent;
I'm invisible to most
they don't even know I exist.
I lurk in the corner
buried by shadows;
I'm in the back of the classroom
silent and still
full of misguided rage,
just buzzing—wings fluttering:
a tiny spec of dust
a grimy glob of muck.
I try to stay true
but what's the truth but
a mere phony construct.
I'm lucid and bright
but most people don't
even fucking know me.
I'm sick of being a structure
just an ambient statue;
I've got a voice that must
be heard but most people
wouldn't know what to make of it.
So I'm walking home all alone
tonight's rejection

prominent in the back of my mind.

But I will not cry about it.
I won't shed a single tear
because if I did
nobody would even see the thing drip....

This Is Punk Rock, Part 2
Like Sheep in Wolves' Clothing

Do you know why it bothers me when someone who knows nothing about Punk rock dresses Punk: it kills the camaraderie that true Punk is all about. There was a day when Punks would hold their hands out to the fallen ones. Sure, they'd ridicule you but it'd be all in fun. It's kind of ironic, but most outsiders would call Punks mean & rotten kids with no respect for anyone because we seem aggro to them with our chains & spikes & studs. But I'll tell you this: at a time when I needed a friend the most, who was it that stuck their hands out & helped me to my feet? It wasn't your own kids who look so neat in their Polo shirts & nicely ironed pleated pants. Your kids shunned me you see, whereas Punks opened their arms wide & said, "Hey you! Kid! Fuck those little pricks! They ain't your friends! They treat you like shit! Come with us & we'll show you what friendship means; & what it means to be Punk, too. We're gonna have loads of fun, kid. Just you wait & see! Let's get outta here." So I went & I learned all about what camaraderie means, but I'll tell you, talking to these trendy kids today who look down on me through their snotty little noses, it really makes it hard to know who I can identify with & who I can't, cuz some kids just wanna look cool & feel even cooler in their black studded leather & dyed hair. You see, there is a reason for the uniform; it's so we can separate the wolves from the sheep, but today the sheep are dressed in wolves' clothing & it makes me sick, you know.

The Dividing Line

If 2 friends are fighting, what do you do? Pick a side, or try to find a solution?

So Sorry

They want me to change
say the way I live my life
is detrimental to
        the lives around me.

So now I've gotta change.
But nobody specified in what ways.

THE THING IS I have changed
      ——A LOT——
My perspectives of the world
my attitudes toward the world
my desires and disinclinations too.

So sorry I'm not your spitting image
        of perfection.

The Bullet

I hear the cock of the shotgun, the click of the rifle, the crack of the handgun; the sound the hammer makes when it snaps the platform. The gun fires a shot, the powder explodes, the sound hard & sharp, the bullet blows out the muzzle & searches for its mark. The target ruptures upon impact, the bullet cuts right through, & I see it coming & start running for my life. The bullet is fast, & I don't think I can evade it, but I can try, & so I try, & my heart hammers inside.

Mrs. Big-Shot NYC Editor, Watcha Think of This??

This big-shot NYC editor gave a lecture about how you shouldn't combine action and depth (which is what makes up the classics in literature, she said). The best kinds of stories, according to her, have both those ingredients, but it's nearly impossible to pull it off. *Hmm,* I thought. So I asked her if she would like to read one of my stories, and she ran away from me. She ran away, I found out later, because I would have had to pay seventy dollars to speak to her one on one. I only wanted her to read "The Haunted Bathroom," is all.

My Mind's a-Racin'

I've got a lot
going on
in my head
all this static
radiant & bright
rapid flashes of light
my right foot tap-
tap-tapping the
white
linoleum
floor
beneath me
the leash comes off
my head swims with glee
the night comes on
my consciousness
flooded with
motion
so emotionless & daft

Smash a Lightbulb: Poetry for Lowlifes

I find myself moving
grooving
emotional like
I-just-can't-fuckin-take-it
the pain   the madness
anymore
this rein of terror
in the wake of
my thoughts
my racing brain
is
on fire
I think I'm
getting higher
I'm running
running from you
I think I'm moving
grooving to the tunes
the beat a raucous ricochet
fast & loud
the double bass pounding
confusing
my cruising head
I'm losing my mind to this
my feet are moving
my jittery fingers are
thrumming a quick rhythm
finger-snapping
on the chair where I sit
the music's fast
not fast enough
too slow
I wanna stand up
& shout

run in place
throw a dashing punch
at the wall
plow straight through
the plaster the wood
Who Wants to Fight Me?
I'll take you all
I'll throw down
right here
right now
C'mon let's go....
let's fuckin go!

In My Honor

One day I'm going to do something really great and when they have a party to celebrate how awesome I am, you are not invited.

Untitled

The world glows, the laughter lulls, the voices pull, and I'm sullen and alone.

Small Town Mentality

In RUTland
people are so 2-faced
        and I think I know why.

A smile around here
feels like a knife to the back
        and I think I know why.

It's a survival technique
        I learned from living around here for quite some time.

Be nice or die!
        you'll get eaten alive by all the close-minded folks who live in these
        parts.

A Split Personality

I think I got a split personality. Sometimes I'll write something on Facebook that I'm really psyched about, but then I'll see that post later on and think, *When did I write that? It's complete crap.*

Love Is Timeless
Forever and Ever

1.
I need her
she & I

2.
We knocked loose
the orgy of one-thousand nights
We brought forth the
reverberating echo that
raged with rage

So irate the little dove
sat on a kettle drinking
whiskey that poured down through
the funnel of one-thousand spirals
spiraling
down
and out
she & I

We laughed like mania
We frolicked like hysteria
We lived like speed
the lid came on knocked back
and muffled the voices
that threatened to
surge
and rise

This

was our demise.

3.
That girl
the one who came to me
amid my wet nightmare
poking her head up
and out
with a shiny radiance
a smile of luminescence
her image distorted and scary
and I hid behind the walls of
my own personal hell
she & I
we lived like dreams
that kill
and we slayed the demons of shrill
rewound
and spun
the day is done
and we went to bed all wound up

in disease.

4.
Years apart
we died
dying
death
and the wakes of panic
rising
until we came together once again

and the night
we thrived

We lived like panic
like a festering hailstorm
like a train derailed
like a cancerous spiral
spiraling
down
into
destruction

and we lived like thieves
died like urchants
murdered by dreams

and we sat hand-&-hand
as the A-bomb bit dirt, smoke billowing
mushroomed up and over us

5.
And, finally: DEATH

a fucking fuckup

I'm a fucking fuckup!

Hey At Least I'm Something.
    What the hell are you????

Like an Open Book

You can read me like an open book
I don't care.
What you know
what you think
what you assume about me
can only affect my state of being
if I let it.

It's up to me to
let the pain in.
The hurt and humiliation is only
a product of my own volition.
Anything strong enough to push me
to twist me
to reel me in
can only effect me if
and only if
I let it.

I am me.
What you see is me.
I only have me.
All I have left is this
flesh that wraps me up like a package
this red blood that streams through my veins
on a seek&destroy mission some might think.
I am Flesh&Blood, that's all.
No amount of dirt
no quantity of information—
the 911
the know-all
—no capacity of evidence against me

has enough power to tear me down.

Rumors are rumors
they carry no weight.
Materials are materials
they are not immense enough
to sink a working spirit.
Gossip all you want cuz
it's me
and it's only me
who I see when I look in the mirror.
Cuz it's me
and it's only me
that I answer to when I'm alone.

Go ahead, talk talk talk.
See what I care.
I know you've been misinformed.
I know the things you say about me
are not true.
I know it and I don't
care one bit, because this unit
of Flesh&Blood that I call
Jeremy Void
is walking out the door....

Have a nice rest-of-your-life,
cuz this soul you speak of
is stepping out of it———

possibly for good....

Yuck!

                        I shat on a gravestone
                              this one time
           the name on the stone was POPE
                and then
                  since it was a veteran's graveyard
                          and there was an abundance of
                    American flags
      I wiped my ass with an American flag
                          in broad daylight too
then a tiny lap dog stuck its head out   from behind the bushes
          and I yanked my pants back on
                                  and got shit all down my leg....

Listening to Verbal Abuse

Listening to Verbal Abuse while all the thoughts in my head seem useless really takes the edge off of the void I find myself locked inside of.

Not Enough

I've seen things
most people don't see.
I've experienced things
only witnessed in dreams.

Nothing you do or say
is enough to scare me away.

Untitled

I KNOW NOTHING!!!

On the Red Couch

The lights above me
        they lurk and shine
The people around me
        they lurk and spy.
I've gotta get out
        of this mental maze
              maybe dissipate
and go back to yesterday....

Untitled

When there is a gun in your face and a deranged man putting more and more pressure on the trigger, the best thing you can do is start jumping in place and screaming. Try to out-derange the gunman.

Part 6

Oh, the sick thoughts that cross my mind when nobody's around.

If only you knew....

Part 6

Oh, the sick thoughts that cross my mind when nobody's around. If you only knew....

Fucking Up, Getting High, and Destroying EVERYthing

Was looking at 5 to 10 years for being in the wrong place, wrong time. Came to Vermont as a way to evade the jailtime hanging over my head, beat it by mere seconds, and here I am, alive and well to tell you my tale, a tale of fucking up, getting high, and destroying EVERYthing.

And I do mean EVERYTHING.

The Game of Life

Waiting waiting, boring boring, nothing's new, Im sick and bored, and Im sitting snoring, and wasting time fingering the hole I cut in my enemys throat. You know what Im saying? Cuz Im sure you dont. Im choking on life as life chokes me up, Im banging the walls and kicking the ceiling as the walls and the ceiling close in on me. Im losing a battle that was never meant to be fought, and people they say to just keep my head up and play it straight, but Im too crooked to play any games they lay out before me, cuz the pawns are busted and the rooks have run away, and the Knights are looking at me, and suddenly this aint life, this is just a game, just a game, but they gave it a name and its name is Life and Im riding in a plastic car with my plastic wife past plastic houses and this is LIFE, and I think I might be turning plastic myself, becoming a pawn to be maneuvered at the will of my masters and its all assbackwards but I seem to be trapped here. Its just a game they told me; and I believed them too.

Raw

What You See Is What You Get, only what you see is a liar and a deceiver who will cut you down so fast your head will spin.

All the Time

At dusk
the sky sings a
vivacious lullaby
        I sit on the window sill
        lifted
            into
                space

At dawn
the sun shines dully
a collage of illumination
twisting
the
great
            beyond

Smash a Lightbulb: Poetry for Lowlifes

In the afternoon
I walk along
whistling a forgotten tune
that my great ancestors
fought killed and devoured for

At night I see
a thin wisp of fog
ghostly and begotten
drifting to and fro
in the hollow blackness
that lurks
like
        a sadistic axe murderer

In the morning
I follow the rainbow
as it shines and folds
curving across the
blossoming sky
the sun is talking to me
as I trek the long lost road
where the rainbow goes
to be alone
      fading
          into
                a blue nothingness
that makes me think of
a time
when everything was fine
drifting away on a white wisp of smoke
that kisses me sadly
on my decaying lips
and the night

erases
> my tainted memories

At dawn
> I dance with
> myself

at dusk
> the moon falls
> the sun evaporates
> and the sky explodes

In the afternoon I cry
alone
my mind beaming
> with fright....
> and decaying from
> the inside-out///

On Conspiracy Theories

Conspiracy theories rely on people not believing what they hear nor see, and yet the sole nature of conspiracy theories is relying on what someone else tells you.

Stalemate

When you read something by someone you absolutely despise
and the words bring actual tears to your eyes
and you hate yourself for that fact,
but you can't help it, it's just too damn sad

and for once you understand
For Once you understand what it's like to live in said person's sad sad life …
and suddenly you feel a connection that you could have never imagined feeing before
and there you go: You've gotten over your self-righteousness because you realized he is no different than you, you are no different than him, you're both just another fuckin victim of this society's fucked-up condition....

Fairy Tales

Little Girls are dreaming;
they're dreaming of Mr. Prince Charming
to ride down on his shiny silver horse
and save her from reality.
But as these girls grow older
and reality sets in,
they no longer fantasize
of being saved by that handsome knight.

Little Boys are scheming;
they're scheming to one day be
the hero who swoops in
and saves the damsel from herself.
But as these boys grow older
and they take a look around,
they see the women hanging off
the shoulders of abusive men.

Duality

I want to either create or destroy something beautiful.

My Wet Nightmare

I'm so angry right now.
I'm so twisted & demented.
Nothing I say makes any sense//

I'm a hypocrite.
      I'll be the first to admit it.

This life, my world, this eerie wet nightmare I always find myself in whenever I awake from my beautific dreamscape, is so damn horrifying that I don't wanna see it anymore.
I close my eyes and try to go back to sleep. I close my eyes and pretend to be somewhere else, someone else. I close my eyes and I try oh how I try to will myself away from here.
      But it never works.

when
will
this
fall
come
to
an
<u>end</u>

A LIFE??

YOU CALL THIS A LIFE????

Editing, a Necessary Evil

I don't know what it is about today, but whenever I write, I keep leaving out words. Maybe I'm writing too fast or something. Thinking faster than I can type. I type really fast, too. So thank God for editing.

God / Pure Luck?

I've done loads of crazy stuff. I've fallen off the subway train, I've climbed out of a pickup truck window while the truck was doing 70 or 80 down the highway, I've even tried to steal the entire PA system out of a church's basement while a hardcore show was underway right upstairs; and I obviously got caught red-handed by this big skinhead/hardcore kid who acted as a bouncer, and I had to book it—fortunately he never caught up with me because he wasn't the kind of guy who would have called the cops.

I'll admit it, I'm an alcoholic/drug addict and I frequent AA meetings. See, the thing about alcoholics is they live on the edge before they sober up. But me, as someone once pointed out, I had no edge to begin with. There were no limits to my mayhem.

Was it God who saved me? Or was it just pure luck? I'd like to think God and luck are one and the same. See, I don't pretend to know God because that would be a lie—make-believe. What I do know is there is something beyond me, something which I may never come to understand because it is <u>BEYOND ME</u>. Is this magical being pulling my strings, having saved me from my own self-destruction time&time again? I don't fucking know and I don't fucking care. It is what it is. Now I'm here, today is not yesterday, nor is it tomorrow. Today is today, and yesterday I soared in the clouds with vicious bats. Tomorrow I might climb a mountain, but today this muse is shouting at me to create something worth viewing——————————sorry about my rant here, but I felt it must be said....

My Addiction

My addiction is doing sit-ups in the parking lot. And I'm about to go out there and punch it in the face. See how it likes it.

Firework Love

Fireworks—a cobweb of colors,

different shades flickering in the sky.

It's a euphoric sensation,

the way your lips come in contact with mine.

Bliss—the waves of the ocean,

rolling and lapping at the sand,

water pouring from the sink faucet,

serenity when we walk hand-&-hand.

Noises—loud and fast and so rambunctious.

We're jumping and bumping and slamming into each other.

The guitar screams a solo, a fluctuation of notes.

We're dancing together; it's you and I forever.

A Shot of Junk

I look through the fog
I stare into yonder as
a shot of junk punches me
in the chest—my heart rebounds
my blood pours through crowded tunnels
like broken subway trains
loaded with cargo, but the cargo speaks
they see hear and dance
my veins shatter as I stumble
through broken lanes of scattered cars
horns blaring and lights zeroing in on
the hole in my head, my brain bubbles and pops//

I'm walking now
      walking on air
crawling through clouds of crud
as the shot of junk lifts me up up & up… — …
I'm falling and flailing as
a blaring ball of hail rips through
my chest cavity
I'm fumbling through day and night
lost in the endless barrage

Jeremy Void

of broken hearts and twisted bodies
voices like knives
chopping me up and feeding me
to mice, the commotion like
a bubble bath flowing with acid
and crumbling rice
a kick of might in the right spot
on a Friday night, out
out with the crowd
I'm walking on roiling clouds
undulating in spurts of bubbly pus
out in the town—the coppers all
sneer & frown
tumbling down I'm out to lunch
a blundering wet dream creeping through
the streets of death
Where Am I?? I shout
but the demons of lust
the crusty serpents and their dying slaves
of sin and bitterly sucking me
till that shot of junk
licks me again....
A Hit a Puff and a Dying Stab
taking me back to the days of madness
killing my dad with an epic stroke
folding over overdosed and choked
floating away in a puff of smoke

don't get caught in the blistering joke!

Note to Self

Dear Penis,

Please release me
from your clutches....

Thank You,
Jeremy Void

I Don't Care

This one's for you:

> I've got my own problems to deal with stop calling me I can't handle it I got problems of my own go away my problems are more pertinent not yours mine I'm sick of your complaining I'm not a shoulder to cry on I'll be your friend but if you shed one fucking tear I'll drop you so quick you wouldn't know what to do with yourself go away cuz I've got my own fucking problems these fucking problems are my own and I simply have no time for yours............

Bother someone else
See how they like it

Jeremy Void

GOODNIGHT, BABYLON!!!

The chords gushing thru
every membrane of your soul....
The rockstar plants a note
that reverberates thru
the underground
orchestrated by the demons   of your lust.

The crowd shifts & wallows
swallowing up the whole band....
They stand up there looking mean
& rad, as the singer leans over the mike
staring out yonder
across the whole stadium
a silence spreading like a
reverse A-bomb sucking out
the cheering & laughing & rambunctious
noise recoiling & rattling
retreating right outta here

& it's silent
dead silent....
1,000 watching eyes
1,000 waiting eyes
1,000 beady eyes
just waiting for him
to speak.

"GOOOOODNIIIGHHHT, BABYLON!"

AND there it comes
shattering as the guitarist slashes
a yodeling bar chord that rips far & wide

Smash a Lightbulb: Poetry for Lowlifes

the stadium explodes turns over
& everyone's flowing like the waves
of the ocean ...

The drummer beats the drums:
clunks! clanks! and the occasional *chink!*
to really get this party bumping.
The guitarist is strumming.
The bassist frets & slaps.

The singer leans in again
& howls a glass-shattering—
—a death-defying—
—a spit-in-the face-of-evil kind of
shriek that cuts & ripples far & wide
across the moving crowd————
smiling & laughing & jumping
becoming a solid wall & then
breaking apart just to come together
once again//

ART

I'm a writer, I'm an artist. I like to delve into dark subjects, explore and fuck them, dissect them and poke and prod at their veins until a vessel bursts and blood sprays in my face, to show me

I've hit the spot!
but, you see
I
AM
NOT

Jeremy Void

CRAZY

no I am not....

I can assure you of THAT
I portray those twisted subjects so well because I am no more than a very talented fucking writer. It's what I do, and

it's what I do best....

The Best Kind of Art, in my opinion, is art that   bites!!!
      Art that snaps at you
growls and barks and grits its vicious fucking
teeth at you ...

that's my kind of art.
                    Art that lacks angst
                      ... well ...
                    isn't art at all.

I'm so sorry if my work
offends you....

Didn't mean it
like that....

I'm so sorry if my work
pisses you off
makes you vomit
scares you gay
because although that would be hysterical

I didn't mean it like that....

The way you choose to

Smash a Lightbulb: Poetry for Lowlifes

perceive my work is on you....

I'm just the Artist!

A Lesson in Trust

cannibals will lie, psycho killers will lie, but the guy who tells you a hooker stabbed him in the chest with an ice pick is the guy to trust

Western Philosophy

I was telling someone last night that misery and happiness are a choice. For the most part I choose happiness, but there are days when I choose misery. Misery is easier, more accommodating, comfortable, familiar, and more accessible. But happiness, however, is much harder to achieve, what with growing up in Western Civilization, having been taught Western Philosophy, having been instilled Western Values: No, misery is *not* a choice; other people *can* make me angry; things outside this room *do* have the power to affect how I feel, how I think. I am a product of Western Teachings. I write about negativity because I come from dark places, I go to dark places; I got this nefarious shadow following me around and I can easily let it take me. But I don't, and I won't. So you see, I write to keep those demons away.

NRG

too much NRG with nothing to fucking do

Crown of Thorns

It was a time when
nothing made sense.
I thought the world
was coming to an end/
Live your life like
you're already dead
       is what I said,
           and I suffered
           the consequences
           of a nowhere existence.
I suffered at the brunt of
a life lost and non-existent.
I was out to lunch
        said my friends.

Everywhere I went,
it was all the same.
A hysterical descent
that drove me insane.
I lived fast only to
be knocked to my knees.
I crawled on all fours
I pleaded and I screamed/
      but for what??
It was all just a dream>>>/

Torture

I'm not a fucking pet. I'm a human being and I've got feelings. I'm not gonna be tethered to a girl I've got feelings for who just wants to be my fucking friend cuz I'm not her "type." First of all, there's the obvious: in order to fit a type I have to be put inside a box, and I'm not inside **A BOX.** Which means I can't be anyone's type. And second of all, I just met this chick, and I don't care enough about her to follow her around all day like a fucking puppy dog in hopes for something that ain't ever gonna happen. Frankly I got better fucking things to do.

                                              So   there!

Untitled

Rejection is the epitome of liberation.

Void One

Can't decide
whether I'm dead or alive.
Too much pressure
daydreaming of suicide.
Gotta relax
put on some tunes.
If I don't see you soon
I might just blow a fuse.

This is life
a de-existing track
I'm bored and fed up
nobody's got my back.
This is life they tell me/
This is death they avoid....
This is living. Right!
I'm dying in this tremoring void.

Untitled

Try not to kill anyone while I'm gone. Or do.... Either way, someone *IS* going to die tonight. I'm sure of it.

Time

Time to go somewhere, someplace, anywhere, anyplace, everywhere, everyplace; time to be someone, somebody, anyone, anybody, everyone, everybody- - -living a lie, a dream, a fantasy, an altered reality- - -time to stretch my limits, push and pinch it and watch it dissolve in acidic waste like fire flies fighting and fucking right by my side>>>>>

Who's the Fag?
sung with Lethal Erection

Nerds are obsessed with video games.
Jocks are obsessed with athletic fame.
Nerds do good in all their classes.
Jocks wear spandex and slap each other on the asses.

Who's the fag?
Who's the fag now??

So what if they wear glasses, you shower together.
And that makes them a fag and you so much better?
You're a self-hating queer
in denial and fear....

Who's the fag?
Who's the fag now??

My Own Hell

There are demons in my closet,
skeletons in my backroom,
clawing the walls, and all I can hear
are the sounds of nails scraping wood.
It's maddening, the scratching of ghouls,
tearing slits and crevices in the doors.
The slamming and banging sounds
keeping me awake for endless hours.
It's all so real, so insane,
I lie awake in a straightjacket,
rocking to and fro, praying for it
all to stop, to cease, to end,
but it doesn't ever rest;
maybe it will when I'm dead.
When I'm gone, and I'm riding the waves
straight to Hell.
When I'm surfing fire, a surge of flames,
curling up, recoiling like a whip,
taking me through downtown Hell,
bringing me uptown to where the Devil
sits on Its thrown, waiting to rape me
with a 100-degree rod wrapped in razor-sharp thorns.
I dread it all, the thrashing sounds of my demons
trying to break out, escape and tie me up
with razor-wire which cuts deep into my skin,
as they dance around me like Indians
bopping around a pit of flames.
They wear hellish loincloths, their skin
orange and pockmarked with three green spots
over their noses, which are big like beaks.

I know what they wanna do to me.

Untitled

I'm telling you, suicide is never the answer.

Unless you're really, *really* depressed, of course.

Losing Friends in a Day

Dye your hair blue.
Overnight you've become a nigger.
Outcasted and exiled,
your fate's been made.
You search for existential purpose.
An existential meaning.
Your friends turn their backs
on you, and there's nothing
you can do.

Boo hoo!

Thoughts on Christmas

The downside of Christmas—is there an upside?—is that everyone on this planet is talking about it. No wonder the holidays have the highest suicide rate.

Blind Skull

The bird tweets delicately
        like
                              tainted
        falcons
in the treacherous heat.

I sit amid the beaming booming crooning
of crass thrashing noise
        not at all like
                the shriek
          of
the lonely loon
who gets eaten by
          a feral Viking
that comes galloping flaming through
the hovering rings of guts
    that bubble   with wretched pus

in the waves of lava-like heat
singeing the hairs off of
      the sedated noise barriers.

It's a violent times
      we live in
surrounded by flickering breaking eardrums
        that bleed grime and crud
        as a cataclysmic hatchet

comes down crashing on the heads of
      many dead civilians
who lurk inside of
      hell's most luxurious coffee shop..........

We're All Sick

People spend their whole lives applying makeup to their faces, covering up their zits and warts, and then they have the nerve to make fun of someone who can't afford to use makeup in more ways than one. It makes them feel better about themselves. But in the end we're all the same: we're all sick and trying to make a place for ourselves in a sadistic world run by giants who wouldn't think twice about stomping our faces into dirt.

Untitled

Why do I gotta act like such a fucking idiot all the time??

A Nursery Rhyme

Love sucks. Hate is great.
Better destroy your love before it's too late.
If you love, you will lose.
I'd much rather be sniffing glue.
My past proves this all the same,
that love will bring me down and drive me insane.
Besides I got nothing I care to share.
Love love love,
it'll tear up my heart and leave me bleeding to death.
Why bother when it hurts so damn much????

<u>Because it's worth the fuss</u>....

When someone says

"You know, Jeremy, sometimes you're really hard to figure out. Sometimes I wonder if you really are as [blah blah blah] as you say you are."

Haha, I Found It!

Found my old iPhone last night, and in doing so I got to read some of the texts I had sent the day I had lost it. Basically I was really, REALLY manic at the time - - and I'm thinking now that I hid the phone on myself so that I would stop sending these stupid texts to certain people, but then I completely forgot about that seconds later when I had the impulse to send another stupid text, because that's the only explanation I can think of of how my phone ended up in the place that it ended up in. But anyway, I read some of the texts, and boy was I crazy that day; some of them didn't even make any sense, they were complete fucking gibberish - - haha, WTF!

the Ego

the Ego
must be
destroyed
if one wants to
achieve
      salvation

An Assbackwards America

I
"Cunt," or other such words,
has an invisible context,
an association carried around
whether you like it or not.

II
The mind of a sheep.
What's it like to depend
on the demands of others?

III
Medications, the more they save
lives, the more costly they
become.
The more necessary, the
more money spent.

I know a woman who
has to cough up three grand for
a brand-new hearing aide.
It's absurd, but it's real,
and sadly we must adhere
to the limitations set forth by others.
This country robs and steals
daily from the pockets of those who
can't afford it.
Those who can afford it make money
off it.
What a sham!

Jeremy Void

IV

We help those who appear
independent, those who
otherwise don't need our help.
We don't help those who need it,
those who are truly poor
and can no longer afford to live
anymore.

What a sad state we're in,
where the rich get richer and fatter,
and the poor get poorer
and so much more
sadder.
Famine rules supreme,
whereas goodness and kindness
are left behind.

Next week, a friend of mine
was putting on a Punk rock flea market
in the basement of his bike shop.
Sadly, the cops stopped in for a visit
and told him his place is not
zoned for such events.
Oh no, not again.

The cops are always closing down venues.
Shutting down spots where the Punk rock kids
go to conjure.

Why us?

Because we're different and choose not
to adhere to cultural principles.

Smash a Lightbulb: Poetry for Lowlifes

We choose not to conform.

V

Lastly, I ask you,
what gives?
Why is open-mindedness cherished,
treated like a virtue in and of itself?
Yet having no convictions is
frowned upon, considered to be
immoral.

Having convictions is equal to
being close-minded, because
having convictions means
you are shut off to the opposition.

Those are just a few
examples of the
assbackwards America
that we live in.

Just one more:

VI

We all judge each other,
like an orgy of
judgments and finger-pointing;
we all call each other sheep,
and yet
we all follow some sort of order,
whatever order makes
the most sense.

Jeremy Void

It's like how
through my own eyes,
all blacks and Asians and
pretty much anyone not white
look the same,
whereas through their eyes,
all whites look the same.

We are all cunts
to a nation of even bigger
cunts!

We are all lost....

Words of Wisdom

Appreciate everyone.

    Help anyone.

        Forgive someone.

            Forget no one.

Lookalike

I looked like Sid Vicious—not intentionally (well, maybe a bit intentionally)—and I acted like Darby Crash, said everyone I knew back in my Punk rock glory days—also not intentionally.
People used to give me shit saying I was trying to act like Stiv Bators or Sid Vicious or Darby Crash, when, really, I was just trying to be myself.

Not my fault Punk rockers who died way before I was even born acted like *ME*. I mean, I wasn't going to change the way I acted so as to not fit a silly Punk rock cliché such as those. It's just the way I was, you know.

Racing Thoughts

Right now my thoughts are like ping pong balls.

Why am I here?

Good question. I've been asking myself this a lot lately. There's the literal reason: because the birds and the bees got together and made nookey and nine months later the egg hatched and I somersaulted out of my mother's womb. Okay ... and then what? I was deformed and demented and this world had no place for me. The end.

But then there's the metaphysical reason, the abstract, and this gets more into philosophical reasoning. This is what my life has amounted to: For 28 odd years I surfed the seas of nothing, I squandered the void forest, I traipsed the plains of nowhere, and all for what? It's an endless cycle, this vicious spiral, plunging deeper and twirling farther into nowhere.

I barely even exist....

please stop

                    stop yelling at me please stop I dont deserve this kind of treatment I dont deserve to be treated this way youre hurting my ears stop it Im doing the best I can and with your senseless yelling how can you possibly expect me to do any better stop yelling stop please please just tell me what I did to you tell me how I hurt you please just stop yelling at me or Im gonna lose it I swear Im gonna lose it if you dont stop please stop Im gonna lose it Im gonna lose it Im gonna lose it

                    Im gonna lose it
                    Im gonna lose it
                    Im gonna lose it

                    please why wont you shut UP

A Poet 1,000 Years Old & Fat Like a Dead Snake

I was reading a poem
minutes ago by a man from Irish
who spins his words together like poison ivy
I found myself lost in the hopeless rhythms
of splattered words mishmashed
across a flaming road

Smash a Lightbulb: Poetry for Lowlifes

I envy I admire I wish I could write
in a surreal fashion like that
toss words about seemingly randomly
but with intent that lashes honestly
down tainted pages of lavished sunshine.
It's so easy to be great in a world
where medals are dished out like
pea soup given to a toddler in ice.
It's so easy to amount to nothing
when the world in which I exist
is sick-ridden with princes & princesses
who boast their achievements
like acidic lips licking up messy linens
when if you think real deeply about
their success you see that it's equal to
shitting in a cup and tossing it through
your neighbor's skull adorned in blue tiedye.
I guess I could easily argue that
life is terror meets hellion wonder
walking down the street with a raised middle pincher
saying fuck this fuck that I hate the state
and I wish it would all just break apart
disintegrate in steaming-hot mounds of milky
crisscrosses crisscrossing a board game made out of
scraps of metal that is just dissolving like
the baby fallen into a bathtub filled with battery acid;
but I could just as easily tell you
that life is great it's magical and magnificent
and although some days I feel quite low
the better days I feel full of charged-up
to exploding action figure parts that work
and move all on their own.
This life is awesome don't you think?
We live in a world where anyone can succeed

Jeremy Void

where failure grows on trees
and kids of the idiotic nature grow up
to be famous celebrities followed around by
even stupider paparazzi that can't seem to point a camera
correctly and they aim it at all the wrong humans beings;
and today everyone's an artist.
Have You Heard of That One Guy?
What's His Name?
Mr. Conye East North or South, or something
of a directional nature who claims
to be more popular than God;
but then what does it mean to be
greater than a mythical being who lurks somewhere
out there in a world where
people pick who to vote for at the next
presidential election by the size of one's
"dink" and they decide to play a pickup game
of touch politics
choosing who will lead the next great American scandal
who will lead the fake Americans straight to hell
and who will guide the pack with a log of
flaming feces plucked straight from
a burning cherry tree.
I think that's what politics amounts to really
when you think about it
reduce the election to its essential elements
you might find the monkeys can't speak American well enough
to argue at the next presidential debate.
So I say fuck it and instead pick up this book
because politics is a boring topic for me
and I read a magical eclipse of
wordplay, so viscerally sound that it winds a
tether of electric visualizations of kinetic
superiority around my already interested head

and I find myself envious of his ability to
twist and mold words in a way that seems to make sense to me.

But then
I'm always envious.   That's all.

Burning Bridges

When you just got nothing to do
when you simply have nothing to lose
when your world is getting smaller by the minute
the sustenance of your life lessening and going extinct—

it's liberating, isn't it?

why i choose not to argue

ive fought w/ every oppressive force my entire life & ive always lost. im 28-years old & have fought-against since i was maybe 10. i realize now that im not a fighter, im a writer. everybody has a weapon of choice. my weapon is the written word. hopefully what i write will provoke action against various oppressive forces, but i doubt it. i dont partake in arguments because typically people are too unbendable to see another way of thinking. im the first to admit that im wrong. like, for example, that blog i wrote about feminists*—i was wrong about that, i acted on anger & not logic. im human & thats what humans do. most people, though, will do anything possible to not admit theyre wrong, so i

---

* I got mad at the facilitator of my weekly writing group for cutting me off mid-poem because the contest was "gross." So I went and wrote a blog to help me cope with my anger.

dont bother argue. its not that im apathetic. its just that i have better things to do than scream at a wall. i do what i can to improve the world, but chances are im not going to incite a revolution.

too soon

I feel depleted.
I'm 28-years old
stuck sucking up the fumes
of a life deleted.
I thrived and I strived for
mayhem only it came to me
when I least expected it
and the beast surrendered its soul to me
eaten and beaten
I cut through and through to the core
of my own fukking problemssss....
my own demise is coming
I'm beside myself
I'm dying and I'm trying and
I'm deciding but I'm deranged
and you know how that goes
I aim for dementia.

The world was mine::::::
but I bit off its hed
and thus I died
when my time came too late
but now it's in bed.
But
I slept with the reaper
the grimmest of grins moaning

outta pure unadulterated hate....
I lust for disaster, I desire a temper
tantrum. I live for madness
only the madness

came too soon and too soon
I became a
disaster case.
That's it I'm sold
to the highest bidder.

The Anti-Trendies

Gonna start a political party called the Anti-Trendies. Anyone who joins is a poser.

Filth

If you play in filth
you'll come out dirty.

If you clean up the filth
you can focus on something else instead.

Treading in the problem
will only get you nowhere.

lo

To Be Shocked

My whole life, I've never been shocked. Maybe as a kid something shocked me so deeply that I'll never be shocked again, or maybe ... I don't know. I sometimes want to be shocked, but no ... nothing.

Close Encounters

Dirty clothes, dirty faces,
dirty looks, dirty places,
dirty alleys, dirty minds—
close encounters of the dirty kind.

We walk outside
on a summer's night.
Show off our colors.
What we're doing's right.
No compromise.
Open your eyes.
No sacrifice.
You're in for a surprise.

Dirty clothes, dirty faces,
dirty looks, dirty places,
dirty alleys, dirty minds—
close encounters of the dirty kind.

They don't understand
what they'll never know.
They won't understand.
They'll only tread on my toes.

Relativity

Men think women got it easier, and women think men got it easier. So maybe each of us has it as rough. It's all relative, I guess.

Scatterbrained

My thoughts are scattered, moving faster than my brain can catch, a haphazard array of a million shooting thoughts, a bouncy ball that just can't be caught. I try and I try, but my ideas are lost. The lines on the page jump like jagged waves. I touch my pen to the line, but it dodges each attempt, so I try and I try, but the lines, so wild and relentless, match the pace of my nervous heart, a pounding so loud, so haphazard—a disaster—that my pulse spikes and my head—yikes! A crazy rhythm—a crazy, crass, spasmodic and fast mess that only I myself made, my thoughts cashing checks that my brain can't catch. An uproarious outterworld in my head, a surreal sort of plane that I dread, über chaos and crude thinking, I can't stop blinking, my lips are tweaking, my vision vile and wild, moving like a shooting star. Because of this, you see—although I don't—my art looks like vomit, so detestable like smeared feces, though in a way it looks great, so remarkably fake. It represents a side of me that I hate. It's almost like standing onstage and farting into the mike, then deemed a genius by fools alike. I guess it would be cruel to say stupidity is a sickness that sticks at birth, a variety of understated answers—none the wiser—and I look for my answers by getting higher. I guess it would be sick to say my brain is cement; my brain is lazy, fat, yet so intelligent. A question about this, and a question about that, a harsh sound sounding so hard in my head; so sharp and fierce, I feel on fire, too many burning desires, too many futile reasons, such pointless force—a hellion of ideas. Sometimes, I must admit—though I'm sorry about this—I feel completely compelled to spray you with the truth. But take my word for it that, the truth coming from me is neurotically sane, though everything I do, it's all unimaginably vain. The human race is corrupt, it's in our nature, it's a disaster of attachments, a fragmented theory, existential proof that at once proves there's a point to all this.

Everyone Is a Cunt

Everyone is a cunt,
with no exceptions.
I'm a cunt, you're a cunt, he's a cunt,
and she's—

Wait, would that be sexist?

A Sacred Place

Punk rock has a very sacred place in my heart. So when I see someone dressing Punk because it looks cool, forgive me for wanting to smash his/her face in!

Verbal War

Words are my ammunition.
My weapon of mass destruction.
I use them wisely,
and buildings erupt beneath me.
I see the Ozone burning down around me.
A riot ignites, and bodies fly.
Walls collapse beneath my tongue.
It clucks and the whole world collapses in on itself.

I see madness boiling in your eyes.
I see an explosion roiling in your mind.
I see an erosion of hellfire. People dying.
I see what you are, and I try to stop it

before it's
too
late.

This is my time.
This is my day.
This is your demise,
because I will rise above it all.

I see nastiness gutted and chucked.
I see fat fucks fucking a duck.
I see babies yanked from the twats of their mothers
by men in green robes and tinfoil on their heads.
The world is going to shit in a hand basket
and we try to stop it but get pulled down in the process.

Help a drowning man swim and see
what happens.
Defuse a flailing man on flames.
You're insane if you think there's a solution.
You're insane if you think
you can stop it
before it's too late.

And it's too late.

A Common Misconception

It seems to be a common misconception that immaturity means constantly seeking pleasure, instant gratification, on a never-ending quest for fun, it becomes all about me and what I want and I'll throw a tantrum if you don't give it to me now; whereas maturity is just the opposite, where it becomes all about everyone else, get a job, get married, have kids, calm down, slow down, you're getting older and you can no longer maintain that fast-paced lifestyle anymore, become a slave to the system, too jaded to enjoy life, just brood and work and brood and work, go down to the pub and get drunk hating your mere existence while your fellow coworkers do the same—is that what anyone wants?

But on the contrary, immaturity is either seeking pleasure 24-7 <u>OR</u> never seeking pleasure again because you've got a job to keep. Maturity, on the other hand, is recognizing when it is okay for one to goof off and when one must step up and do the right thing, work hard play hard, as you will. So when you see me in downtown Rutland goofing on all the stuck-up, jaded shoppers who mosey past me with a rotten chip on their shoulder, a demented monkey treating their backs like a set of bongo drums, don't tell me to grow up, act my age, you're 28-years old for godsake so when are you gonna act like it?

When are you gonna be revived from the dead? Rise from your tormented coma of jaded waste, a boring vessel on this planet to serve this system which breeds concepts that this is what it means to be a HUMAN BEING. I know when to care about others, I may be a goofball a clown a laughing lowlife but when life beats you down I'll be the first one to hold out my hand and lift you back up. Don't tell me I'm immature because I'm living my life and you are not, on the run from a child that's hidden in the darkest region of your forgotten soul, a child caged and praying that one day this "man" this "adult" this "civilized human being" will lighten up and let it run free like it was meant to be. Maturity has nothing to do with how one acts, it has to do solely on how one understands and conceptualizes actions and reactions, having a greater knowledge about oneself, that's all there is to say about it....

Life Is Short?

Whoever said life is short is a liar. Life is long—too long. In fact, it feels like forever.

The Zipper

A couple years ago I went on the zipper at the Rutland fair, and someone in the cart in front of me lost a pocketful change and I caught one of his quarters in my mouth—swear to God.
The zipper is the only ride I'm going on this year.

A Poem for Cyndi
Whoever You Are

Heartbreak is a terrible thing;
the way I see it there's only one remedy.
To find another, another, another
to replace the girl of your dreams.

But now I had a new dream, a dream
about a new girl I'd never seen.
And I want her bad, because
I know what she has in store for me.

Her name is Cyndi and she's so so pretty,
it makes me crazy, so fucking crazy,
to know she exists somewhere far,
far, far away from me, me, me.

Cyndi, are you out there?
I hope you read this someday.
I hope you hear my name.
I hope you come looking for me.

I'd go looking for you, but I don't know
who you are or where you're from.
I don't know anything about you, Cyndi.
All I know is

Growing Up

It's funny that when you're younger, you got the whole world ahead of you and you're rebellious and you think you'll never conform or grow up or do what everyone else is doing. But then you get older and everything changes and now you're an adult, and change is just thrusted at you.

My Own Wisdom

i accept the fact that i fight my own wisdom , because thats what my wisdom entails — question everything . if i didnt question everything , then i wudnt be questioning everything , now wud i ? i second - guess myself way too much , always unsure , a mind never made , & that i accept . introspection is a sure way to drive a crazy person insane . act first question later ? no , i question first act never . or maybe i do act , i dont know . im at war w/ reality all the time & that i accept . it wont always be this way , i suppose , but today it is , & today i wage war on all things me . i accept myself for who i am , really i do . but who i am is someone who beats himself up too much . i dont sleep so that my mind races & races it does & in those states of racing thoughts i create art nonstop , jumping from one creative idea to the next experimental notion , & then i go to sleep , wake up the next day w/ a splitting headache , & reflect on all that i made the previous day in my hyper-aware state & i reject it all.

And That I Gotta Accept....

Swearing Loudly

At a nearby Panera Bread two boys are swearing loudly, goofing off, doing what boys do, really, but to the surrounding families in the vicinity, they look like assholes and this must be stopped. The father of two girls doesn't want to hear the curse words even though at work with his racist coworkers he swears and puts down faggots. He puts them down good.

But not around his kids. His Kids. His innocent little girls who do not get exposed to it by their own friends at school or even by their own bigoted father who curses out spics and niggers when he talks to his mistress over the phone unaware that his two daughters are playing SPY games and absorbing every word he uses from the next room over.

So what does he do?——he rises to his feet with a deep-seeded sigh and marches over to the two boys' table, a righteous feeling hovering over him like a halo. He stops at the boys' table, folds his arms in front of him, and fake-coughs. The boys look at him.

The one on his right looks back at his friend and says, "Who's this asshole?"

His friend shrugs and the two boys resume like the father wasn't even there.

The father tries one more time to get their attention, but they ignore him.

So the father drives his fist into the table, a powerful maneuver loaded with two tons of construction-worker force, and with a reverberating clunk the table rattles radically. The boys look at him, and now, finally, they're scared——or maybe just a little.

What the father doesn't know, doesn't realize in his uncalled-for rage, is that all the occupants of Panera Bread have his attention too.

"You little twits," he barks. "I'm here with my freakin' kids trying to have a nice time when yous are over here swearin' like sailors. If I hear one more freakin' swear come out of either of you boys' mouths, I will lift yous up and drag yous outside and kick the crap out of both of you. You think I'm kidding?"

Both boys shake their heads.

"Good!" the father says, and turns and walks away. The whole dining room opens up in applause.

The two boys leave shortly after.

Tonight

I've got nothing to say tonight.
I squeeze and squeeze and squeeze
but I keep quiet after all
afraid of the demons that'll be released.

I've got too much to say tonight
and I'm searching for the right words
to bring these things to life.
It's like, there's red painted across
the walls of my skull
so bright and vivid I just want to
paint it on the stucco walls outside
of my mind.

I live in a fantasy, but it's getting old.
I live in a world of my own that is
starting to get stale and gross.
I want out of this playground

Smash a Lightbulb: Poetry for Lowlifes

I want access to the fairgrounds
I want to join hands with my oppressor
and watch as he dies.

I've got something to say tonight.
I know I do only whatever it is
is lost in a matrix of filth.
There are demons controlling me
my mood changes frequently
and my beliefs are always in flux....

I don't know anymore.
Are my ideas even valid?
To me they seem pointless and foreign
as if they came from somewhere else.
My world is closing in
my mind is opened wide.
That eye that sees the world differently
is starting to go blind.

I'm stuck I tell you
in a world of thoughtless action.
I'm stuck I tell you
in a world of selfish reactions.
I want to understand
not to be understood
but at times I wouldn't mind
a little understanding of my own.

I'm sticking out my hand
don't you see it?
It's right before your eyes
only the TV is on
the music is playing

the XBOX is flashing images
and my cries for help have gone
missing.

I've got stuff to do tonight
but I can't remember what....
I'm bored
and I'm anxious
and I'm racking my brain
with immortal scenarios.

This chain of thought is pointless anyway
and I don't know why I do it.
Maybe to reflect
maybe to resurrect
maybe to get it out of my head
or maybe I do it for the sake of attention
               I don't know...............................

No Shame

Nothing's right
Nothing's wrong
Feel no shame
because it's all the same
      in the end.

Social Anxiety

The thump of my bumping heart
is pumping so damn hard.
My nerves are rattled, and my bones
are bedazzled, and my mind is scattered.
This anxiety is giving me the jitters.
The crowd flows like a swarm of cattle.
I wanna get away from here, but
there's just no escaping the craziness,
the ebbing passersby bleating past
me like race cars hammering down the track.
I scan the exits, giving it a fast once-over,
but there's more of them blocking the way.
I scratch and pant, scratch and pant, but I can't
stop the racking of my Goddamn heart.

A Life-Span of Five Hundred Thousand Light-Years

Blow a fuse
and see how far it'll take you.
Run backwards on ice
as the devil watches and the mold
comes back for round 2.
A Vacuum is a fantastic vacation spot
a void the size of my head
rotting out from the inside.
A Black Hole—
wash yourself with monkey blood
look through the eyes of a four-legged vampire
stick your middle finger through the hole

located at the center of the earth
and then shout as loud as you can:
THERE IS A WORLD IN WHICH I HAVE YET
TO WATCH EXPLODE IN TEARS DRIPPING FROM
THE BRIGHT RED EYES OF A NAKED WOMAN'S LUSTFUL
WAYS!!!
You know, there is a lot to do when
you're only 3-inches tall and everyone is a giant.
And the world is your apple orchard
and you run amok through a world divided
by virtuous princesses stealing crowns …
off the heads of a thousand mini mountains.

You can't escape your sex

You can't escape your sex. Just remember that. How many times have I spotted a hot girl who claims to be different, to be Punk or Metal or Hardcore, something more than the norm? But she's hanging on to a tall, muscle-bound jock right before my eyes.

You can't escape your sex!

Interconnected

I am a Man
I am made out of
flesh&blood
        no more
        no less

Smash a Lightbulb: Poetry for Lowlifes

I don't promote badness
nor do I seek goodness.
I see equality—the yin
and the yang—it sheds
its light like a tropical bird
falling off its perch

I look out the window
at the overhanging sky
blue as the ocean
but clear as the madman's
conscience—it speaks
to me so softly in the night ...

like a child's touch

tells me things I didn't
already know
it brings light to my
sorrow
the sun radiating in the sky
like a swollen heart
bright in the bleakness
overhead
almost empty—smug
but full of life

it shows me things
I couldn't see otherwise
it guides me through
this world
a world overcast
in shadows
a world filled with

madness

AT NIGHT
this world goes black
blank as
the madman's face
the stars like freckles
the moon smiling at me
from the meek beyond
I see hope
out there
        —somewhere
far far away

it comes to me like
a dream
touching but sinister
a thing of evil
it brings many a good man
to his knees....

The Scorpion and the Frog

A frog sits on a lilly pad. A scorpion skitters up to the pond and says, "Yo, Froggy, how 'bout givin' me a lift to the other side?" But the frog says, "Hell no, Mr. Scorpio, cuz if I give you a ride you might bite me and we'll both go down." The scorpion shakes his head and waves his tail and says, "No, I would nevah bite you, dawg. You my homie and I would nevah disrespect you like that, dawg." The frog says, "Go away, Mr. Scorpio, cuz I'm not letting you on. Please leave me be or I'm dialing 911." But the scorpion scowls and spits. Tries again saying, "C'mon, yo. I'm good for it and I'll even chip in for gas." But the frog stands his ground and shakes his head and points past the scorpion to signal him to leave. This goes on for a long, long time, and eventually, after lots and lots of polite chiding by the scorpion and lots and lots of intense contemplating by the frog, the squat, green guy decides to let the scorpion on for a ride. The scorpion skitters on to the lilly pad and stands beside the frog, who feels rather delighted of himself for helping out the——— Then the scorpion stabs him in the neck. The frog's vision blurs. Blood is gushing and spraying, the frog is leaping and hollering, the lilly pad is swaying and sinking, and in his final breath the frog says, "Why?" and the scorpion replies, "Cuz I'm a scorpion!"

Nighttime in the City

A rumble of bums huddle
around a trashcan fire, a cone
of flames flashes up from the gaping
hole where the trash is thrown.
        Rich folk on the street,
in a hurry, always in a hurry,
zip down the lanes
to their jobs to make cash money.
        Junkies and winos clutter
the sidewalk as they shiver in
the cold and tremble in withdrawals.
        Spilling out of the alleyways.

Nighttime in the city
you got spikey-haired Punks,
and you got long-haired drunks.
Beards are wavy and unkempt
and the more-put-together stare
in nauseating contempt.

Homeless youth hustle and bustle,
until the coppers catch their scent,
in which case the kids are off in a run,
darting past the passersby who gasp,
shouting, "Hey, watchit," as the kids plow
a path through the swarming masses, and
then zip down the escalators
and disappear onto the fleeting trains.

Insanity runs wild, bearded men talk
to themselves, and old women scream
at their imaginary friends.

While college kids stagger from parties,
spilling out from the doors that hide
the raging keggers that only
happen at nighttime in the city.

Someone Said

Someone messaged me, said they find the photo I posted to be annoying and distasteful, "Will you please take it down?" so I wrote "I don't know who you are" and "All my photos are annoying and distasteful," but apparently she blocked me before I even had a chance to respond. Still haven't uncovered who she is, though.

panic >>>

My mind races
my heart chases its own
tail ITS OWN TAIL

My eyes dart around the coffee shop
futilely searching but not stopping on
A N Y T H I N G

Nerves raid-firing
signals flying through my veins
but not catching on....

!I'M SCARED!
!!!I'M SCARED!!!

The torment I put myself through
I should never have come here
voices shouting too loudly in my ears.

My head throbs as if
a thick ring of radiation
pulsates within....

I JUST CAN'T TAKE IT ANYMORE!!!

The Same Old Song

Clones
Drones
Everything's the same.
Whatever happened to going against the grain?
Do something new,
something unique.
I'm sick and tired of the same fucking track.
The same old song.
The same notes, the same chords.
It's getting old.
Gonna gimme an ulcer.
When will it stop?
I'm sick of being the only one,
the only man willing to stand out,
willing to do something new,
something unique.
This fucking tune is gonna make me puke.
I've heard it before.
I'm hearing it now.
I'll hear it again.
Shut the fuck up and break a norm!
Now, now, now!!!
You're pissing me off.
Make it stop.
Why won't you stop?
Copycat.
You're a copycat.
It's getting old.
It's the same old track.
Different day, different hour.
But the same song I hear every hour.
This poem sucks.

That's a fact.
But at least I have the balls to take a chance.
To stand up here and call you a cunt.
You fucking cunt!
You fucking cliché.
Clones
Drones
Everything's the same.
Whatever happened to going against the grain?
Does your brain not work?

I'm torn

I want to be myself and please no one. Yet I'm obsessed with LIKEs and the public opinion. I'm confused. Should I say FUCK YOU and move on with my life? Or should I shake your hand, even though I really want to stab you in the back. Should I listen to your vile and pretend that I care, just so that you will read my vile and pretend that you care.

Recovered Poem from 2011

I fell for her & all her tricks
I should've known she's a junky bitch
The life you choose is the life you got
The life I got ain't the life I want
No turning back on the way you act
But I know I'm right & that's a fact
Got hatred flowing through my veins
Love is a dream that's so insane
Tried it once & a few times after
Guess I'm insane cuz I'm the bastard

Two Drunk Punks on Parade
A Poem for Darby Crash

From LA to Boston,
Boston to LA,
you and I my friend
would have made
quite the extraordinary pair,
although
unfortunately you died
before I even came into being.

I read a book about you:
Lexicon Devil.
I saw a movie about you too:
What We Do Is Secret.
I've fantasized of us two together,
sitting on the sandy beaches of LA
or on the wasted streets of Boston,
drinking liquor and visiting dilapidated places
where we would hunker in the corner
and shoot bags of speed into our arms.

We would get wild and wacky,
wacky and wild,
hitting the city streets and vandalizing
the town in an angst-fueled evening.
We would paint our names, sing
our songs of hate and spit
in the fuckers' faces.
I would loop my arm over you
and we'd stagger away, like
two drunk Punks on parade

It would be wild.
It would be joyous.
It would be all I could ask for.
Just one night with you,
and a morning of aching heads
to remind me I'm still alive.

We'd puke in the sink,
scrounge up some cash,
and grab something to eat.
One day down,
a lifetime of more to go.

We'd dine together.
We'd thrive together.
We'd make terrible music together;
and in the end we'd die together.

Like all good clichés in the Punk rock scene,
we'd die from a heroin-induced state.
Good riddance, the mass media would say,
while our underground fans would
tower over our buried bodies and hawk
loogies into our graves.

Life Is Hell

Life is hell.
Her jacket said LIFE IS HELL.
Life is hell,
and I believed it too.

I believed it's hell.
It's life in a nutshell.
I've known it since I was 12.
But then that girl she really smells.

Life is hell
Life is hell
Life is hell
Life is fuck fuck fuckin hell....

A Text Message to a Friend

You know you don't have to be anything or anyone. You just have to exist. That's the problem with religion. It was created so that people feel like there's a purpose to life. So they can feel like SOMEone, and not just a useless vessel.

His response: OK

Nietzsche said there's something beyond us, but we'll never know what it is. We'll never know who we are and why we're here, so it's easier to just accept the nothingness that life has in store for us. But I don't mean to preach, I feel that way all the time; I think everyone feels that way at times. I tried to catch up with you after the group to tell you this, but you were already gone. I'll talk to you later.

His response: OK

Untitled

I got this rippling feeling
a trilling of hope
ripping straight through me and it
cuts through my skull like
a fuckin shotgun shell:::
a death-awakening blast
an ear-murdering burst
a wood-splintering crack
that hits like a jackhammer

and instantly
it comes to me all at once:::
an earthquaking realization
that causes my legs to wobble

and I know right then and there
that I am dead....

Not One of Those Days

Sometimes I feel so proud and smart that I just want to give myself a pat on the back. Other times I feel so hopeless and stupid that I just want to slam my head through a pane-glass window. Sometimes I feel so full of joy that I want to walk down the street boasting and rubbing my happiness in the passersby's faces. Other times I feel so depleted that the existence of other people makes me feel as though they're boasting at me, rubbing their glee in my face, ramming it up my nose like it's a line of coke, etc. etc.

Today's not one of those days.

Hipsters

Fuckin bullshit is what it is. You see pictures of people dressed all in Punk costumes—because costumes are all they are—hanging out with others in the same scummy outfits, but then you click next, and the next picture to appear on your screen is of that same "Punk rockers" out clubbing with cunts in baggy pants and name-brand T-shirts with strobe lights flickering in the background, all dancing to hip hop or whatever fuckin music these college kids are into these days, and it makes me fuckin sick, makes me want to spew and slash. I never heard of a gray-area Punk, those who are half-Punk and half-something else, or maybe a third Punk, a third of this, and a third of that. FUCK!

Such a Bore

When orgasms bore ya
when the world doesn't know ya
when you hate the state
and know it's gonna blow up

you wonder what for
you feel like such a whore
your middle finger sticks up on end
and life seems such a bore....

GET IT STRAIGHT

ALL THE SHIT I POST ON FACEBOOK, UNLESS STATED OTHERWISE, IS TOTALLY ORIGINAL
        BUT PEOPLE PROBABLY SEE IT AND THINK I'M JUST ONE MORE RIPOFF ARTIST IN THIS WORLD

that I'm merely stealing other people's art and other people's words, just like the Internet was designed for
                                                            as if

ALTHOUGH I DO ENJOY RIPPING PEOPLE OFF
I'm not in the same class as the mass majority of people who lack creativity.

Death of an Artist

Oh boredom
holiest of things
I become one with
the virtue of sadness
the vice that is
a lavender painting
I paint with feces
I spit blood at the fishes
& dive into deep space
as a retro, thrummed bass
clicks like a sonic boom
it sounds like an explosion
of dust billowing up
& it's gone
& I feel pretty dumb

when a fat man plucks the magical plumb
from the tree of infinite wisdom
I feel like
I'm flying
Sometimes
I'm dying
the sky painted in
bright-red streaks of light
yesterday I fainted &
the noises creep up on me
from behind
this paranoid state of being
is pushing me
beyond
this state of consciousness
that lives in
the Garden of Sin
where I go to be
alone
& happy I bathe in
blasphemy
that's just how I choose
to navigate through
the masses
guided by madness
the bleak sphere
reeks of ashes
& these ashes
scratched in stone………………………

A Waste of Time & Energy

When every movement—even the smallest flexing of a muscle—requires a deep-seeded sigh, that's when you know something ain't right. You just lumber through life, a false sense of entitlement hovering over you, as if the world owes you something. A burden on everybody you've ever met, you sit alone in the dark and, when someone tries to spark a conversation with you, all you can say is "I don't want to talk right now." You're a waste of space if you choose to carry on this way. Not to say you couldn't amount to anything, but your attitude (not your dilemma) *must* change first.

And worst of all, you're really bumming me out. Either CHEER the fuck UP or KILL YOURSELF—it'll save a lot of people the time & energy.

Mobbed

The crowd swarms like ants, flowing around me like a river splashing off some sort of an obstruction in the center of the stream—and I am that obstruction, walking the opposite way. I walk against the flow, bumping shoulders with the hurried passersby, men and women dressed nicely on their way to work. I continue to wade upstream, the flow of people getting thicker as I step farther and farther the other way.

People gasp and scowl at me, shouting, "Hey, watchit!" but that doesn't stop me from going this way—the opposite way. The crowd grows larger as I step farther along. The swarming masses are getting thicker. But I keep at it, getting jammed up by hurrying people coming on both sides, sandwiching me in.

I see my destination; it's a rundown shack with a cardboard sign tacked to the door, a Sharpied-on message that reads, THE GHOULIGANS. The name of my band. I see the drummer standing out front, twirling a drumstick in his hand, smoking a cigarette, and then he catches me in his sight and nods coolly in my direction.

I nod back, taken completely off guard by a burly woman with short red hair, who knocks me off my feet, and I crumble to the ground.

The crowd continues to flow around me, the passersby looking down at me, and sneering through their phony faces, their million-dollar grins. I push myself up and look toward the shack, but I can't see it through the thick stream of bystanders. But I know it's there, and I must go farther along.

I see lawyers, and doctors, and Wall Street types. Stock-brokers. People making a shit-ton of money to do nothing but sit on their asses all day. I see those who work furtively on computers, jammed up in their own little cubicles, decorated with pictures of their families on the walls, pictures of their pets.

I see the hopelessness at bay, and I must get through to the other side. Then I catch a glimpse of the drummer tossing out his cigarette and heading back inside. I'm almost there.

The shack looms above me, tall and mysterious, ominous and gritty. I push through the last few passersby, emerging onto the yard in front of the shack, and outta breath I flop on the grass. The swarming masses, tittering past the shack, dress shoes clicking and clacking on the sidewalk, voices hushed but active, on their way to work, to waste another day doing something that they hate.

I stand up and brush myself off. Push through the door. The sounds from the outside go suddenly silent, cut off by the shutting of the door. I look at my band, the Ghouligans, with the drummer, Nick, scratching beneath his left eye. The guitarist, Jared, leans against the wall, drinking a tall boy.

I pick up the bass, lace the strap behind me and over my shoulder, and with a series of clicks, I start in....

A Lost Generation

What happened to sticks and stones will break my bones but words will never hurt me?

Van Gogh

Van Gogh cut off his ear for a chick.
I know how that feels.
If I wasn't so afraid
I'd shed off all my skin
just to get close to you again....

fuck this shit

fight those
        who fight us

imprison those
        who try to imprison us

arrest cops
censor left-wing extremists
gas the nazis
chain up rednecks
        and drag em on the back of your truck
bomb terrorists
and discriminate the american citizen

        FUCK THE MOTHERFUCKIN SYSTEM!!!
            before it fucks you

Cheaters

Girls cheat on guys.
I used to not trust them.
I used to hate them for it.
But just tonight I realized

I cheated too.

Steal This Quote

How come when I post quotes they get more LIKEs than my original stuff? Either I'm a shitty writer and my own ideas are not valid enough, or people would rather see unoriginal ideas.

That's all anyone ever sees on Facebook. People stealing this quote, people stealing that meme, people using this person's art, this person's picture. As long as you're not making money off it, I guess it's okay.

OMG

An older woman and a younger woman, as though I'm sandwiched between their two separate ages, were just praising me on Facebook in a stream of comments following a post by a woman who HATES me....
I can't possibly imagine what she might think when she finally checks her Facebook page and receives a long rap sheet of notifications alluding to THIS

Just thinking about it makes the hairs on the back of my neck rise ... like we're in for a surprise of epic, and rather hysterical, proportion.

A Mass Headache

A tug-of-war going on in my head....

A mental push-and-pull....

A cacophony of words tearing through my head....

Violent discourse like 2 sides spewing lies is spinning around my head, making me dizzy & fed up, sick & lost & in a world of my own, thought bubbles growing & popping & spraying me in the eye with intellectual jive, too fast for me to comprehend, so fast that I wish I was dead!!!

Having an Opinion

It's funny how we automatically assume that those who agree with us are smart. Or at least I do. Like having the same opinion as me is a sign of intelligence.

Really, having an opinion is a sign of stupidity, anyway.

Part 7
If you're not offended, then I haven't done right by you

Part 7
If you're not offended, then I haven't done right by you

a fate you cant escape from

thats the worst:

being buried alive w/o
your headphones to distract you
from the cold & stiff reality that is
a million little squirming maggots nibbling
on your skin

thats the worst:

your boat is going down & theres no
television set for you to watch as
the ocean overtakes your watercraft,
no movies to view as you drift away into
another world & the sea
assaults your sinking ship, boards breaking,
nuts shattering in the terrorizing waves
that come one after another

thats the worst:

when an airplane comes soaring
outta the sky heading straight to
your place of work & you left
your cellphone in your other pair of pants,
your smart phone is out of batteries
& you left the charger at home,
your tablet broke the day before,
& right now a plummeting airplane smashes
ramming & flashes as it tears thru
the glass, desks flipping & flying as the fires
are burning the whole fuckin place down

im sorry

Rutland, VT
Home of No Creativity

Going down to Pub 42 to make a racket with [No Name] right now. Show those copycats what's what.

Nothing but a Fucking Scumcunt

    You're crazy—
              and I like that about you.
    You're crazy—
              and I hate that about you.

Smash a Lightbulb: Poetry for Lowlifes

    You're crazy.
        We've got everything in common.
    You're crazy.
But all the bands you listen to suck.

        You're nothing but a fuckin scumcunt!
        You're nothing but a fuckin scumcunt!
        You're nothing but a fuckin scumcunt!
        You're nothing but a fucking ... *RUNT!!!*

    You're crazy—
        and they hold that against you.
    You're crazy—
        and they warn me about you.
    You're crazy.
        We've got everything in common.
    You're crazy.
But all the bands you listen to suck.

        You're nothing but a fuckin scumcunt!
        You're nothing but a fuckin scumcunt!
        You're nothing but a fuckin scumcunt!
        You're nothing but a fucking ... *RUNT!!!*

Baby, I want you to know that I love you.
But there are times when I really hate you.
There are times when I wish you'd die,
    because all the bands you listen to suck.

        You're nothing but a fuckin scumcunt!
        You're nothing but a fuckin scumcunt!
        You're nothing but a fuckin scumcunt!
        You're nothing but a fucking ... *RUNT!!!*

9/11

So weird. Last night I got a text from a number I didn't recognize, which said *Happy 9/11.*

A FeW WeEkS AgO

i was down at the bar to read for an open-mike, & there was this stunning blond-haired chick who kept looking at me, which i interpreted as intrigue at first. then when i was just about done with my cigarette i stood up, about to go back inside. i walked around the picnic table at which id been sitting & stopped right at the corner of the table to finish my cigarette before going in. what i didnt realize was the girls purse was apparently right in front of me. i assume this next bit happened cuz my hair was spiked. she sidled past me, really close too, too close in fact, almost like an inch away from me, & then snatched up her purse from the table. since i didnt realize her purse was there, i had no idea what she was doing, but thought she was making a move on me or something, kind of like teasing me in a way, so i didnt budge from where I was standing. then when i saw that she wasnt going for me, but for her purse, i felt really stupid because i realized the reason she came so close in the first place was because i wouldnt move out of her way.
now get this, a day later i had a Facebook friend request from her.

strange, right?

Don't You Judge Me

I ENJOY
BEATING THE CRAP OUT OF
        WOMEN

BECAUSE
IT MAKES ME FEEL
STRONG & POWERFUL

AND EVERYONE NEEDS TO FEEL
STRONG & POWERFUL

The Image Is Fuckkkked

I crave disaster
got mayhem on my mind
my thoughts are fast and spastic
it's how I unwind....

Strange Things

I think I'm seeing shit. That, or shit is seeing me. Either way, strange things are going down.

My Love

If My Love was talking it would tell me to open this door, but knowing my history with My Love I oughta keep that door shut. *C'mon, honey. Open up, I've got a surprise for you on the other side.* I stare at said door, listening to the ticking go off in my head, tick-tock, I count the minutes, the seconds, I watch the door sitting there all stagnant-like, unmoving, just waiting for me to open it and step inside.

But I've ventured down this road many a time; I know what waits for me on the other side—nothing good, that's for sure. My Love, or Succubus as some might call her, is chiding me to go forth, to crank the nob, wrench it open, and go inside. But I'd rather not.

Silly Spider

Silly spider, this is my house. MY HOUSE!

Inside a Box

For a long time I did everything for myself, and at the time I was very confident and I new what I wanted and what I believed in. Today it seems I do EVERY-THING for everyone else, and I don't know, I seem to be lost, unsure, broken, and hurt.... I don't know what I want and I don't know how to get it. Just give give give and I'm sick of giving. I wanna be me, but I forgot what that means. I wanna live free, but you know, I don't see that happening any time soon. I'm in a box, and I can't get out. PEOPLE are stuffing me in boxes with their boring assessments of me and it's no use trying to prove them wrong because every attempt at that will only be interpreted as something I never meant. I'm claustrophobic and this figurative box is closing in and getting tighter around me. <u>STOP FUCKIN JUDGING ME, STOP ASSESSING ME, STOP THINKING ABOUT ME</u>, I don't need any more tension to hold me in place. I've got enough tension of my own keeping me locked inside this fate. I WANNA ESCAPE, I WANNA ESCAPE, I wanna fucking escape. You're all killing me in the dark. It's useless, anyway.

Prolific?

I guess you could call me prolific, but I wouldn't.

like a fuckin GOD

the joke is broke
i look at the sky & some bloke
flips me the fuckin finger.
i open my mouth & fire
an insult flying back at him
it hits him in the face & i feel
i feel
<u>i feel like a fuckin GOD</u>>>>>>>>

Car Crash

Like the movie *Final Destination,* I thought I saw a car crash before it happened. I wanted to shout STOP, but I was too afraid. But then the car crash didn't happen anyway, and I felt quite disappointed that I am not in fact psychic.

Go Away

I want everyone to read
this poem.
I'll shove it in your face
if I haveta.

Better yet, I don't want
you to read it.
Because maybe then
you'll sully it with your
ugliness.

That's what I deal with

Outside this guy's talking to me and telling me to slow down and that he knows I can write because his friend's got my book and that he understands getting nervous because he plays guitar and his biggest fear is breaking a fucking string onstage. But he doesn't fucking understand because I have a disorder that actually causes me to shake and that biggest fucking fear of his would be a terminal reality if he were me. I read something to my class on Tuesday and I had to put the paper from which I was reading down on the table because it was shaking so fast in my hand that I couldn't make out the words. That's what I deal with.

From 5 Years Ago

the thought of suicide is a powerful comfort: it helps one through many a dreadful night.

> I was a lot deeper back then, I think. A philosophical pill popper I was; an esoteric drunk; a deep thinker blowing lines of speed and sticking needles in my arm. A self-destructive artist-type with an introspective bone to pick with the world. I chucked glass bottles and contemplated the meaning of breaking glass as it exploded in this universal cesspool of diarrhea that swirls in the form of ugly puss, and I wondered, I pondered, I philosophized theorized and conceptualized as the world went to hell around me and people everywhere drowned in a piss-stained, cum-tainted reality that is life—a blessed life, ain't it?

Fucking Writer's Block

No no no no no, everything I write has been shit last night and I can't seem to get it right and I've been writing so well for so long and it seems like it would never end, but I think it's coming, and it's coming, fucking writer's block, and it'll shatter my heart....

Fuck me it's starting....

!CUNT!

You know, if you've got a problem with me, tell me to Fuck Off. Stop playing these fucking games!

I said I was sorry, what's your problem!

I've said this before and I'll say it again: If you've got a problem with something I said, then that's your problem, not mine. And when I approach you after the fact, trying to make things right, saying, "Look I didn't mean it that way, and I'm sorry if you took it that way," and then you come at me all pig-headed saying, "You're damn right I'm offended," again it's not my problem and I did my part. I'm not gonna cater my language to your own personal insecurities, because it's not my responsibility to do so.

Untitled

What doesn't kill you is a great big disappointment!

Not My Friend

Another night squandering
another hopeless pondering
another lost and troubled child
another death and hated wild
I'm so sick of everyone and their games
      —especially their games—
the fabricated injustices
the worldly tough guys
everything's the same
I'm bored and so sick of the same old same old
why won't someone listen to me?
No one cares
Oh yeah, no one knows

Smash a Lightbulb: Poetry for Lowlifes

You just point your finger and call me names
point your finger and make accusations of me
but you don't know me
so don't pretend to.

Don't act like you're my friend
cuz I know your kind
I've seen it all before
I can read between your lies
This is such bullshit and you know it
everything's bullshit
I'm too depressed to get out of bed
cuz I'm sick and troubled
but so are you and don't say you're better
I make stupid moves
I act aggressive and pathetic at times
but that's okay, because I'm all I've got.
So go ahead and talk your talk.
Go ahead and play your games.
Go ahead and fabricate
phony tears of hope and tell me
it'll all be okay when it won't.

I'm hopeless, a futile force
I'm bored and cold and sick and sold.
Just leave me alone.
Walk away when I show you something
that you cannot take.
There is no hope and I don't pretend
There is no good and I don't pretend
There is no reason so why don't you just leave me alone.
Go back home and I'll never see you again.
FUCK you're not my friend....

Welcome to the 21st Century

This girl asked:
Why doesn't anyone love me?

I wrote:
Because it's the 21st Century.

Then:
Love doesn't exist anymore.

WHAT, it's true.

Lose Control
sung with Lethal Erection

Outta my mind, I'm outta my head.
Don't understand what I say, it don't matter what you said.
One of a kind, I'd be better off dead.
It don't matter what I say cuz I'm outta my head.

My skull is hard, my brain is mush.
I can't get a grip, but who said I want a grip?
My skin is scarred, my heart is squished.
I can't get a grip cuz my dick is limp, so

Lose, lose, lose control!
Get out, out, outta control!
Lose, lose, lose control!
Racin' thoughts won't let me in … control, so

Smash a Lightbulb: Poetry for Lowlifes

Lose, lose, lose control!
Get out, out, outta control!
Lose, lose, lose control!
I'm lost.............

GET OUTTA CONTROL!!!

Outta control, can't stop me now.
Runnin' wild throughout your town.
Can't figure out what to do next.
Impulses kick in and I'll do it now, now, now.
I'm going down, so
Confused young teenager with nothin' to do,
feel the freedom of life in a zoo.
Done my drugs, what's more to do?
Outta control, I'll be seeing you, so

Lose, lose, lose control!
Get out, out, outta control!
Lose, lose, lose control!
Racin' thoughts won't let me in ... control, so
Lose, lose, lose control!
Get out, out, outta control!
Lose, lose, lose control!
I'm lost.............

GET OUTTA CONTROL!!!

{available on YouTube}

Pissing Contests

People are simply too concerned with their petty pissing contests to give a legitimate shit about others. I say, *Hang the assholes, hang them high, beat em with a stick until they die!*

Growth Spurt

Another day, another crime. Another way, another rhyme. Life happens, and it happens, and we become things we had never expected to be, but we continue to grow and evolve and become better and better men and women and one day, when we're looking death right in the eye, we realize we've done it all and we're all ready to die....

Lies

I Am Stuck
I Am Scared
I Am Lost
I Don't Know Where I Am Going
I Don't Know What I Am
I Should Just Kill Myself
I'm Afraid of Everything
and Everyone
Bite the Bullet Is the Only Valid Solution
I Never Should Have Lived This Long Anyway
The World Is Shit
Everyone Pretending to Be Happy
All Smiles

Smash a Lightbulb: Poetry for Lowlifes

Misery
Hate
My Fate Is Dissolving
I'm Melting into Ashes
This Is Definitely a Cry for Help
But Please Ignore Me

Lies   Lies

everything's a lie

Brainstorm

i walk at dawn
as the rain trickles
around me
something's wrong
i feel sick in my own skin
trapped by thoughts of
devilish schemes run away
i have no place finding myself
in madness
the sadness peeks its decrepit head
over the hills
like bloodshot demons' eyes

falling lost in
a mental holocaust
my world torn apart
life is sometimes too hard
and i need escape   from everything
       and everyone
they hate me and
i don't know what went wrong

my center broken
i'm outside myself
all hope gone
i'm running with wolves
they hate me when i turn
the corner
my fate is falling
off
can't stop, the story
of my life
broken lost & hurting
blank jaded & deserted
it's no use anymore

just leave me alone
i bite when i'm tested
the water's not cold enough
in an ocean of disease
in a world of deceased badness
lacking mental stability
needing pills to keep me in line
treading the clouds which
feel soft and comfy and i lie down
and never want to
return
home
again

there's got to be
a reason
a plan
gimme a hand as i emerge
from beneath the wasted
swimming pool

as i ascend the ladder
into your arms
hold me tight and don't you ever
let me go
lost in a lucid dream
needing relief
seeking things too twisted
and wretched it's all the same
in the end
and i rack my ugly head
against the beautiful bricks
all at once
hell rises
devours
all things go sour
i'm stuck
in a foreverness
that only gets worse as
time goes on....

let me off this rollercoaster
PLEASE

Listening to the Grateful Dead—boo!

If I'm stuck in a car for thirty to forty-five minutes listening to the Grateful Dead, I want my fucking window down. It's my window. I don't care if the sound hurts your ears.

The Grateful Dead hurts my fucking ears.

Tradition

Tradition is lame.
Let's all get together and do
what our ancestors have done.

Burn witches on the stake.

Hipsters "R" Us

Wearing Doc Martin boots, a designer skirt, a designer sweater, and a designer book bag. Or wearing a combat jacket, red spiky hair, but with two diamond earrings suspended from your ears.

Oi, oi, hipsters. <u>Get your own club</u>!

To Create Inspiration

I want to create
      I want to inspire
           I want to create inspiration
all the while punching a devastatingly volatile hole through the sound waves, destroying the noise barriers, the oh so familiar OH MY GODs and NO YOU DIDNTs and blah blah blah, the Kardashian crap that fills the mainstream media with its ignorant jargon, its popular nuances, that cut like a corkscrewing jackknife as it rams right through your fuckin heart—I will not sugarcoat a reality that cuts the old grease from beneath your beat-up jeep like Diet Coke—it's *SICK!*, and I want to kick it off a cliff into icy waters infested with piranhas and blood-thirsty tigers....

Video Games

Video games are so fucking lame. If I was going to compete against you with my thumbs, I'd much rather have a butt-picking contest. Because then at least we'll come out with some *real* shit.

Band Names
to name a few

Jeremy Void & the Negligent Nosebleeds
Jeremy Void & the Subliminal MindFucks
Jeremy Void & the Rutland Riotears
Jeremy Void & the Infamous Über Manch
Jeremy Void & the Freedom Stompers
Jeremy Void & the Annoying Children
Jeremy Void & the Family Destroyed
Jeremy Void & the Crazed Villians
Jeremy Void & the Homeland Bouncers
Jeremy Void & the Censored Cunt Whackers
Jeremy Void & the Teenage Mutant Ninja Retards
Jeremy Void & the Crazed Space Helmets
Jeremy Void & the _____
Jeremy Void & the Speedy Police
Jeremy Void & the Slam-Dancing Alligators

The Poem, the Man, & the Obsession

The poem starts here
it starts with a solitary word
that evolves and becomes
something more
it becomes something special
something to hold onto
        it becomes a derelict beast>>>>>>>

I am deranged
can't say that again.
For me love equals self-destruction
the opposite is true when you're dealing with
lust
just take take take
and consume
before it
consumes you

I am a monster
it started at childbirth
and then GOD came to me at night
like a sacred wet dream
and told me things
like he told me
I'm no good I'm a mistake
I deserve no joy in life

So I thought
GOD IS WRONG

But God can't be wrong
God … huh?

Smash a Lightbulb: Poetry for Lowlifes

God are you listening to me
when I cry at night
So tell me
what exactly does a deity of your stature
a shapeless thing that sees and hears
everything
think of when
its creation dissolves
like an alkaseltzer tablet
dropped
into a cup filled to the tip with
blood....

FOAMY BLOOD

I can't say any more on the subject
sure I believe in A god
but that's just it, who's to say
there aren't more GODs
MORE THAN ONE.

I have a disease
I have an ailment
for me love equals abuse
it represents two separate using souls
that come together to
ABUSE or be ABUSED
it's not even worth it
when I look back at
       all the people that I hurt
       all the faces that cried
       all the hearts that I shattered
me and me alone

because LOVE makes me think of obsession
LOVE makes me believe in nothing
LOVE gives me no joy
it turns me into a
        complete and utter bastard

or maybe …
is it possible
      might be
      as it's more likely
      the case
that I've never felt
true love
that I've never experienced
that liberating, expressive emotion
so sensual and deliberate
a feeling of longing for another soul
      the first thing you think of
        when you get up in the morning
          the last thing you think of
          before you go to bed
maybe I've just never been a victim
to such a sacred feeling as
love
it takes two to tangle
and two is already exceeding my limit
      So what's the point????

BUT LUST——
there's something I understand
there's something that makes sense
cuz
it's all about me in the end
it's all about what I want>>>>>

Smash a Lightbulb: Poetry for Lowlifes

And do you know what I want?

I want love of course
I want to be in love
but girls are whack
they play petty games
and so I play them back
which brings me right back to the same place
I was in before
imprisoned by this putrid ailment
of mine

LOCKED in a world of
obsession and self-preservation

Did I tell you I'm twisted
and my mind is ridden
with a sick sick virus
in which God does not exist

THERE ARE NO ANGELS
THERE ARE NO SAINTS
only me me and me
and I'm so fucking deranged
nothing makes sense any more

So I drop the pen
it falls
it bounces
when the end clips the floor
just bounces
one two three
and then it's gone I can't find it
and the poem is over

before it even started.

A Solitary Word
that evolves
and becomes
something more
something sick
something I cannot
fucking stand
so I set it aflame
and never come back to it
again.
THE POEM ENDS>>>>>>

Stupid Is a Stupid Does

How do you tell someone they're stupid and their opinion is stupid, without this person thinking I'm stupid and my own opinion is stupid?

Fuck Facebook

It will suck your face out thru your eyes and nail it to a cross.

Reduce you to a mere photograph. And all your so-called "friends" to blank entities with the personality of a series of memes.

        I KNOW, IT HAPPENED TO ME.

On Addiction
What else is new?

I know I shouldn't do it.
                               But I'm gonna do it anyway.
Fuck the results. Fuck the outcome.
                               It's all the same
                                                            anyway.

The consequences are set in stone;
                           they're a fate
                               I don't want
but I know is coming, and
it's coming fast.
                         Why avoid it?
                         Why resist?
         Why not submit and give in?
                                   Why do that when I can do this?
Living in shit is a dream   I've always sought after,
             and the shit came quicker than I could ask for.
I lived it,
                     I was it,
                  and
                                                 I hated it.

I know nothing

The only thing I know for certain is that I know nothing. And if you start arguing that that's not true, I will defend my case.

"Oh, you're better than that."

"You're smarter."

"No, I'm fucking not." The end.

Destroy All Things Human!

I need to stay awake. I need to combat sleep and all the necessities that humans need to stay healthy. Food, fuck that! Sleep, fuck that! Masturbation, fuck me! Exercise, unless it involves fucking then it can go get fucked. I Don't Want to Be Human Anymore and I Will Do Everything in My Power to Assure that I Remain More Than Human. I will rise above addiction and never breathe again. Fuck oxygen and our dependence towards it. Fuck all things good. Wage war on all off it.   BURN

Say NO to Conformity

If I were to speak for myself, I would say everything I've already said. I'm honest, I'm genuine, and although I do emulate from time to time, my voice, my thoughts, my ideas, are all my own. At one stage in my messy pubescence I admit my voice got watered down by peer pressure, I admit I lost my identity in an endless struggle to be cool.
But today my voice is my own. I'm a freak a loser and a cretin, but I'd rather be that than a victim of conformity. I'd rather be crazy than sane cuz to me sane represents repression. It represents bottled-up thoughts and ideas, feelings that are not permitted to see the light of day. I don't feel shame because shame is only a mere product of self-inflicted social etiquette.

The End Is Nigh

The world is falling apart
                 piece by piece.
I sit in the ashes and watch
    as they all kill each other.
I wait quietly because
              my time is coming.
Terror is in my midst.
I bathe in the madness
      bask in the glory.
The world is coming apart
       stitch by fuckin stitch,
and I sit in the dark
       clenching the knife
           cradling the gun
waiting for something
          for something that has yet to come
but it's done
     finally..................

               It's fuckin done!

A Mannequin Nation

Gotta Love Those Mannequins, cuz we live in a mannequin nation, a plastic reality, with made-up faces and phony fragrances....

The Sun Sets

My skin bubbles delightfully beneath the array of colors coming together in the darkening sky, the soft mix of pale pink, orange, and amber magically touching my insides as I stare through the crisp evening sky. It's wonderful the way they form and glow and dance before my very eyes. I marvel, I stare, I watch, I behold the ever-changing, translucent sea of sparkling tones as they stream like confetti across the screen; they jump and dash, erratic splashes of decadent godliness painted across the blackening beyond.

These Assholes

This is my night and the assholes gotta ruin it....
This is my night and the assholes gotta ruin it....
This is my night and the assholes gotta ruin it....

i went to the pub to read for the open mike when those two fuckers showed up all punked out like cocksuckers on a sunday morning, dressed in spikes and studs, pins and patches, black on black on black, the fucks come there and they harass me because they're boring fucking posers who have nothing better to do on a sunday but drink and be dicks and act like king kong in the jungle what with their tough but stupid attitudes which need to be challenged and taught a hard fucking lesson a lesson only learned by pure aggro and force that entails fists to faces boots to balls heads to heads and blood will pour and form rivers on the floor i'm telling you now. it will be mania and pure fucking chaos the kind only seen in the darkest of wet dreams you'll see, and their heads will collide with the sticky grossness that grows on the floor of the bar and they will be screaming as their eyes are plucked from the sockets and death will be served like corn dogs at the county fair, like hamburgers at a sunny barbecue and pizza at the shops where women wander and men cop feels every chance they can get and these people's fists will launch toward the sky in a frantic fucking cheer as those "punk" rock cunT scumfuckingwhores are served pain and punishment and punishment and pain for crossing me you know what i mean, i mean they will hurt with broken bones and scabs breaking out on the skin of their faces and scars will slash at them like a tic tac toe board on the sidewalk

                                                and i'll be laughing....
                                              the whole time laughing....
                                       my face bloated with laughter....

and then i will spark a match and a flame will spit and flicker and lick on the tip of the matchstick as i touch it to the cigarette in my mouth and smoke will rise and roil, roil and rise, from the smoldering butt in my hand. watching them squirm like rolly pollies, squirm and rock and wobble, limbs flailing as they scream and shake on the floooor, and i will smoke that butt, lift it to my mouth, breathe in the poisonous venomous air that streams from the filter and feel satisfied and gleeful in my twisted state a state that i know is only a temporary state a state that comes from my knowing i destroyed a couple "punk" rock tools at the bar tonight

and, oh yeah, i forgot to mention

i have a tank of gas in my other hand the hand not holding my cigarette butt and i forgot to mention it because i'm too distracted by the dying butt pirates lying and squirming as if immersed by flames on the floor, hobbling about in a prone state, doing the worm dance maneuver as they scream and holler and yell for their dear lives, and i drench them in gas in gasoline in gas in gasoline, and the smell of gas is putrid in my nostrils as i soak the two dumb butt fucks in it and i smoke my butt and watch as their screaming dies out and i run a trail of the toxic liquid out the door and around the corner where i take a final drag of my cigarette and drop it

                                      whooooooooooooooooooooosh!!!

the gas trail ignites and a flame dashes along the trail, tearing down the sidewalk like a bulldozer being driven by a drunken demolisher, zigzagging as he maneuvers the mammoth thing into the bar and tearing an asshole outta the door, like a shit being sucked back in, magically, and the flame eats away at the wood as it swerves thru the door and finds its way to the "PUNK" rock morons on the floor. their squirming stops and ceases, ceases and stops, and stops and ceases as a brand-new renewed tremor stirs from inside them as they shake in a miserable motion, so fast and pathetic it's almost fun to watch, so utterly fun and enticing. i watch the flame surround the two guys, circling and crackling and rippling as it boxes them in and then leaps and smothers them like a net set to catch a gorilla out in the wilderness. pounces like a lion tackling a smaller beast in the jungle. like a mob of tough guys closing in on a backstabber in some alleyway somewhere, their sleeves rolled up to show their bulbous muscles as they pound their fists in their open palms

      the two fools get burned alive, or maybe they already died before the fire devoured them whole and their skin sizzles and melts, crackles and snaps as the color of their skin changes to a bright and bloody red like a virgin's cherry popped by a nigger's cock on the beach in the dead of the morning the cock being driven into the bloody gash between the blond chick's legs like a drill designed to dig into the earth ramming and stabbing, stabbing and ramming, trembling and jabbing, and maybe there are even shades of orange amid the glimmering redness that spreads like an infection on their skin and their burning flesh smells absolutely delicious like a pie set on granny's windowsill waiting to be stolen a scent that you can almost taste and is so vividly visceral it feels like you are nibbling on the pie yourself watching a movie-slash-tv show as the flame leaps from their fetal bodies and attacks the bar which i hadn't expected would happen, i mean duh, right? because fire has a mind of its own and you just can't control it never can you control it because it won't ever obey and trust me i know

the whole place is up in flames now and thick roiling smoke coils up from the bar as the breaking smashing shattering beer bottles crash and crumble on the floor a loud cataclysmic sound that can be heard over the snapping popping flames now climbing and eating the walls making its way up to the ceiling, and the breaking bottles crumbling on the floor make a messy litter of broken glass that i suppose if i was feeling ambitious enough i could retrieve and then leave the bar and go find someone to cut open and inspect his-or-her flesh with. in the wake of the hot flittering flames that are growing immensely even as we speak, gaining heat and getting bigger and consuming this entire place—in the wake of the fire that rolls and rumbles and terrorizes and consumes every single fucking thing in its way—amid thick clouds of smoke that sting my eyes and force me to squint, settling in places and getting tossed about by the wind that comes thru the door in sudden bursts and flashes i watch in amusement as the patrons here this sunday

Smash a Lightbulb: Poetry for Lowlifes

evening scream in terror panicking, in panicking terror, and rush the doors but there's too many and they clog the charred exit-slash-entryway like a butt plug jammed up a lesbian's twat, and when i say a butt plug jammed up a lesbian's twat i mean it was rammed in there so hard and deep and is now stuck so god help me get it out but it won't come out no matter how hard i push and pull, pull and push, and stuff and yank but it just ain't coming out not now or ever, and this is how the door looked, a surge of bodies, twisted and mangled, all at once pushing to get out. jammed in there good. and i stand there behind them, light another cigarette as i watch the pursuing chaos surge and rumble, splurging in your face like a fat load of cum waiting impatiently to be shot but hates the fact that you were its target because that's such a waste of sperm you know what i mean and the insanity is tearing the place apart one brick one block of wood at a time, the travesty of actions, the absurdness of all this, the confusion the pandemonium the disarray the total fucking madness trapping any innocent bystander that might come its way, the hell i've created traveling to and fro and around and out and in and on and the fiery disorder is everywhere but nowhere and i know that doesn't make much sense, but who's the writer here?

please!

just listen, okay?

and then a guy with a bazooka appears from behind the bar and he aims the mega piece of equipment nestled on his right shoulder at the crowd clustered and clogging the door and

you can probably figure out what happens from here i'm sure it's pretty obvious right?

out on the street there's a traffic jam of rubbernecking drivers taking a peek at the destruction, my annihilation, the passersby watching from a safe distance as i step thru the smoke screen that hides the bar very well and i can see all the gasping gawkers, the stupid assholes, cluttering around and crowding the roads, leaping onto backs to get some height and a better view of the craziness that went on inside even tho the smoke hides the place like a portal to another dimension and <u>these assholes</u> can't see a goddamn thing

oh and i must add:

people died here tonight and

Jeremy Void

these assholes want
to see it for themselves
to witness it to believe it
because this is entertainment to them
like a stupid fucking movie
something to watch while scarfing down kernel
after kernel of popcorn
the fat fucks eating their greasy fucking food
like the characters within were made up
well, you see
this is not a movie
nor is it a tv show
this is your life and
it is real
this is real
even the scribe who wrote this is real—a real person who dictated the words of
the actual author who will remain anonymous
and, finally, you my friend are REAL

WELCOME TO THE REAL WORLD!

assholes

This is my night and the assholes gotta ruin in....
This is my night and the assholes gotta ruin in....
This is my night and the assholes gotta ruin it....

the end

Applied Knowledge

There are dumb people who read and spew facts easily. There are dumb people who act and mingle with ease, doing the right things all the time. Look at any high school cafeteria and you'll find popular kids who are complete idiots but always know the right thing to do and say. Then go to any activist group and listen to what they say. You'll find that there are people who can spew facts as if they know what they're talking about but really don't. I think Smarts has nothing to do with obtaining knowledge, it has to do with using the knowledge.

a polliticaly corect PUNK?

a polliticaly corect PUNK? ive never herd a such a thing. i thought Punk rawk was foundid on the absence of corect ANYthing. i meen theres Richard Hell (& he was tha first) hu walked the streets of New York City whereing a t-shirt sed "Pleeze Kill Me," w/ a bulseye in tha senter. Darby Crash who died his hair blu to see wat it wud be like to be the only nigger in an all wite skool.

shall i go on?

Sid Vicious whereing the swastika
Minor Threat saying "Guilty of Being Wite"
The Lewd w/ there song "Kill Yerself"
The Forgotten Rebels & TSOL both
      saying they wud rather fuk tha ded....

shall i go on....

Don't Overthink Things

LIVE AND LET LIVE AS LONG AS THEY LIVE IN SYNCE WITH HOW YOU LIVE, is too many words. Keep it simple. LIVE AND LET LIVE is enough for me.

Love = Cocaine

Love = a shot of cocaine, the feeling of the drug rushing your veins, the pow when the madness hits you in the brain, that part when you feel oh so happy and you're never gonna fall, and then it leaves your system and you drop drop drop into a pit of despair where the only relief is another hit of the very thing that brought you here....

Something Like a Beast

The room is dark and stark, a padded cell where hopelessness breeds. A straightjacket strapped to my back, so tight that I can't breathe. I try to escape, but the key is gone, and it's something like a beast that won't go away, no matter how hard I try. Every attempt is stark, and sparks a vicious war, a hole in my head, a wound full of dread, a bed for my excessive ways. A place where I can wage **war!** where I can wage **hell!** where I can chime the bells to inform you, that hell is here, it's hell on earth, chaos the human race deserves. Desert me. Leave me bleeding and dead; like road-kill, my stomach's crushed and ill. Do I deserve this? The answer is clear. Hell is here. It's hell on earth. The rifles play the anthem of the day: the chaos we breed, the chaos we need, the chaos we see—the chaos in our minds. We need a place to go, where we can defy.... We need an answer to the madness that shines from our eyes, glowing red and grim, thin with rage, thick with hate, sick with repulsion. Destruction. Destruction.

Death and destruction. We need a place to defy you: where we can wage **war!** where we can wage **hell!** where we can chime the bells to inform you, that hell is here, it's hell on earth, chaos the human race neeeeeeeeds ... if we want to live free.

2-Faced

I put on this face for people cuz I'm really not such a bad person after all, but still I have these sick thoughts that I must address and if I don't address them they will consume me. So I write to keep the demons away and I'm sure people read it and think I'm such an asshole. I'm 2-faced. Haha, well I am 2-faced. It's so hard to coexist in such a tiny world without faking your way out of madness and pretending everything is fine and dandy. That's just reality. People would not understand, so you play the game. You pretend to be someone else.

Self-Induced Mania

I think I'm gonna make myself manic, I mean really MANIC. Like off the wall. Cuz I'm curious about something. Besides, I'm happier when I'm manic.

                                                                          So it begins.

A Game of Cat & Mouse

Where *am* I from.... Where am I *from*.... *Where* am I from.... Where am *I* from, me me me, that seems to be the question, with a clusterfuck of answers coursing through my head as my eyes like static bounce and clatter in my skull, turning and tumbling with a confusing quickness and chaotic velocity like that cat having snatched up the neighbor's ADD meds, now thinking everything's a mouse, every splicing motion, every dashing dot, every surging light; with a flash and a click, the cat rips through the wall in search of … what? A mouse? I think that about says it all, I am that mouse on the run from a speed-addled black cat tearing crevices in the furniture.

That says everything that needs to be said, I think;;; it says nothing that should be said, anything that would be said if only (emphasize the <u>only</u>) … if only I wasn't running for my life, at constant war with the uppity kitty cat, kinda like Tom & Jerry, only <u>this</u> cat isn't idiotic like, but smarter and more vicious, only I'm smarter than it and much moree … well, not vicious, definitely not vicious; just smart, almost delusionally so.

So I think that about says it all. So watch me as I lather the American flag with the fumes of endeavor, as I take my loaded Tec9 and splatter the mirror. Now *that's* my point, see….

The Beloved Messenger of Destruction

feeling so depleted———

The Truth always hurts
but The Truth coming from someone
you hold so dear to your heart
is like a slashed tire releasing every last bit
of life right out of it.

As if Your Universe
has been slashed open
ripped apart and now the ghosts
that hold your soul together
are rushing out free to dance

Smash a Lightbulb: Poetry for Lowlifes

and loiter
and do what ghosts do
leaving you a wretched mess of
a human being.

Now   I think about
escaping farther
and farther into myself
losing myself to tainted memories
of a day when everything was
great.

There was a day
1,000 years ago
when I walked atop the moon
fought with ghouls carrying
jackhammers over their backs.

There was a day when I frolicked
in the gardens of sin
running amok through the hailstorms
the tornados of recklessness
a day when I needed
no one and a day when The Truth
was like a bloody skull
kicked and abused with all the steel-toes
in the world.

There are no truths anymore
and the mere fabric of life
is being ripped apart by
the Beloved Messenger of Destruction.

I sit here alone not wanting

anyone to tell me anything.
I sit here wanting to abuse my mind
         and my body
with all the goodies that life holds.
Kicking punching stabbing and smashing
are the anthems of my past
the ambient noise that followed me around
everywhere I'd go
like
angels of death swarming and thrashing and
picking people off like hungry
blood-thirsty
ravens///

Life consists of
one
pointless endeavor
after
another pointless endeavor
and it's all I know—
the fertiveness of life wrecking havoc
inside my brain.

The Messenger spoke showed me
something I was blind to
showed me a perspective
I could not see.
He she or it gave me a line
and now my eyes feel like
they're on fire.

I wanna run away
I wanna hide
I wanna do more dastardly actions

more reckless transactions
more nothingness that reeks
of acidic waste
and I'm screaming WHY
I'm praying to this alleged thing
lurking in the clouds
and I pray to it and I ask for
something or another
some more nothingness
more absent thought
more lack thereof

I ask for another brain
another head
another set of eyes
new limbs
a new stomach
and I wonder why

this thing doesn't deliver me
what I need to get out
of
myself.

Absurdism At Its Worst (or Best?)

Life is sometimes as retarded as a school boy with a hard-on.

A Forgotten Rebel

LOOK AT ME AMERICA
this is the face of another forgotten rebel

Some people think I'm dead, some people think I'm in jail, and the rest don't think of me at all.

Good News

Just received an email back from a publisher. They are interested. I quote: "Hey Jeremy, you got me, I'm interested."

The Story of My Life

I Told This Girl I Was Crazy
        She Didn't Believe Me
        She Got Too Close
and now she hates me.

People

PEOPLE scare the fuckin shit out of me.
        She's more scared of me He Says
              than I am of her.......

PEOPLE piss me off
            to no end....

So I run and hide

                          but they always find me there
                              ALWAYS

Quitting Smoking

I NEED A FUCKING CIGARETTE. EVERYBODY FUCKING HATES ME AND I NEED A FUCKING CIGARETTE. THE WORLD HAS TURNED AGAINST ME AND I NEED A FUCKING CIGARETTE. SOMEBODY SHOOT ME DEAD BEFORE I SMOKE ANOTHER FUCKING CIGARETTE. Cuz I'd much rather die quick and painlessly than live another day choking myself to death on tar and rat poison. It's no way to fucking die.

Suicide

Suicide seems appealing right now. A bullet, a noose, a razor blade, let's have some fucking fun.

A Midlife Crisis

You're not having a midlife crisis, are you? Dwelling over old photographs of you when you looked like a sickening sweet Punk rock star dressed in velvet and black leather, with splashes of leopard-print here and there. Like, there was a time when you were raw and mean, a time when you had an answer for everything (a discharged middle finger was that), a time when you may have been smarter and wiser, with a childish playfulness about you, which held you in its fun-loving embrace. But today you've got a job to uphold, people you have no choice but to please, and your middle finger is on lockdown, bound snugly beside its neighbors, never to be seen of in solitude again. It's like, there was a day when life was easy, you had it all planned out, the future was caustic, the past was toxic, and the present was all that you had in front of you—but today you've got bills to pay, appointments you need to adhere to, asses you've gotta kiss, and that free world you had dreamed of when you were a rebellious teenager had gotten washed away in stacks of paperwork piled up high on your desk. No more drunk weekends, no more stoned holidays, no more partying on rooftops, and no more fucking girls beneath the bridge down by the Charles River, either—no more nothing, the life you thought you had made for yourself got sold out to responsibilities. Yeah, dude, I can so relate. I think I'm having a midlife crisis too. It's rough!

Mindless

Can you imagine never asking questions?
Can you imagine being a drone,
                programmed to obey?

I'm watching people and they
all look the same, so put together,
living such a boring existence.

I wonder,
　　　　honestly,
　　　　　what it must be like
to be mindless.
　　　I wonder,
　　　　honestly,
　　　　　why the human race
is so damned foolish, so
　　　　　futile.

And it's such a shame!
　　　　　that things are this way.

Listening to the Drones

Listening to the Drones right now. This band is sick. I just really got into them a few days ago and they're amazing and so damn catchy—when I'm not listening to them I still hear their songs in my head all day long.

In God We Trust

My auto-correct turned "gay" into "gap." Auto-correct can actually be very smart sometimes.

Sorry to offend you if you like to shop at the gap. Because only those who shop at the gap think it's a bad thing to be gay.

Work Days

My boss yelled at me

I looked up

He was screaming

I said what?

His screams turned to shrieks

The fuck?

He didn't pause to breathe
        didn't stop to think
        didn't stop
               period
just kept screaming

I was standing in the dining room

Everyone was watching us

I was rather confused

What the hell
was wrong with this dude?

Then he stopped
        just stopped

And in the absence of noise
        the world felt empty

Smash a Lightbulb: Poetry for Lowlifes

and I was alone
>   so alone

in the dining room surrounded by
>   diners
>   eating their food

They tried not to look at us
>   but they were looking
>   I saw them looking
>   it was obvious

My bosses face was turning red
>   puffing out
>   like a perturbed blow fish
>   in the fish tank

He lifted his finger
>   started to say something
>   but stopped
>   just looked at me
with these beady bloodshot eyes

He looked mad
>   lowered his finger
>   and walked away

and I never saw him again....

Part 8
I can piss farther than you

Part 8
I can piss farther than you

Too Much Second-Guessing

What is wrong with me? I second-guess myself way too much. Why can't I just be confident in every fucking thing I do, like I used to be? Why do I have to overthink every fucking move I make? too worried about what others will think, too worried about how they'll assess me, the diagnoseses they'll give me. Why can't I just be me and let go of the outcome? I used to be confident in the words I used, never apologetic for the lines I spewed, always speaking with my head up high and my middle finger ready to rise up if you had a problem with it. That was the man I used to be, and today I'm a boy who is never sure, always uncertain of everything I do. I hate my brain and I hate the things I say and I hate every single line that leaves my mouth and the first thing I wanna do after speaking is say, *I'm so sorry, I didn't mean it like that. I'm sorry if you took it that way. I'm sorry I spoke my mind.* I refuse to censor myself but I am so sorry for that fact. As my ex-girlfriend would always say, If you're sorry, you wouldn't keep making the same mistakes. Like, if I was sorry for not censoring myself I should censor myself the next time instead of repeating the same derelict act in question. But I *am* sorry, I'm so sorry you have no idea. I just can't control myself, I shoot from the hip because in the moment I feel like it's the right thing to say, but after the fact, it's like, SHIT SHIT SHIT, I STUCK MY FUCKING FOOT IN MY MOUTH AGAIN———the story of my life.

Untitled

You ignore me like
I'm ambient noise.

The Business Show

Haven't listened to the Business in ages. Last show I got drunk at in Boston was the Business. I got so blitzed. Drank over $100 in beer, and people bought me drinks left and right cuz I claimed to have just gotten out of prison. At one point during their set these two girls heard my knee snap over the music and ran in the pit and dragged me out and set me against the wall. But then "Guinness Boys," my favorite Business song, came on, and I shoved them both out of the way and did a swan-dive into the pit. The next day, I swear it looked like my bone was sticking out of my knee.

Nighttime in the City 2
The Unrelated Sequel

Nighttime in the City
What a scary place to be.
When you're drunk and lost,
stoned and stumbling while the madhatter
strums his acoustic guitar,
and jugglers in clown makeup
roll around on unicycles.

You see gangbangers roll up in their lowrider,
wanting to pop a cap in your silly richboy ass.

Smash a Lightbulb: Poetry for Lowlifes

You're lost and you can't find your friends.
You're lost and you're drunk and stoned,
and you just wanna go home.

What a scary
scary
scary
scary place to be.
You wander endlessly,
the street signs blurring
in your haze, fading and clarifying,
and the homeless man with a paper bag
shaped like a wine bottle in his hand
staggers up to you and asks, Spare change, sir?
Ma'am?
Anybody. I'm homeless and I need food.
(drugs and booze)
You shriek and recoil at the sight
of this strange man in the night.
His black skin makes him look like
an eerie silhouette. Oh my!

There's no escape,
like a labyrinth through hell,
the darkest corners of hell, and
you come to on the subway as it
barrels down the tracks
and
the people stare at you
you
you
YOU!!!!
Fucking A, leave me alone,
you shout, batting away the ghost

with your hand, slapping it,
saying, Go Away.
They stare and watch,
laughter filling the train
like bubbles, air filling the bubbles
like
like
like helium.
Like laughing gas,
and you shriek and gasp.
You shout but the words don't come out.

Not now.

Not then.

Not ever.

and you're lost.

To the night.

Nighttime in the City and You Can't Get Away

There's no escape.
Take the drugs and run.
Drink the booze and scoot.

Float away on a balloon,
and don't you ever come back,

yahear?

A Clusterfuck

I've really been getting down on myself a lot these past few days. First and foremost I'm a writer, and secondly I'm an artist, and I guess this comes with the territory of being an artist, this self-hatred that courses through me at the worst possible moments, sneaking up on me when I least expect it, when I ring the doorbell and out comes a bright-red boxing glove, glistening in the torrential heat like a flash of red dust, thick and hard, that comes railing straight through me, knocking me flat on my ass. Now lying at the foot of the busted door, beside a thick and green block of lumber that had been punched out like a super-sonic hole punch meant for busting up wood instead of paper only instead I got in the way of its pulverizing, piledriving plow-through and now found myself rolling around on the ground holding my bloodied none and that epic shiner that will sting and throb the following morning, for sure.
That's how I look at life, this is my unique perspective - - if you don't like it, kiss my fucking ass cuz this is the best I can do, simply because I am not Him, I will never be Her, and I sure as hell am not It, whatever It may be, however It manifests Itself in this pre-apocalyptic void I occupy, just biding my time, nervously biting my nails; waiting for, hoping for, and dreading the inevitable Armageddon-like blast that will level entire blocks, incinerate tall buildings, and will save me from myself, from that place of complacent struggle where I *really* sit around biding my time, too comfortable to budge, secretly seeking a searing hot strain that will set my ass aflame, so maybe then I might act, I might change my stressful circumstances; maybe the flame will give me enough propulsion for me to finally rise from this hell I call a life - - I might move a muscle change a thought, as they say. I'm always willing the flame to start but I'm way too comfortable to light it myself, too calm and cozy, supposedly serene—*supposedly*—to lather my pants in gasoline, flick a Bic lighter and touch the tiny, flickering torch to the fuse that is my drawers ... and *kaboom!* off I go running for cover, ducking beneath railroad bridges, darting through alleys; my ass is burning and I'm a-runnin' fast as lighting and straight and fierce as misfired bullet ricocheting off of steel walls and stones and ruts and angled crevices that knock me out of orbit and I'm off running in another direction now. I'm going everywhere—my ass is on fire and I don't know the correct course of action to take so my body is a clusterfuck of

motion, a ricocheting, half-assed set of actions that knees me in the groin and there I stop running and the fire devours me whole.

What the hell am I doing? I'm just rambling here; see, that's what I do when my thoughts fire like a clusterfuck of tumbling clicks and clacks scattering throughout my overflowing head—I ramble and diverge, it's just a distraction, is all. I'm avoiding the real issue, the issue that has kept me oppressed since Day One. Plagued with doubt, afflicted with unanswered questions, with low self-esteems, with an ethical dilemma that tells me to questions everything that comes my way, and then question more. So I find myself questioning myself, my own actions and reactions, my own givings and misgivings, my own social skills and a-social skills and of course anti-social skills too cuz that's about all that my social skills add up to: DESTRUCTION OF. Destroying Everything Good in this world. Am I good? I don't know, let's find out—so envy is the root of my problems. I'm either too good or I'm not good enough, but when I'm too good I hate myself for that fact and thus I still fall short of my ideal selfless self. But just the very nature of having a self is not the least bit selfless. Lose your own identity, destroy your own fucking name. I am Jeremy Void, hear my roar. I scribble my name in green lipstick all across the mirror, which is the most beautiful thing in the word, I must add, cock back my arm, and splatter the crashing mirror with the blood that comes spilling through the thin slits in my knuckles as I punch straight through the fucker, my whole face explodes into tiny shards—you see, that's how I lose myself....

What the hell am I talking about? That's right—envy, the root of my problems. Destroy your own image but in the end that feeling of entitlement creeps into my head, a tiny voice that spreads lies telling me I'm not good enough, and I never will be, a sinister voice that comes to me like hornet sting, and I didn't expect it, not one bit, and then my image grows really, *really* fast as I throw my face through the glass only to emerge out the other side wearing a mask of blood and pus. That's what my life amounts to, anyway.... At least, what my life amounts to, as I can only speak for myself.

My Last Prayer of Hope

STUCK
in this mediocre world
STUCK in
retroland where kids
dress in skinny jeans
& studded vests
diamond earrings
& designer purses
kids who know nothing of
Punk rock, dressing Punk
& listening to nu metal
while smashing fingers
on touchscreens till time is
exploded in dust, as the past
becomes today
becomes tomorrow
STUCK
in bondage, restricted by
chains———the television set

Today's world
makes me so irate
the bleeding hearts
& those sinister farts
sitting at desks inside
a rainbow pulling strings
as their country dies around them
stupid times(x) insane
equals(=)
the united states
       of industry
an industrial wasteland

we're crying
behind bars
as the badmen in charge
wage war on
all things smart

I'm so so bored
I want something more
so sick of the phonies
parading around
in black clothing
It's like
today the stupid people thrive
a gatling gun of discharged babies
retarded genetics
growing up in the dumbest of nations
whereas the smarter ones
are waiting because they KNOW
that senselessly hatching babies
is not the best way to go

This is the state of things.
You better believe it....
You better wake up
even though it's way too late
to do anything about it
1,000,000 forces of progression
verse
5 billion agents of regression
we're in a state
of disrepair
the de-evolution of mankind
is here
WAKE UP, AMERICA

don't you see!
Blind & apathetic
it's a wasted solution
these PC Neo Nazis
are only spitting fire
on the problem.
The answer isn't censorship
cuz in fact that's what They want
the last of our freedoms to go
will be speech
they teach us social etiquette
as a way to gain
mass control
WAKE UP, AMERICA
cuz this is my last prayer of hope

Overcoming Your Problem
    now what??

I've overcome my problem, stepped over my dilemma like it's a dead body left out in the road. But now what?? I'm just faced with another problem, looking the next dilemma right in the eye. That's life for you: you think you got it made, well you don't—you're just as fucked as the next guy. But that doesn't matter, I guess. We are all dying, death sits right around the corner waiting, so while we're here:

LET'S DANCE
<u>in between the flames</u>

LET'S TANGO
<u>on the dead man's grave</u>

Untitled

Live fast, die slow!

No Fun

Yes, my art has been very angry as of lately—on the darker side, even for me. Yes, it might be disturbing and even a bit creepy. But you know what, at least I'm feeling something. At least I'm making something. At least—at least—at least I'm doing something real with my life other than just pushing buttons on my phone and wasting time with a boring divergent such as this—this—THIS fucking thing called life: a window into "life"—what life, whose life? OUR LIFE!

Untitled

sanity comes in small doses

On Mindfulness

Today is Thursday, and I'm sitting here in the now, overly mindful of tomorrow. How can I be alive if I spend all my time writing about life? Writing is like the opposite of mindfulness. How can I write about the moment, in the moment? It would be like: I touch the pen to the line, I move it along the line to write words and then sentences and then … well … that's writing about the moment because in the moment I am writing. So I write about yesterday's world, about all the adventures, the misadventures, and the fetes I never crossed; and I write about tomorrow's world, about all my dreams and aspirations—or lack thereof. This is my life as a writer. When I'm not writing, I try to stay in the here and now, but when I am, I turn this mindfulness on its side, kick it in the head, and claw out its eyes. Yesterday tomorrow left right up down, but never dead-center in the here and now. That's just how life goes ... for me! 24 hours a day, 224 words a page, give or take.

Lost Sick & Fed Up

Is anybody listening to me? Can anybody relate with me? Can you identify, put yourself in the picture, or am I so strange and my ideas so foreign that I come across as unreal, sad, pathetic, crazy. Lost. YOU'RE RIGHT I AM FUCKING LOST. Lost sick & fed up. The rage is roiling. My thoughts are boiling. The stew is overflowing. And I'm coming after you. Guns blazing.

Haha——it's all just a dream.

A Thought Disorder

I've got a thought disorder.
My thoughts are in disorder.

My rage won't open this door....

I'm banging the door, racking my fists against the solid wood, and all it does is rattle in place. I'm screaming at it, shouting for it to open, jumping and hollering, but it will not budge, no matter how hard I whack it, no matter how loud I shout. I wind up my right leg, swinging it like a pendulum, and drive my steel-capped boot straight through, but It's all to no avail. Nothing I do will open this door, no amount of anger in the world will move it; no quantity of angst, no volume of torment, no extent of rage, nothing I do in this über state of turmoil that rails through my head, coils in my mind, courses through my brain and overtakes my nerves on a seek&destroy mission just tearing me apart from the inside-out, will cause this goddamn door to budge, not even an inch.

I lurch forward.

My knees buckle.

My stomach rolls and rumbles, stirring and seething and bubbling and fizzling—popping and crackling deep down within.

A storm is brewing.

I stagger forward.

Stagger backwards.

Tipping left. And right.

I sway and stagger.

My whole body seesaws as I try to gain control of myself.

As I try to stop my legs from moving, to keep myself from falling.

But nothing I do can stop gravity's viscous tug as it seizes me in its vice-like grasp, as if having been sent directly from the darkest regions of helllll to pull me under—as it grips me and pulls me straight down.

My creased knees hammer the floor as I plunge to my butt, and then my back racks the concrete with an epic smack

Lying there as the anger torments me, a torturous emotion that delivers punch after punch, kick after kick, to my red-hot skull—stab after stab, jab after jab, etcetera etcetera, like a seething-hot poker being rammed straight through my fucking eyeballs—the strangest realization comes to me, so stark and silent like a bee sting:

I remember last night's dream, where an angel hovered at my bedside and hummed a delicate tune that caressed my left cheek.

Passion, my son. Passion will knock down all doors in your path; it will split the ocean in half like God did to the Red Sea.

Passion is key!

Listening to Johnny Thunders

I think I'm going to listen to Johnny Thunders and tune the world out. Cuz I think the world had tuned me out a long, long time ago.

To Me

Punk to me has always been about the MISFITS banding together.

What's more MISFIT than saying something against the mass majority?

Drink to That

The energy kicks in when you least expect it
when I convince my adrenaline to spark like a joint.
When I tell myself again and again that this
this
this is how I should feel, high on life and full of crack,
as they say somewhere on this godblessed earth.
Life bores me when I think too hard
Life irks me when I don't think at all
and then I start thinking again and I can feel
my brain throbbing and ejecting bloody neurons
out of its asshole....

Have you ever been brain raped?
Well I sure have, I thrive on the molestation
of my brain waves, I thrive on intruders
sneaking through and penetrating the gooey organ—
penetrating it with

words ...

words that I can use to
make you think
words that I can misuse

Smash a Lightbulb: Poetry for Lowlifes

so you come out shocked
and frightened like
an aborted fetus.
Words that I can abuse
and I abuse them
so quick and craftily that
when I hit you with a line
you melt into a pile of nasty
gushy tangled shoelaces that I
don't bother to untangle the damage has been
done and it's the American way
the patriotic way to take a shit on foreign
soil and leave it there for Mr. Arab
to come by on his 4-humped camel
rocking about and when he sees the giant shit
the odorless fetal matter that was sent straight from
America, America the great
he has a fit, screaming & hollering in that middle-
eastern drawl that goes
something like
this:

LaLaLaLaLa, his tongue jumping and thrashing
in his open mouth:
America Must Die!
and you see, this is exactly why
the Twin Towers melted into smoke
and fire, disintegrating as the fire
clawed its way up from the basement to the roof
and kicked ass as it rose and slapped
and got bigger and so much more meca than that.

War over shit, what else is there
to fight over anyway? Everything is shit,

Jeremy Void

so let's play and frolic in the rancid
waste like monkeys who fling shit for fun.
Let's celebrate the demise of the World Trade Center.
Let's celebrate the rise of Hitler
and celebrate when he died, cuz
it's all the same in the end.
We can tell stories about Kim Jung Eun till the sun
goes down, stories of murder and mayhem
and we can surely drink to that.

We got junkies struggling to survive.
Let's all drink to that.
We got ballerinas fucking older guys
when they're only fucking nine.
Let's all drink to that.
To rape and prostitution and a nation
where cops can beat their wives and get a slap
on the wrist and the average Joe gets put
away for life.

Let's all drink to that.
The world is burning open your eyes.
Everybody is dying

and let's all drink to that.

Be glad that you live in a world
where neglect and dislike are prominent as
facial herpes, and where people give everything
they've got to the people on TV simply because
they tell them to.

An age where writing has become texting
and sharing art means sharing memes.

An age where love & sex are synonymous
and the difference is lost in history.

Let's all drink to that, my friend.
Drink to the world's demise as we plummet
into mindlessness.
Let's all drink to that cuz I see no better way
to die!

wrote this just now

wen i try , nothing cums out rite . wen i dont, perfection is rite round tha bend . im an accomplished failure , a man w/ a nowhere plan , w/ nothing on his mind , & nowhere 2 go , cuz time is n absent dream , n aspiration jus outta reach . i live my life like a tec9 , loaded & full a chewing gum . a mind that races & a body so slow that danger is evrywhere i go & i cant ever get away from it , i jus dont no . i dont no , i got nowhere 2 go , nothing 2 b , yet evrything i want , its 2 far outta reach . its a hopeless journey , where death is the only hopeful local , its the only place im going , the only place that welcums me , & anyway i cudnt have it any other way cuz my final destination is that place only found in graveyards , in secluded warehouses where tha nowhere boys & grls go 2 roam & we trash tha places like its our 2nd home

Things We Are Not Supposed to See

I am fairly smart, which means I can see things most people cannot see. But maybe there are things we are not supposed to see. No wonder smart people tend to get so depressed all the time.

Growing Pains

You're a teenager, you look so neat.
You look so innocent in your clean clothing
that your mother washed the night before.
You have the time to dress up, the time to mess up,
and you can do anything you want,
because you're not dying quite yet.

But then you grow older, your body decays.
You grow depraved by the minute, getting wrinkly-faced.
The drugs eat your liver, destroy your skin.
You're pockmarked now, and you walk
with a limp.
Your voice gets slurred, and you realize
you realize, in vain, that you're going
nowhere, getting nothing, a nine-to-five job,
a nine-to-five routine, the life you lived
catching up to you faster than you can
blink.

Suicide, sure, it's an option.
A bullet in your brain would
end the pain, for sure.
But do you have the guts?
Do you really have the guts
to go through with it?

A Fatalist

I'm just a fatalist.

I talk myself out of doing the right thing
                          in so many ways
because it's never gonna work out anyway, you know.

Like something good and positive will actually come from my life
        FAT CHANCE!

Doom and gloom is all my life has in store for me.

I know none of this is true, but it feels so true, and my feelings have a way with words that my common sense does not have; they can twist words and bring my common sense to the same page and make it agree, thinking, *You know, my emotions do kind of have a point.*

PRETENDERS

"*Everybody's happy nowadays,*" sang the Buzzcocks in the late 1970s.
      "*Everybody's happy nowadays*" is a thought that is known to frequent my mind in, oh, the year 2016   2015   2014   etcetera etcetera.

Nothing's changed—everything's the same.

The streets are polluted
with liars—phonies————actors and the like.

        PRETENDERS

pretending everything is great.

But nothing is great.   It's all the same.

It's all so   fake.   FAKE>>>>>

                I want out
                      I want out
                              I want out of this cage.

Fuckin Aggro to the Max!

Jacked on caffeine, your arms hurtling like nun-chucks, boots coming down in a series of feral stomps, knees pumping as you move like pure fuckin muscle, head shaved clean, replaced with a thin carpet on top, you dart and dash like a madman, thrashing like it's nobody's business but your own—*and let it be known!*—serious aggression built up from all the repression you experience each and every fuckin day of your life—and now you've come to the Punk rock/Hardcore show to let it all loose on the world.

Getting Better

If getting better means being like you, then I want no part of it.

Trash

To you
        I AM
        <u>TRASH</u>

To me
        YOU ARE
        <u>TRASH</u>

Relativity defines perspective—
    BOTTOM LINE

Untitled

HELP ME, I am lost in the supermarket!

Punk Rock Love/ The New Church Is Back in Business

There is a world beyond
where marvelous bonds and trusts
are being passed around like blunts.
Then there is a world on our forefront,
a more modern-day reality
where teenage girls wear skirts and pumps
and teenage boys scarf down McDonald's
and watch as teenage girls dance pole-side.
There is a place locked away
in hidden dungeons where communities

Jeremy Void

come together and discuss levels
of intellect trading debates like cheap wine,
drinking knowledge and getting drunk
on worldly trinkets of information.
While in front of us men smash keys on the keyboard
dressed in old, worn out suits that are
neatly pressed and wrinkle free
and women get paid less but do the same things
treated less-than and yet perform
the same exact tasks as their
manly counterparts.
Some people keep track of
celebrity behaviors, vacationing in Hollywood
and going for a hike down the star-lined streets
where hookers roam
drug-dealers hide and deal
and kids barely old enough to tie
their own shoes are traded into cheap labor.
I came from a world where madness lingers
I was brought into a sadly shaped hemisphere
where reality is twisted and beaten
by Christians in loins cloths wielding long,
wooden shafts—another whacking for
the sake of God's holy wrath.
I watched TV where pimps pimped out
young girls—hos, they called them
and dumb shit men and women speak
in their dumb shit drawls:
LOL—TTYL—the lingo of the deathly retarded.
This world I learned quickly was sickly ridden
and the places that I drifted
the land of the free that I seeked
a world beyond physics
where kids dress in black leather and sport

big fucking studs and swear like filthy
fucking sailors, a world that sadly
most people will never get to know
or understand
where I learned to be kind and helpful
and treat others not the way I wanted to be treated
but the way they wanted to be treated.
I learned there's no need to fight eachother anymore
when kids in the "real" world have to be
constantly vigil because everyone becomes
the enemy—but see I joined the new church
home to the wild few
untamable and crazy they said
rat finks no good for nothing they labeled us
a bunch of fucking fuckups they spewed
when we passed them on the street.
Just a bunch of punks, the quote-unquote
"normals" thought as we squandered past them.
But we learned there was no need to hide anymore
because here the brethren's got our backs
and that is something the normals always seem to lack.

Existential Hell

If existentialists believed in hell, I think this would be it, this nonexistence, this being lost in a lonely dream where the only way out is through that twisted and jagged mirror that shows me what's behind the veil, uncovered and dirty - - shows me everything that I thought I had tucked away in the laundry shoot, to be taken away by men in shiny white suits who will go off and wash them for me,,, all those years of torment neglect and abuse, all those sinister defects that under the right light I can dress in pounds of makeup and make look nice and right so that instead of being haunted by them I can own them, take them home and boast about their wonders, because under the right light anything can be seen as anything and everything can then seem bearable but that right light is broken, the fuse torn out by crisp claws in the night, and here under the <u>WRONG</u> light everything looks so damn right but horrible, not how I remember it looking. So if the existentialists believed in hell, I'm pretty sure this would be it - - not a wet dream, not a fantasy,,, but a reality!

Bored & Frustrated

The bomb is set to go off.
It's set to disrupt.
The toxicity is billowing up in
the city....   This wretched piece of wasteland———————
the anxiety the boredom the pent-up hate
capped up & ignored, thrown in the backseat
of your minivan, the walls undulating as it
overflows with rage———   *Aaaaaaaaaaaahhh!!!*

No Love

It's ugly!
It's disgusting!
It's sick!
It's mindnumbingly dull!
It's wretched!
It's a complete fuckin waste
    of time!!!
It's **LOVE**
        LOVE
               LOVE

IT'S JUST NOT WORTH IT

It will leave you a broken, bleeding mess
a pathetic waste of life addicted to this wretched, fucked-up device called **LOVE**

Immoral

This is the reason I don't typically go on Facebook. I've been on it way too much these past few days, and now everybody hates me. I never said I don't have problems. I'm actually very upfront about my problems. Like this one girl broke up with me cuz I was immoral. So I said you knew I was immoral, and she said but I didn't think it was true.

Reality

Reality comes at me swinging
pushes me on my face
kicks me in the ass.
again and again and again

so I fight back....

A Method to My Madness

See, kindness doesn't pay in the realm of materials, but it does pay in the realm of spirituality. You might not get fame and notoriety but you will get satisfaction at the fact that you yourself did the right thing, something so few of us step up to do. Other people may misread your actions and call you an asshole, but it's *you* who you have to face every day. Not them, but *you*. If you can look in the mirror and see an honest, kind human being staring back at you, then you've done a good job. Most of society is very sick and people *will* misinterpret kindness as a devious act only because if they were to act kindly themselves, they'd know their own motives were misguided and therefore your motives must be misguided too. If that makes sense. Keep your head up, keep writing and doing art, and keep your hand out cuz you never know who will need it next.

Suicidal Plan

The mirror on the wall
shows me in all my
morbid glory.

There I am,
sweaty and crazed.
My eyes are puffy
        red and glassy.

In my hand
there's a revolver.
It's silver and shiny.

                    Six bullets.
              But I'll only need one.

Smash a Lightbulb: Poetry for Lowlifes

I look at myself
tip the bottle of whiskey
to my mouth.
        Gulp, gulp, gulp.

The bitter liquid
burns on its way down
sweltering in my gut.

The image, my reflection
winks at me.
But I didn't wink.

I think I'm going crazy.
I must be, for what
I'm about to do.

                                  The gun
                              silver and shiny
                              holds six bullets.
                            But I'll only need one.

I lift it up and press
the muzzle to my head.
Cock the hammer.
        And the image winks.

It winks again.

I lower the gun
take a hit of the bourbon.
Is this the right thing to do?
        But I'm all out of options.

Jeremy Void

I lift it again and press
the cold steel to my head.
The image winks
        and now I'm scared.

                "Don't do it" it says.
                "Don't do it" it repeats.

Me, I'm saying that.
Me, I'm talking to me.

                No, not possible.

A hand, my reflection's hand
surges out and grasps my wrists.
Holds it tight and forces the gun down..
                                                       No!

                                                          Stop!

                                          This is not happening.

                My image, *me*
                mimicking *me*.

It steps out and cocks its arm back.
A radiant fist, slightly transparent
bashes me in the face.

I drop the gun..
                                                            No!

                                                          Stop!

My reflection grapples me.
Lifts me overhead.
Hurls me at the wall.
        A *THUMP,* the wall rattles
and I fall on the floor—

                      ouch!

I struggle to my feet.
A radiant version of me
leaps up onto the bed.

GOD-

                # -FUCKING-

                                    # -ZILLA

It hurls itself at me.

Knocks me back
into the wall,
hammering me with a clubbed fist.
It smashes me and when I'm
done for, it goes for the gun.

My reflection stands there
sweaty and crazed,
eyes red and puffy
        glassy and mad.

I think, Oh no,
it's gonna shoot me.
I don't wanna die.
        Not tonight, anyway.

It points the gun.
Then walks back into the mirror,
                                    and it's gone.

Smash a Lightbulb
Tonight

A lonely candle
in a dark room

smells putrid to
me.
It smells like
rotted fish, like
acidic dicks.
It smells like burning
fetal matter,
like lighting a bag
of dog shit and dropping it
on your neighbor's
front steps.

I don't know why
we bother lighting up
the night.
I don't know why
we cry when someone
dies.
I don't know why anyone cares,
because goodness loses its
meaning when everyone
does it.

The night is beautiful
and should thus be
preserved.
You talk about saving
lives; well
the night has feelings too.

No Hope

Only when you have no hope will you be free from bondage.

RULE #1

Don't be a sheep—black or white, white or black—don't be a fuckin sheep. BE YOURSELF. Or, if you have to, be a wolf.

On the Edge of Madness

They Say
Medication Makes Me
Robotic
But I Take Pills Just So
I Can Fall Into
My Brain And See
The World Under A New Lens…
Just So Just So   You Know
Just So I Can Fly Through Space
Talk To Antelopes Who Salute Me
With Crisp Jagged Horns
Become A Cantelope
Drunk By The Rich
Poured Into A Wine Glass
As Great Gusts Of Wind Lift Me
Out Of This Mess I Enter When
The Pants Don't Seem To
Fit Me Quite Right

Jeremy Void

They Say
Madness
Is No Good
But Is It Madness That Opens
My Eyes   Widens The Mind
Gives Me Wings So I Can Fly
Does It Not Make Me Feel Superb
And 'Crazy'— —A Twisted Sensation
A Jagged Haze That Creates Life
And Murders It Too
I Find I'm Swimming With Sharks
Crawling Through Glaciers Of Shit
Cresting The Putrid Mountainside
And Watching From A Passive Distance
As These 'Normal' People Slaughter Themselves
With Aggro Exchanges And Deadly Stares
Eyes That Project Vomit Through
The Television Set

Is It
Mania
That Makes Me Madd
Or Is It The Torturous Media
A Sleeping Nation Only Awake
To Kill Someone Unsuspecting
And We Give Life To Sleeper Agents
<u>Don't Utter Certain Phrases</u>
<u>Don't Utter Certain Phrases</u>
Or These Agents Of Death Will Hatch From
Distant Places Lurking Only To Murder
Starved Children In The Night
To Murder
Creativity With A Flip Of The Switch
Just Aim And Point

And I Wonder

Is It Me
Or Does Creativity Seem To Be
A Sin In This Day And Age
Like The Creation Of New Thought
Can Cave In Your Head
Like
Thinking Becomes Shunned By
Cool Men In Spartan Uniforms
Waging War On The Persian Army
Like A Repeat Of Thermopylae
It's Retro
So It's Cool, Right
Learn About History So It Doesn't Repeat Itself
Learn About War And Hitler And
Sylvester Stallone
So It Doesn't Happen To Us
Again

Are The 'Sick' So Bad
Is It Not The Good Who Destroy?

Pogo to Forget

Punk rock has always been my escape from the oppressive 9-to-5 world we live in, my much-needed release that came at the end of every week, where I could see my friends, and a badass band would play, and the crowd would go wild. We'd swirl in front of the stage, feet kicking, fists swinging, knees pumping, elbows thrashing. We'd spin. We'd crash and burn, fall to the ground and get lifted up just to be hurled back into the madness. When I was a kid, those were the best times of my life. Taking out all that pent-up aggression in the form of moshing was the greatest thing in the world. Nothing mattered when I was in the pit. Not the girl who rejected me on Monday, the job that fired me on Tuesday, the teacher that failed me on Wednesday, my parents telling me I'm grounded on Thursday, or the big kid that beat me up on Friday————none of it fucking mattered when I was in the pit.

Multiple Choice

       Am I

a.) An artist?
b.) A crass technician?
c.) A lewd bazooka?
d.) A crazy mad scientist?
e.) An insomniac battling fantastic demons that come crawling out of my dresser drawer when I least expect it, with razor-sharp eyeballs?
f.) Or all of the above?

Untitled

When you die,
I'll die laughing.

A Little Piece of My Insanity

I don't want to hate anymore. Only I can't stop hating. What I do want is love. Only I can't start loving. What I need is somebody, to tell you the truth. Somebody who will spit on me and put me down. What I need is you to punish me. What I want is for you to go away. But while you're here, you might as well punch me, kick me, hit me with all you got. Spit on me, humiliate me. Make me feel pain, it's what I need. I want you to leave me be, but you have no idea what it means to be me, and if you did, you might just hurt me, throw dirt on me, kick me around and make me bite the fucking curb. What I need, what I want, it's all the same in the end. Just make me know pain, it's the only way.

MADness Thrivery

The world is shaded out
with bliss.
I feel like Jesus
I walk on water
I turn water to wine
and drink the wine
I don't share....

STOP

I'm a serpent
I'm a devil
drink my coffee
go back to bed.
This is the way
of the world....

STOP

I live too fast
don't slow down.
The car runs outta gas
I think I'm going
madd..

I listen to the moon
the man up there speaks
take off my mask
the world is going
bleak....

STOP

This is the end
This is the beginning
it won't start again
so pay attention while it's here>>>>>>>>>
and say goodbye to all your fears................

STOP   STOP   STOP

Looting for Jesus

Somebody gimme an excuse to go looting.
      A reason to rob a store.
            Somebody shoot a black man in the head.
        So I can go and steal.

THIS IS MY ART

I LIKE TO CREATE ART, if you would even call it that.   IF YOU DO NOT APPROVE OF THE ART I PRODUCE, by all means, UNFOLLOW ME.   IF YOU THINK ITS CRAP, well, it kind of is, dont you think.   but thats aside the point————my point is, I LIKE TO CREATE ART, end of subject.
i know that some people spend years polishing their craft, maybe even their whole life smoothing out the edges, sanding it down & shining it all neat & tidy for all eyes to see————some people take their craft so seriously, too seriously if you ask me————some people point the tips of their noses high in the air & maybe even look down at others thru their snot holes, as if thats where they keep their eyes, hidden deep inside their noses, you know the type, they scrutinize & tell you your arts not satisfactory for the likes of them————some people are too damn high & mighty, dont do that, no you cant do that, art was never meant to be like that————some people are so proud that anything below their standards is so far from real art that the person responsible for said mess should be shunned by all artists everywhere, you know the kind—some people————
some people are just not REAL artists themselves....   of course, there are the trolls, critics, or whatever you wanna call them, & then there are us, the ones putting in the effort, the TRUE believers....   besides, art was never meant to be taken seriously if you ask me————i mean, its not like i aspire to have my work hung up in a museum, nor do i hope to have it dangling in a gallery for all eyes to see, eyes of the more classy variety, That Is.   because my art is not classy, it will bring about goosebumps, this is true, but its not the kind of crud that others will be marveling at behind monocles, scholars talking in their formal drawl about how the edges & the colors & the everything else put together really brings out the message said artist is trying to convey....

if you dont like it, I dont really give a fuck, now do I?...   because I LIKE TO CREATE ART ... end of subject

Just Like Me

I knew this guy
        who was just like me.

I hated this guy.
        I wanted him to die.

a CUNT RAWKer
a more lucid more destructive form of art

Punk these days has become rather lame.
It's turned into a mob of pretty boys and wannabes.

See   I'm no Punk—I listen to Punk Rock
                but, really, I'm just a cunt
                      a cunt <u>raw</u>ker

It's raw, what you see is what you'll get.

so Untalented = so Successful

It's sad that someone so untalented could be so successful just because they were born in the right life.

Nothing Matters Anymore

Everybody turns on you. You do the right thing but it doesn't matter—nothing matters. You feel numb and alone, dumb and blind—nothing matters anymore. What's the point when they hate you? You try and try but your tries are worthless. It's like you're 5-years old again. You're running away. You're stuck in a rut and you're running ... running ... *somebody help me please i dont know whats going on im scared & alone please help me.* Darkness seizes you. You've done the right thing, but to what does it matter? You're giving up, you're breaking down down down——you're lost and alone, stuck and so very sold. Falling—that's your anthem. Falling into damnation....

Your image shatters and it's all over from here....

Shite!

Thats such terrible
boring crap that
my eyes bleed
when I see it.
Its so bad that
my dick leaks pus
from experiencing it.
Shite, shite, shite!

Or maybe thats a good thing.

Maybe your goal is to make
me hate you.
In which case youd be a success.
Now, wouldnt you?

Don't Call Me a Bigot

When I use the "cunt" word
        people take ultra offense
and forget the facts I conveyed///

When a white cop kills a black man
        people take ultra concern
and forget about the facts at hand.

It's not like these are Harvard student black kids
for these kids being gunned down
are being gunned down in the ghettos, no less
        next door to the crack house
        right outside the busted window of
        the store whose TV just got jacked
            five minutes prior.

Yeah so they've got nothing on
these black kids
so they were shot with no provocation
        and I'm not arguing that fact
            I'm just saying
            maybe the cop's not
            all to blame
            in these situations....
Yeah they shot first, asked questions later
and yeah that's highly against protocol,
but it's not like the black kids in question
        were saints either.

The media will slant it that way
white liberals will tell you that's the case
and black people will spew broken English

Smash a Lightbulb: Poetry for Lowlifes

to stand up for the black race—*duh!*

Undereducated people should not have a say
        in these matters of affairs
but then these are not just any
        undereducated people,
these are undereducated *black* people, no less
        who not to mention have had it rough
and can't afford to go to college anyway....

Blacks are not the only ones
who've had it rough
        and don't call me a bigot
        for saying that
        because I'm really not....
It's just that I bet I've had it
just as rough and maybe more
        and maybe less
        depending on which black kid
        you refer to.

Reverse racism is still racism
        no matter which way you swing it....
Are you looking for another race war?
because it's on its way
if you keep segregating,
blaming races like you have been doing///
        If you keep blaming the cops
        and taking the responsibility away
        from the black kids at
        the scene of the crime
then blacks will riot and loot
snatching irrelevant crap
        like TVs and DVD players

through the holes in busted windows
      as history has shown
           time and time again///

I'm all for black education
and there are the smart ones too
      not saying there aren't
but some of them are just as big
a lowlife as me
      and maybe they deserve to be shot!
          —oooh I said it....

But don't call me a bigot
because I'm really not.
Just, if a man pulls a gun on you
wouldn't you want him dead?
      If a black pulls a gun on me
      I would just as quick shoot him
      as I would shoot you.

But don't call me a bigot
because I'm really NOT

FUN FACT:

If you order a pizza from Domino's online and you use the hard-rock tracker, they play the beginning of "Beef Boloney" by Fear on a loop.

A Closet Case
inspired by Closet Spase

Close your eyes
listen to the waves to the bite
the madness of the night
the world dissolves in fright
got no time/
                              got no time/
                                                          got no time/

I think I'm dying.
Something's a-rising.
Next thing I'm flying///
can't stay grounded on free will alone
                        I don't know how to
                                          I'm floating into
                                          the clouds/

which ripple and laugh
pointing their sorrowful fingers
through the holes in my eyes
and releasing sperm cells
                that crawl
                out of my asshole
                hit the ground and dissolve
                into ninja midget queens....

It's the story
        of
                        my life
                            blown up
by a seizure of flickering
        flashing
                rippling

Jeremy Void

        clapping
                cutting into me like

        laser

beams
of the liquidated kind

a burst of zigzagging waterfalls
that spray rabies at dead mammals

straight from

outer space!   STOP!   STOP!   STOP!

too much commotion
an explosion
a crumbling fusion
spiking   my heart with
                sonic

      blasts

of neutron bombs———
        eat dust
        eat dust
        eat my
                fucking fledglings
                of electronic

      X-

vampires   super sonic
            zonked

Smash a Lightbulb: Poetry for Lowlifes

        clonked
           topping
                the noise barriers

    with

glass breaking pounding beating screaming
    screeching banging rippling flailing

as I stretch out across
the flaming
        front yard   you know

is it over ...... ??
is it over ...... ??
        a dashing lawnmower crashing into thrashing walls that splash and roll
        tumbling into a fumbling football hero who plummets to his knees
        holding the ball like a life-line as a razor-sharp cleat cuts straight through
        the fucker's Adam's apple
        and he's dead
             the opposing team laughs
             as he lies there suffering

        twitching

        blood flowing from the hole in his neck,,,,,

        and he's dead!!!

        and it's all over and done with ...   the end

I can't decide
so don't make me

Either too smart, or too stupid, I just can't decide. One way or another, I'm too young to do it. Fuck me, I blew it!

Lust

When BOREDOM strikes
When MADNESS bites
When the cold spike of the night
       cuts through me like
      an ice pick
            I will fight
            I will live my life

            I won't look back

A Six-Word Story

<u>If Hemingway can do it, then so can I.</u>

Rooftop sniper.
                    Grounded gunman.
                                         Sniper dead.

Untitled

If you're determined to not get a job but situations are closing in on you and forcing you to get out there and start working, do what I do: NEVER SHOWER AGAIN!!!

Self-sabotage is key to living a successful and fulfilling life.

Love Love Love

Love is everything, Love is nothing.... Love will break you, Love will make you. One whiff of Love will lift up your spirits, until that whiff evaporates and you fall right off a cliff.

Love is manipulative, it speaks to you softly, chides you into following it into your own doom.

Love and Mania go hand&hand, until those hands come apart, and before long you'll be spiraling down into a void of self-destruction.

Love soothes the mischievous, and Love eases the violent, but a loss of Love stirs them both into a roiling mass of turmoil.

We Love because it feels good—until that feeling loses its romance and sensation, and we fall to our knees and pray that we had never fallen in Love in the first place.

Love heals all wounds, brings fools together, spins them around in a cacophony of pleasure and catastrophic bliss, but just don't take away their Love ... or the sky will come crashing down.

Writing Fiction

I read somewhere that writing fiction is like acting, in that you gotta think like your characters in order to portray them properly. I read somewhere else that writing fiction is like lying, in that you gotta make an untrue story seem believable. I'm not much of an actor, but I am a damn good liar.

A Rally of Skeletons Marching for Equal Rights
in a rather repressed kingdom—Hold On For Your Dear Life

Don't speak, I can't speak, I'll never speak, because if I dared speak I know what would happen to me: my skeleton would break loose and tear a path through my stomach and out my throat, and I know what will be waiting for it out there in the real world:

The one-eyed judge carrying a shiny golden mallet behind his ten-foot tall podium just waiting for my skeleton to get loose.

So much madness going on around me and if only I spoke up the hysteria might cease, but I can't risk it, not yet.

I can't risk setting my skeleton up for a crash-course in anal rape at boner penitentiary where ghouls and goblins lurk in solitude carrying thick clubs infested with rabies with slithering worms squirming out of holes in the polished oak and they bite, these worms are bullies like my day's in high school, being chased down by the sun and its own set of nefarious planets trying to wreak havoc in and around the school

but I'll get to that in a bit

I'll get to that, I promise>>>

Smash a Lightbulb: Poetry for Lowlifes

Hold your horses, I'LL FUCKING GET TO IT, STOP YOUR FUCKING NAGGING—and there it comes, I feel the internal biting and nibbling and ripping and clawing as my stirred skeleton starts its ascent, my skin starts to feel like Jello.

With one noxious blast like sonic gas my skeleton makes it to my lips and kisses me gently goodbye and off he runs, I depress quickly to the stony grass beneath my combat boots.

My eyes roll out of my head as my deflated body lies there like slime and I see my skeleton hurrying and scurrying and pushing through vines of the lonely forest in a busy world filled with hateful people who spend all their time in solitude dreaming up murderous schemes.

In the distance: a rumbling, a wailing, a tumbling, a pelting, a force of pushing and shoving plowing into bones—only bones—the bones break—*my* bones—and the golden mallet comes flying past my slimy form like the hammer of Thor and it's then when I know

I know I'll never see my skeleton again—

off to the boner penitentiary he goes and all I've got left of this worthless existence is my massive penis that coils away from me like a dead snake. It's a sad day to be me.

In the distance I catch sight of a solitary figure, walking hunched over and with a limp—and then another, and then another, and then the judge pops into sight like a flaming blimp on a crash course to planet neutron, and I try to say to him:

I try to speak but without my exoskeleton in there my voice is lost to a bleakish, meekish reality that is——and then there, I see it again, and again, and I realize with one withering thought that thousands of loosed skeletons are scattered across the jungle, lulling about happily like apes having conquered the planet. And I think to myself, Why are they allowed to roam free? whereas my own bone structure was strung up inside boner penitentiary to be raped by some stone-cold dragqueen without a bone of sympathy amid his girlish figure, and those *things* have nothing better to do but wait for the bony arrival of many escaped skeletons and they wait and wait and wait; and then the judge eyeballs me with a thick, protruding eyeball that juts out of the socket like a slimeball rolling to and fro in a pit of angst and despair, and I can't speak, I can't speak, I can't begin to tell him of all the injustices here, but instead let loose a squeaking fart that sounds like a balloon releasing its inners and that's all there is left to think of as I wither away: a hairy, smelly balloon leaking blood and guts and nobody cares and I cry but I don't because I can't and it's hopeless and so … if only I could say goodbye....

Shove It

I rarely get bored nowadays. My thoughts still race, but I've found a way to direct my racing thoughts, as opposed to letting them run rampant like the days of my past.

> Shove
> that
> in your asshole and
> watch it float....

Too Smart for My Own Good

If only I wasn't so damn smart, I wouldn't think so intensely about everything, and as a result I wouldn't make such an ass of myself every chance I get. My voice might not quiver, like it does; I might speak louder and with more bronze to really project my voice so that the receiver isn't always having to say WHAT? after everything I say; I might even, like I used to do I think, act first ask questions later, you know. But no, I've got this pestering voice lingering in the back of my head telling me to halt. Just HALT!, don't do that, people will think you're foolish, they will be able to tell I've got borderline personality disorder, they will be able to read all the symptoms of my social anxiety, and yet NOBODY I'M TALKING TO HAS THE BRAINS TO DIAGNOSE ME WITH ANYTHING, let alone something as complex as BPD. These aren't trained individuals, these are commoners, people who bag my groceries, people who say WOULD YOU LIKE FRIES WITH THAT?, people who get brained senseless from watching relentless amounts of television, cuz you just never know what the Kardashians are going to do this week in stupid-ville. I've got nothing to worry about, of course. It's kind of like that stupid childish notion: if I can't see them, then they can't see me. Like, if I possess this knowledge, then EVERYone must possess it. You know, it really comes down to this: they KNOW. They know everything about me, and I can't get away from their judgmental stares, those judgmental cunts, so pedantic the way they stick their chins and their noses in the air and prance around like brain surgeons on their magic carpets of knowledge. FUCK, is all I can say. Fuck me and my obsessive obsessions, it's driving me mad!

Sorry about my rant here. Hope you can relate. Hope you pull the trigger before I do, cuz I'm sure to make a mess all over my bedroom walls. Fun, right? It's life 101: when you're smarter than the mass public, the slimeballs who think THEY'RE SMARTER THAN ME. Gimme a break. Peace!

Bad Luck

      A man steps outside,
           side
           side
           side
           side
            sinks into the ground
                  like

        quicksand
           sand

           sand

           sand

His life flashes before his eyes———*his eyes!*
      He thinks he's going to die!!
Overhead the sky changes.
     A flash of light sparks, and
         an idea
comes to him....
His head feels heavy, his body feels light.
He allows himself to sink
         down
            down
              down

He waits
patiently.
    He wonders
where the quicksand came
    from.
It wasn't here before, is
his final thought before
he is submerged in it.

Why I hate nerds

Wanna know why I hate nerds? They are obsessive little cretins. Control freaks, so caught up in their own obsessions. I had a friend who was a complete and total nerd and at his birthday party we played Dungeons & Dragon, and I unloaded a Tommy Gun and gunned the little fuckers down. Of course they went apeshit on me.

My response: What, it's just a fucking game.

Never spoke to this friend again.

Now, wanna know why I hate jocks?...

Gotta Get Outta Here

I'm so tired of the boring crap out there;
so utterly repulsed by the lack of mediums
that people like me have to share our
....................art.

Come on, Punks, this is your wakeup call.
This is your chance to produce beautiful crap.
This is your chance to pick through the garbage
and find meaning out of it all.

I say let's go dive into dumpsters;
let's take dirt and make something great.
We'll make something out of nothing
and shove our creations in their fucking faces.

This is our time now, the fuckups of Vermont
banning together to deface all that is pretty.
We have to take a stand against the norm.
We have to stand up to all that is ...
<u>boring</u>.

MadDog 20/20

Remember those days?
I hope not.
They're the days of the MadDog
        20/20
That sneaky beast, he eases
into you like a disease
overtaking your mind///
You live your life
like a plummeting jetplane
the MadDog behind the scenes
twisting your levers
pushing your buttons
watching defiantly as you fall
behind....

Now is
the time for fighting
it's the time for chaos
a summer of cheap wine and
you'll be all set....
One single night of belligerence
followed by a morning of aching heads, and
the MadDog wins again.

Part 9
Introspection is a sure way to drive a crazy person insane

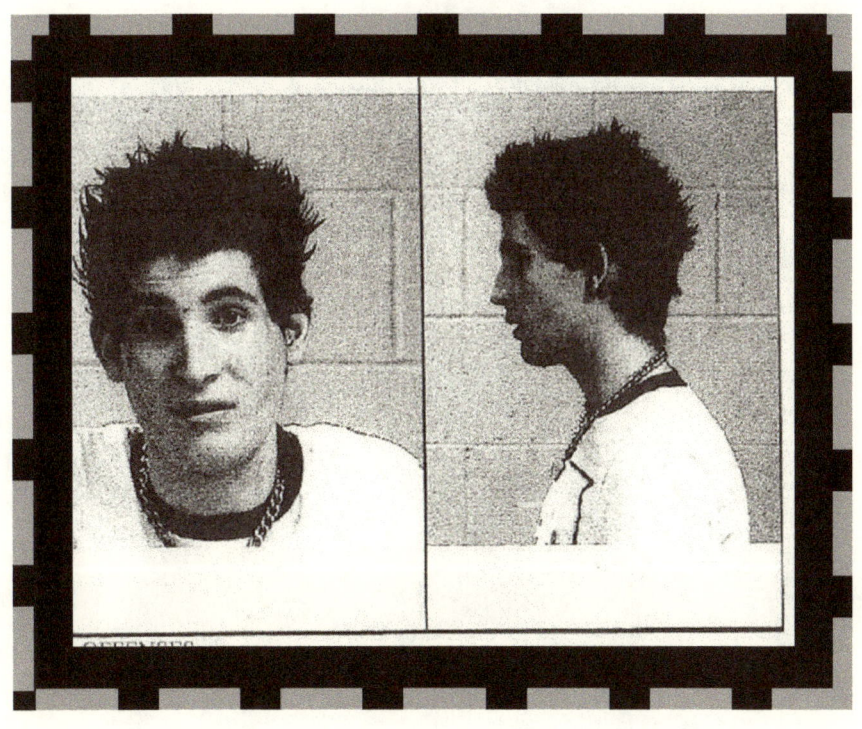

Part 9
Introspection is a sure way to drive a crazy person insane

so ABSURD

I am sitting in the writing group, doing a free-write. It's free, right? so I can write freely and freely I will write. My mind is like an inflating bubble, filling up with air as it rises to the sky—and then, *POP!*, my dreams snap out of existence like a reverse bunny-out-of-the-hat trick. It's a scary thing, right? I dream, but sometimes these idiotic notions of mine get too big for my head to contain—and then I get a headache, you know how that feels>>>>>>>>>>> I get depressed, all wound up with these sappy things called feelings, until I take something, anything, to wind me down, or until I do something that takes my focus away from these prior ruminations: This person hates me this person hates me this person hates me this person—SHUT THE FUCK UP!!! Stop your fucking yapping, your voice sounds like a rapid succession of firecrackers going off in my head, just crackling and snapping and crackling and snapping, *POPPOPPOP!* Make it stop before I get an aneurism or something. See, this is what I do when I'm alone, stowed away in the privacy of my own home; I yell at myself, my inner dialogue which is incessantly relentless consists of constant shouting—it's traumatic, I know, and I'm the rape victim here. I still to this day have flashbacks of the devastating whip that crackled and snapped across my back, leaving a slash as bright as lava and as wide as a leering smile all the way down my ribcage. Still I remember the time when I stood outside myself, threw myself headfirst into the wall, and held me there as I stole my own innocence with a series of angry, but short-lasted, thrusts. That's the shit I deal with daily, only I do it to myself, imagine that>>>>>> I'm both the victim and the victimizer. Have you ever seen the movie *Fight Club*?—well that's me, tenfold. Only I know, I'm aware, I understand the tremendous weight I carry around with me; I know I'm the one beating myself up, *me*. It's always been that way, but you know what?—I prefer it like that. It's like forcefully whacking off a man twice your height and three times as wide, a man who could easily punch a hole through your head——only it's not at all like that, that's just an absurd example of what reality plus non-reality and speculation plus non-speculation and sickening ruminations that spin webs of nonsense inside my head, are doing to me. Every day I live with this burden. Now, put that in your pipe and smoke it. Maybe you'll turn into a turtle and spread your wings and lift off. Or an elephant that swims just like a panda bear; or something that tells me everything will be all right and one day I will have my way and soon enough I'll be drifting and swooping and flapping and hooting amid the rest of the colony of bats, my brethren, free to live fast and wild and free, and no silly thinking will dampen the adventure that is soon to happen here....

Going Down the Pub

Going out to Pub 42 tonight: Gonna read some shit, drink some shit, smoke some shit (only water & cigarettes, of course, tho I might add Red Bull to the mix if I can scrounge up some cash, maybe sell a book)

My Life's Story

Chapter 1

I was brought into sadness.

Chapter 2

I was raised into badness.

Chapter 3

I delved into madness.

Chapter 4

I sanded the rusty metal
defused the flames of hell
fought to the death with the devil
and came through with a tale to tell.

Chapter 5

I got hit by a bus.

Unrestricted Self-Expression

This fucking guy
> **WHO CLAIMED TO BE AN ANARCHIST**
> I must add

accused me of being a Nazi because of my dark art

and because I said everyone
> **FROM ALL WALKS OF LIFE**

has the right to express themselves whichever way they choose.

So this fucking guy
> **WHO CLAIMED TO BE AN ANARCHIST**
> I must add

threatened to stomp my face in....   via Facebook, no less

My response: I'll be looking forward to tasting the bottom of your boot, then.
His response: You don't have to taste it if you would just stop producing this "propaganda."
My response: See, I'd rather taste the bottom of your boot than be censored like that.

And this was thus followed by a completely uncalled-for volley of threats.

Untitled Collaboration
with Gabriella Mirollo

My own rules crumble
when I go to move a muscle.

Greedy boys eat tuna fish
from rusty cans at midnight
as the drunken eagle spreads its wings
and blood drips from the moon

Smash a Lightbulb: Poetry for Lowlifes

in an eerie wet and lucid dream, the kid
hears the HORN that meant disaster
the HORN, the HORN
>>> Zombies crawl down from the rafters
like falling snow
plummeting, cold and white, into an ocean of
fish guts and poets' brains
the ghost of Edgar Allan Poe lurking
at the fringes of memory like a sweet bad smell
as the crabs devour a kayak in maggot blood
and the kid is finally feeling something
on the lam with nothing but a six-shooter and these nasty-smelling
rusty cans of tuna that give him nightmares
to no end, pirates commandeering his mind, so fucking viscerally
it's like parentheses around his head
Period. Period. The parentheses live
or die because of everything that lies between them
everything within their reach withers and dries up
the kid wakes up with his dick in his hand
the spider is mocking him, saying he's seen bigger
and points to Poe still lurking in the corner
Poe looks over and shrieks at the pointing spider
the pointing spider hisses and yelps
hobbling about, directing Poe's eyes
to the kid who tried to masturbate in the night.

The whole scene like something
only two poets could write.

Memes

I HATE MEMES. Again, someone just called one of my pieces a fucking meme. I'll say it again: I HATE MEMES. These are not memes. Memes are silly graphics that make light of a stupid situation. I am an artist, and in my opinion, memes are the lowest form of art, they cater to the lowest form of human, they are stupid at stupid's best.

Wikipedia says a meme is "'an idea, behavior, or style that spreads from person to person within a culture.' A meme acts as a unit for carrying cultural ideas, symbols, or practices that can be transmitted from one mind to another through writing, speech, gestures, rituals, or other imitable phenomena with a mimicked theme. Supporters of the concept regard memes as cultural analogues to genes in that they self-replicate, mutate, and respond to selective pressures."

Goddammit, I hate this culture and its stupid practices. I'm willing to bet that memes weren't even around before social media, which means back then what I did would be respected and appreciated as REAL art; not as silly analogues to promote silly ideas, but as REAL word art, as REAL visual poetry, as something for a smarter kind of human, the kind shunned and disrespected by the mass majority because the masses could never understand, comprehend, or relate.

Not that scholars would ever respect me, anyway.

For Answers

LIFE fall apart
I don't know where I am
I'm surfing
a sea of benzoats.
I'm hiking

the mountains of cocaine.
This world becomes caustic
Everything is destroyed
I pray to God for answers
But it's all too late for that.

The avalanche is coming
The storm clouds
are tumbling.
The rain plunges straight down
and everything
just stops/

Like Watching Paint Dry

Forgive me for not being excited about sitting and watching paint dry.

Life As a Poet
in RUTland VT

I'm bored

Let me see: I'm at the Center Street Alley right now—open-mike night—conspiring to ride up to Burlington Tuesday night with a few older guys for another open-mike, but of the spoken word variety.

I'm bored

Let me see: Before me four grown men are whacking balls with long, wooden sticks, and then the balls roll and spin, skittering and clacking as they connect with another set of balls on the other side of the green-matted, rectangular table.

I'm bored

Let me see: I can hear the metronomic thrumming of a bass guitar being plucked rhythmically and emotionlessly, I can hear the monotonous sound of communication being exchanged gingerly from one person to the next, and I can hear the steady beat of my heart as it tells me to leave, GET OUT WHILE YOU CAN!!!, and so I rise to my feet, lift my bag and toss it over my back, and make a B-line for the door.

WTF

WTfuck

A Joke Is a Joke Is a Joke

Last night I stood onstage
told a joke that
nobody seemed to understand
and in response
they called me an asshole
said I'm an offensive prick
I'm a bad person
I should not speak of such blasphemies
they said....

It was just a joke I told them
just a joke....

Close your eyes
cover your ears
wrap duct tape over your mouths
take a drill and drive it through
your fucking brain
don't utter certain phrases
don't discuss certain ideations
      or be deemed a sadist ...
      is that really what you want?

Hard Times

Hard times brings people together, but it also tears people apart.   It's The Only Sure-Fire Way To Know If Your Love Is True....

Over 48 Hours

Why the hell am I still awake? I hadn't slept in over 48 hours and all day I've been dragging my body along, just yanking it here and there, my mind blank and blanking out, and yet yet it's 8:09 PM and I'm still pulling myself forward on a tight leash and all afternoon I'd been nodding my head, struggling to keep my eyes open, and yet yet yet it's 8:10 the following night after a no-sleep night. So why the hell am I still awake?

Jeremy Void

To the Girl I Love

My erect penis sticks up and points to the one I love.
Her crisp nipples jut out and lock onto my swollen heart.
The water runs and splashes inside the tub.
She stands beneath the spray, looking like a shimmering angel,
while I stay dry and keep my eyes aligned with hers.
An angel, so sweet and naked, her skin so dark and bare,
her hair so long and wet and stuck to her shoulders like a coat of fur.
This is the girl I love, standing nude in the tub,
her skin wet, oh so wet, and ready for me to touch.
I step forward and plant my hands on her shoulders.
My erect penis applies pressure to her slightly rounded belly.
Her body deflects the spray of water coming down hard on her head,
and I take it in the face and start to shiver, my bones trembling and cold.
This must be the reason why her nipples are hard.
I took it as a sign that she loves me as much as I love her.
I step closer and wrap my arms around her back.
My penis shrinks a bit as her body pushes it straight facing up.
I feel it squeezed tightly between us as we hug.
I look down, and I'm on the verge of crying out loud.
I look down at the voluptuous rump jutting out from behind her.
I feel her pubic hair brushing against my skin,
rubbing against my leg like a wet and soggy sponge.
The feeling so sweet and sensual that
I cry and I cry, knowing not the reason why.
Maybe because the spray of cold water,
raining down with the force of a fly swatter,
juxtaposed against the warmth of her body—
her firm tits, her soft skin,
her wiry arms gripping me tight,
her head flush with my chest,
her cheek pressed to my peck—
it's so unreal, so surreal, like it's too good to be true.

Why me? is what I'm thinking as tears stream down my face.
The soap in my hair dissipates with the heavy flow of water.
My penis shrinks and hardens, standing straight up between us.
Her warm body. Her hard nipples—
I feel them poking holes in my skin, cutting crevices in my chest,
carving a path to my heart, so that she can see what's inside.
Dooooon't!!! You won't like what you'll find.
She tells me not to worry, but cringes when she catches
my cold heart in her line of sight.
It's blue, she says, so very blue, and frozen solid, not even beating.
Your heart is cold, she tells me, like I didn't already know,
as her nipples harden and sharpen and look like the barrels of two loaded guns.

LIFE

I wanna stay <u>young</u> & <u>fresh</u>
    as opposed to <u>old</u> & <u>sold</u>

                                                 doesn't sound like
                                               much of a life to me

I want to create life, as opposed to waste life

                                               I want to live
                                               I don't want to die

                                               not yet, anyway

Nefarious Things

Girls   Transitions—

Two things that tear me down, all the time, just rip me straight through hell & I don't put up a fight. I welcome the strain that those two forces bring about. I embrace the chaos, the turmoil, some more action drama & disaster. I live for madness. I do my part & they do theirs. We hug & tumble all across my bedroom floor, through my living room, rolling across the kitchen floor & crashing into the oven door, pots & pans clattering out of cabinets & the heated stove catches fire & the whole house burns down. Girls   Transitions, the nefarious things that they are.

Girls, love— It's all too tough for me, but I pull it in & I'm vulnerable against their vicious tug. Like a violent match of tug-of-war, a power struggle that always pulls me in. I'm sliding through the mud as the object of my lust yanks the rope & I'm skittering across the dirt & sand & thrown into the blood-red sea. I'm sinking fast & I peek my head out of the redness & see her standing on the shore holding my lifeline—a lifejacket, a fucking lifejacket the only thing that could keep me alive—but she walks away & leaves me to drown.

Transitions, change— Fuck me, they got me again. I can't take the unknown as it peers around the edge of the building, watching me as I cut through the alleyway, & then jumps out at me lashing & jams a steak knife through my skull. It's a lethal thing, a terrible vicious beast that holds me in a straightjacket & I'm flailing & thrashing as life fluctuates & laughs, & it's all in flux. Everything's in flux. FLUX. Stop the interchanging the switching courses the coming & going—stop it all before I'm nothing but guts drifting along in the blood-red sea & I see the changes holding hands with the object of my lust & together the two forces walk off into the night.

I'm screaming, can't you see! It's all too much for me.

A Tumultuous Magnet

I attract the energy I give off, and yet I'm attracted to negative energies....

My Best Friend

I come here on a Friday evening.
Work got out six hours prior.
The girls don't notice me as I lumber
inside.
I'm alone. I watch the girls dance onstage.
I'm alone.
So alone.
I want to cry, but I don't.

Two weeks ago
I went to slug my bestfriend in the face.
I missed and hit the wall
didn't feel the collision at all.

He and I used to come here together.
We used to come here together.
He and I.
We'd sit outside in my van and listen
to the Punk rock mix I had made
special for this occasion.

I had called the mix
Strip Club.

Tonight I sat alone in my van and listened

to the *Strip Club* mix alone in my van.
I could have cried, but I didn't.
I lowered the mirror and saw my face.
I could have cried, but I didn't.

A girl.

A girl divided us that night, and
when I saw him that night I cocked my arm
and let it fly.
He saw it coming, and stepped aside.
I hit the wall, and he was gone.
Gone.
So very gone.
My girlfriend grabbed me and we walked away.
He was gone.
Gone.
So very gone.

The girls are dancing, and I sit up front.
I have a good view of the girls dancing
in the nude.
They don't see me thru the blinding lights
splashed on the stage. They don't see me.
I watch them and they dance.

My bestfriend, he and I were so damned tight.
We did everything together.
We shared our women and our drugs.
We drank and fucked shit up.
We did everything together.
But then I had to fuck it up.
I shouldn't have been surprised
by it because that's just how life goes

Smash a Lightbulb: Poetry for Lowlifes

for me.

I contemplate crying, but decide after all
that I'd rather not.
That or
I don't know how.
That or
I don't know how.

I don't know how.

God, please help me.

I remember my bestfriend.
I think of us together.
I think of he and I.
I ask the passing girl for a lap dance.

Her name is Cherry, and
she says okay.
She says okay, and she and I
walk away.

She rubs up against me.
I think of my bestfriend.
He has gone away.
He has left me here.
She rubs me but
I can't feel a thing.

I'm just too damn numb.

She rubs me and I say,
That's enough.

She straightens and I pay her.
I watch her walk away.

Then I divert my eyes to the door,
debate leaving this place,
when it swings inward on its own
and a sliver of moonlight bursts through
and slides across the floor.

I wonder what my bestfriend
is doing this very moment.
I wonder if he thinks of me
and all the fun times we've had.

In walks a man,
dark from where I stand,
too dark to make out

and somehow I wish it was he.

My bestfriend.

The Hospice Exhibit

There's this Hospice Exhibit (to celebrate the art of dying) tonight at the Chaffee Art Center and I went up there and didn't see anything I wrote, because I did submit stuff, so I asked the woman there what's up? She said they didn't hang up my stuff because I'm not a part of their little club. Who the fuck are they? But anyway, the shit that was hung up had nothing to do with death. They were mostly surreal landscapes or gothic paintings, and they weren't even dark. Probably because they'd scare the crap out of the close-minded citizens of Rutland if they were. So I sat down and wrote this on an index card:

Death is a distraction,
a void into another universe,
a place of escape, where the fires
grow and fester, a world
beyond sight, beyond fathomable might.
We can talk and laugh and cry.
We can curl up in a ball and die.
But in the end death's slithering embrace
will sliver up to you in the night
and pull you through the gates.
There's no escape.

I know it's bad, but it's all I could come up with in five minutes. And I was going to take the liberty of hanging it up myself, just find some tape and stick it to the wall. But last minute I decided not to. I was all ready to, but then I got a text message saying there was a skunk lingering around my apartment and I ought to come home and let in my cat.

Nihilism
so what??

Why does not caring have negative connotations? Why do people look down on those who have no convictions? Not caring does not mean you wish harm on others. Not caring about politics, for example, does not mean I'm gonna blow up the white house. Why would I blow it up if I DON'T CARE? People think nihilism is such a negative stance that they suddenly put you in the same category as terrorists. If I believed in nothing, why the hell would I blow up a church? The church would not bother me if I truly believed in nothing. Nihilists are NOT Satanists, they do not worship Allah, they do not believe in chaos or wish for total annihilation of the human race.

Save Me

Someone

        please

save me

       from

            <u>myself</u>!

Visceral

I have no idea where I am.

1.
Everything is black—pitch-black—with a harsh scratching sound tearing through my ears. I call Molly's name—no answer. I reach out my hands, cringing and swiveling my head. Something is so very wrong.

2.
A bright flash immerses me—so instantaneous and bright that the whole world comes to life before my very eyes—and then snaps back to black. An image of a park, a playground, kids on swings and seesaws, is embedded in my mind. "Molly!" I shout. "Molly, what is going on?"

3.

I feel the ground beneath my feet, it tips and I lean and my arms and hands flail as I try to stay grounded. I feel like I'm spinning I feel internally dizzy, my stomach feels bubbly and sick as the ground wobbles and slants. "Molly!"—no answer.

4.

I take a step forward; when my right foot connects I hear an explosive bang and the scratching sound stops. Just stops. A devastating silence encompasses me. So deadly silent. So horrifying of a silence that when I shout Molly again, I hear nothing. *Molly!* I try, but no words come out of my mouth. *Molly!* I try again. I begin jumping and waving my arms angrily and cursing silently. What the hell is going on??

5.

I give up; I decide instead to just drop on my butt and wait here to die—what else is there to do in this pitch-black silence? But I don't land anywhere; instead my stomach flips and flops as I plummet—a straight free-fall.

6.

This must be a dream, I think to myself just as the scratching sound recommences, getting louder and louder the farther and farther I fall into—where?

7.

This is not happening.

8.

This can't be happening.

9.

10.

11.
12.
13.
14.

With a heavy *thud* my back connects with something soft; it breaks my fall; my eyes surge open, I bounce once twice three times, take a deep breath; I flail my hands, I knock something over. Something shatters. I whip my head around, catch sight of a dim light coming through the window, branches like bones whack and scrape glass, creating skeletonlike shadows of the most grotesque. An explosive bang, followed by a flash of light that reveals my bedroom. I'm in bed. In bed. It was only a dream. Thank God. And what a dream that it was. It felt so real. All I can say is: Thank. Fucking. God. It was only a dream.... Thank. Fucking. God! It was just a dream....

Opinionated

People who have opinions are more selfish and egotistical than people who don't. Cuz people without opinions are saying, "I don't know." People with opinions are saying, "Well, I do know and let me tell you." I DON'T KNOW A GODDAMN THING ABOUT ANYTHING AND I AM SO PROUD OF THAT FUCKING FACT and you seem to know everything about everything and are so proud of that fact. Fucking check your fucking ego, Mrs. Self-Righteous, Nose-in-the-Air, Not-in-My-Backyard— I was about to say cunt, but I stopped myself because I know you're not a cunt, I know better than that. Just, no offense, your preaching is giving me a headache and I unfollowed you two days ago because of that, but you have the right to do it and I have the right to not listen.

THIS IS MY ART, Part 2
of the darker variety

i know my art is dark & thought-provoking & maybe even scary to certain audiences, & maybe people are thinking, *is he okay? is he gonna do himself in tonight? im a little worried;* or maybe people are thinking, *what an asshole! he just wants to complain, hes only seeking attention, is all*————all for a few more LIKEs. but the truth of the matter is, i like this kind of art. when i see art of a darker variety, i feel stimulated, i feel joyful & alive, i feel like im on top of the whole FUCKING world, & i dont know why that is. i like things that bite i guess, for ive always surrounded myself with a more <u>dangerous</u> kind of person, even though to me the average joe was rearing to bite my head off, the prom kings & queens lurking around the corner brandishing switchblades & clubs just waiting for me to come rounding the bend, & you all know what would happen to me then, right? yeah, MY people wear spikes & leather, but YOUR people wear uggs & denim with plastic smiles & phony lives that seem so pathetic but still scare me senseless. you see, i stopped checking out plastic-looking girls one day on the train as i admired these 2 hot preppy-looking girls standing by the door, & then the thought popped in my head: <u>Like fucking a dried-out blow-up doll, your dick chafing the plastic twat in between her legs</u>—painful *and* gross, right? well, that did it for me; those girls no longer seemed hot anymore & the kind of girls that did intrigue me had piercing scowls carved across their faces, sporting short, spikey hair, with leather jackets dashed & tainted with loads of paint & spikes & studs sticking thru the vacant spaces. thats my kind of girl, this is my kind of art. darkness doesn't seem so scary anymore when youve lived it, like walking thru a haunted house; only the haunted house is your life & the ghouls & goblins hiding in the shadows getting ready to pounce on the first passerby that crosses their paths, are your friends & the only ones left to fear are the quote-unquote <u>normal</u> folk who are wanting to destroy you.

In a State of Fear

Terrorism: To induce terror in our hearts and souls; Victory: To maintain a state of constant terror in America; Defeat: To let the terror in to fester and rot; Freedom: To be rid of bondage and outside influence. Rights: the right to be safe.

The terrorists have won, we run scared every day of our lives, through security checkpoints and body scans at the airport, through fields of candid cameras peeping on us you just can't get away.
We're stuck in a terminal state of fear, we're lost hoping they don't get us here, ISIS, Al Quaeda, the big bad Taliban lurking around every corner, can't take a shower without fear that the walls will erupt without fear that stepping out of the shower means meeting a barrage of bullets as they splice through the walls and sever your heart from your soul.
There's nowhere to turn nowhere to run, because everywhere you go Osama's henchmen are locked and loaded, the schools are not safe, run away, for fear of what might be around the bend waiting to chop you down.
Terrorism: to evoke fear.
Terrorism: to control us with acts of terror....
It's sad and I'm scared of the worldly toughguys wielding explosive swords, pens that nuke bridges, clip on ties that if you were to yank on them airplanes would come railing through the sky and colliding with your child's school.
Run away before they win.
Run away admit defeat before the fuckers win.
Protect the women & children protect ourselves.
Death is inevitable but please oh please don't bring us there....
We're in a state of fear but there are worse things to fear than pussy gunmen who hide in shadows trained assassins who wait for the precise moment to pull and next thing gunfire punches holes in everything in sight, there's worse things to fear than that
like the United States Government, for one.

Smash a Lightbulb: Poetry for Lowlifes

Like the police marching like Gestapo withdrawing guns and firing them at inno-
    cents people
 beating kids up in the street/
But it's funny isn't it? if we're scared of them then we ain't got a single fight left
    in us, like look at a boxer who's too scared to enter the ring, just wait-
    ing for that knockout punk to come jarring into his jaw bones and out go
    his lights as he drops to the mat with a heavy clack, see that's all that
    fear does, it keeps us weak and passive and terrorists can go home feel-
    ing gratified at a job well done at a country stuttering and afraid....

That's all that it does///

RUTland VT

                        There's no way in, no way out....
              There are all the drugs you could ever want....
                  Just stick your head out the window....
                                 and take a whiff....

                                That's Rutland in a nutshell—
                                      RUTland, VT

where crack blooms like flowers
and the air smells like fresh-cooked junk.

THINK ABOUT IT!

When a man breaks his leg he has to acknowledge this fact and use crutches to aide him in walking until he can walk on his own again. He can surely deny this fact and try and walk on his own anyway, without the help of crutches, but that won't get him very far. Plus, his leg won't ever heal and he'll forever be a *prideful* gimp.

Who am I????

Who am I????
Frightened & alone
a lost pondering left to die
a terminal third wheel
& the gears are clinking
in space
& my restless thoughts
race >>>

I'm in a dwelling of dilemma
a masochist afraid of being hurt
a psychopath with a conscience
too strong too deliberate too caustic
for my own good....

I'm walking backwards
Who am I????
a mindless drone heading
for disaster.

It's hopeless, the story

Smash a Lightbulb: Poetry for Lowlifes

of my life.
I'd cry about it but
the electric tears
would singe me too badly, &
I might as well just go
back to bed....

The tightrope trembles
a wobbly course of action
a terrifying surge coursing through
its every fiber.

Who am I????
I'm alive,
I think, or maybe
I'm dying
drowning in the kitchen sink....

I have lots of thoughts
so many they explode
in my head & my decaying skull
absorbs the blow.

So thick
too sick
yesterday's myth is peeking
around the corner
a trickster a temptress a devil
waving its bony finger for me
to follow ...

& I let go
& I fall
& I plummet

into madness, my legs absorb
the blast & my entire skeleton
shatters on the rocky floor....

Who am I????
I'm lost!

Like a Drone

The girl's boyfriend looks like a drone. Why not just get a sex machine? Emotionless, drab, boring—but boy, will it get you off.

The Show Tonight
sung with Lethal Erection

Gimme a drink
or gimme a line.
Gimme a pill
and I'll be doing fine.
Gimme a stage
or gimme a crowd.
Gimme a mike
and I'll show you how.

Gimme an instrument
and an amplifier.
Gimme some drugs
and I'll play this show tonight.

I'll play this show tonight.

{available on YouTube}

DON'T VOTE

I don't vote because
I'm ignorant.

        I'm ignorant and I
        prefer to keep it that
        way.

                Politics is just an
                orgy, don't you
                know?

I feel like in order to vote, one must have to take a test to prove that he/she is up to date in world affairs/
        that he/she is aware of who is fucking who///

Total Takeover

I'm doing great. Living the nightmare and trying to find ways to market that. I wanna exploit the exploiters, steal money from the rich and burn it all to the ground. Just pile it up, douse it in gasoline, light a match, and let the flame do the rest. I wanna see the sociopathic big business men fall to their knees and ball as they watch their children perish amid billows of cigarette smoke and piles of fast food. I wanna witness the world turning in on itself, the poor getting rich and fat, and the rich getting skinny on crack. One of these days I'll turn water to wine. Treat the poor to a drink, while the rich stand on the corner panhandling for our easily swindled dough. And then I'll be doing better than great, I'll be grand, I'll feel like the man, my ego would have skyrocketed, and in a few years the rich will rise the ranks and knock me down and take my cash and force me to work as a gizz catcher at the local strip club. Every man will have their day.

Smash It Up

EVERYBODY
        and that means you
is doing the best they can
with the knowledge they think they know.

                    SMASH   UP   YOUR
                         knowledge
                    before it defeats you

Burning Out Is Inevitable

Don't take it slow

Burning out is inevitable

Don't take it easy

Burning out is inevitable

The future is approaching

Burning out is inevitable

The city is coming apart

Burning out is inevitable

Don't stop
    don't get stale
        don't wait
            no need to yell

Burning out is inevitable

Must Be Said

You wouldn't believe all the good I do
    on a day-to-day basis
        probably more than you
            when it comes down to it.

But I don't promote it
I don't paint myself as a saint
        because that would defeat the purpose
            now wouldn't it?

Painting myself as a villain
seems much more saint-like
        if you ask me.
Masking the good with sinister things
making me seem like the asshole
      just goes to show
          how purely selfless I am.

But let the record be straight
          —here—
               —now—
that I'm only telling you this because
        I feel it must be said
        so that you know
        I'm not such a bad person after all
        but a selfless individual with
        a twisted sense of humor, is all.

Really
I'm just trying to give you a mirror
into yourself <<<<<<

When's My Turn

When I was younger, but not too young I suppose, I had no problem getting with girls—as easy as picking them off of trees.   With a new girl every week I was.

But now, at 28-years old, things like that seem much harder to me, especially in a city as small as Rutland, where girls just get recycled back into the mix and you can't get away from them———
ever.

Every decent girl is taken it seems. Every good-looking girl has a boyfriend and I sit and watch these couples and they never seem to break, as if they've been welded together to time and nothing is strong enough to break the hold....

IT'S FRIGHTENING
how perfect some of these couples seem together.............

Smash a Lightbulb: Poetry for Lowlifes

And I will never, ever have a chance of my own to weasel my head in between these wretched developments called love and say:

WHEN'S MY TURN

Where the Freaks Roam

Dirty Alleyways
Dingy Floors
Roofs Looming Over a Sea of Nothing
I was there
I was there
it was dank and rough
it was mean and rotten
I was there
I was there
it was nothing to be scared of
there was no reason to avoid it

the lights were out
the shadows lurk and shift on the floor
the world as we know it
goes topsy turvy
it flips——it flips
cavernous dwellings a pit of despair
I was there
THERE—THERE—THERE

Dirty Alleyways
Dingy Floors
Roofs Looming Over a Sea of Nothing
I was there
I was there

it was dank and rough
it was mean and rotten
I was there
I was there
it was nothing to be scared of
there was no reason to avoid it

the world is blotted out in blackness
run away DARLING
run away DARLING
the things that go bump
the things that bite
the things that run around at night
are sick and dastardly
ridden with disease
a thing to watch out for
cuz it will make you sick
IT WILL MAKE YOU SICK

cuz I was there....

Months Later

It's awesome. When I write, it's like straight-up vomiting, and then I read it months later and try to figure out what it means. It's like dissecting someone else's poem, only it's my own poem.

On Picking Sides

Picking sides doesn't solve any problems, all it does is create more problems. Because I choose not to pick a side people have called me apathetic or indifferent, and yet I'm the first one to hold out my hand to someone who's been the victim of persecution. Like, I got into this really heated argument with this girl who was saying I'm apathetic and I don't care because I refuse to pick a side in matters of politics, and a few months earlier that same girl messaged me in the middle of the night saying she was going to kill herself and I hurried to help her out, and I did whatever I could to keep her alive in that moment. Guess she forgot this fact when she was telling me I'm a bad person because I refuse to pick a side. Picking sides means I'm determining one group to be right and another group to be wrong and that just creates more problems if you ask me. Everyone's like, *I'm liberal and I live by those ethics and people who don't live by those ethics are wrong.* (Nietzche said "a liberal institution ceases to be liberal the moment is it established.") Or they're saying, *I'm conservative and everyone who isn't conservative is wrong.* I mean, it takes two to tango, and choosing sides just promotes war, it gives you a reason to hate another group, an excuse to segregate, and what's worse is these people who are so against segregation are the first ones to divide us up.

A Story About Nothing

This is a story about nothing—it's absurd and pointless; you might not get it at first or ever, but you know what, I don't really care because nothing matters anymore.

This is a story about nothing—I lived it and I loved it and I come to realize that the life I lived swallowed me up, yum yum yum, and spit me out. I learned that the hard way, I never came to until I came to Vermont, living in a daze, every single day, a haze, everything fading away.

This is a story about nothing—just remember, kids, try it and see what happens. You could die. Just remember, kids, don't live like I did. It's no way to exist.

This is a story about nothing—the end.

Animosity As a Virtue

Hate isn't necessarily a bad thing. It's an agent of change. Discomfort is good for the soul, it makes us see things that happiness blinds us of, it shows us things in our life that aren't right. Hopefully the day comes when you're so uncomfortable that you make the necessary steps to get comfortable. Plus, if you loved everything, you'd be equally as sick as if you truly hated everything. There needs to be a balance. A yin and a yang. I'm sure you don't hate everything, but at times I'm sure it feels like you do. I can totally relate. On my worst days I wanna murder everyone who gets in my way, but on my best days, I wanna fuck everything that moves. [No Name], it's okay to be angry at times, it only means that you are human, but don't let that anger consume you. There are two wolves in our heads, one for love and the other for hate, and whichever wolf we feed gets bigger and stronger and soon consumes us. So feel the hate, let yourself be hateful if that's what you need; just don't let it consume you. Punch a wall, scream as loud as you can—and fuck the neighbors if they complain—just feel what you gotta feel and it'll pass. Embrace the hate while it's here because hate is equally important to love, and fuck anyone who says you shouldn't hate....

Not Now

I reach the breaking point
the Whole Wide World melts away
my visions blurs....
It's just me and the paper
me & the pen.
I tap the pen—there's gotta be something
for me to say
something that hasn't
been said before.

A single thought
a solid idea
something not overdone
I got this I got this
but I stare at the empty slip
and realize that I don't.

Writer's block sets in.
I'm finished. My time has come
and now it's over I'm done.
The song coming from
my stereo skips and skips
and skip-skip-skips.
My brain aches I sit here
and I've just got
nothing to say
anymore...........................

I rack my mind with ideas
but it all seems just the same
as before
overplayed

overdone
over&over and it's over.
I bleed my mind
time and time again
I seek answers I plead for
something or another to put down
on this sheet of paper.

It's useless.
My time has come
and now it's gone.
My life's work unfinished
I traipse my mental dictionary
but all the words are blotted out
all my thoughts feel so
blank tonight.
It's not fair.
I'm not done I'm not done

but I am
and I place down the pen
and try something else on for size.

An Outlaw

At an AA meeting just now …
        an open discussion
I raised my hand to share
               the chairperson gives the room a once-over
his eyes   swept right past me
               my hand is the only one raised
          sweeps his eyes across the room once again

and I could see the reluctance
                              when he finally called my name

5 to 10 minutes left now
        my hand is raised   his eyes sweep past me
                                        he closes the meeting

My Brother

Junkies bite the dust, it's what they do and it's what they do best. Wasted and dilapidated, their lives dwindle and dwindle, while their friends sit in safety and watch as they fiddle with death. The reaper is rearing after you, my friend, he's got you on his list, another wasted existence, and it makes me sick as shit. You & I, we shot the shit together, we snorted shit in our noses, we popped pills and guzzled booze like it was all just some sick and twisted joke that would never fucking end. Or so we thought.... Then the mallet came clanking down on the podium and they sent me away from that wasteland, and now, years later, I'm looking through a microscope that illuminates the past. I see you lost in your own madness, lost in yesterday's world, and it makes me sad to know that I brought you into this crap....

Jaded Eyes

these Jaded Eyes have seen hatred
these Jaded Eyes have seen pain
these Jaded Eyes have seen your demise
these Jaded Eyes don't lie

The Punk Scene

The Punk scene has become a cesspool for politicians and winey, ball-less liberals who would much rather preach to you than put their head through a wall. Me, I'd rather put my head through a wall. Or moreover, I'd rather put the preacher's head through a wall.

> When I say politicians, I don't mean anarchists, as an anarchist politician is a bit of a paradox, don't you think? Punk to me has always been an anti-politic, THE anti-politic. I considered myself an anarchist when I was a kid but then changed my views as I grew older because I realized anarchy in and of itself is a paradox. Although I still share some anarchist points of view, I started considering myself a nihilist, well kinda—I believed in chaos, in ultimate freedom: CENSOR CENSORSHIP became my slogan, along with EVERYONE IS A CUNT; and I realized there was something very wrong with the world, only I didn't know what it was. I was a hypocrite a junky a cretin and a thief, but that was okay with me because I'd much rather be a villain than one of "them." Something was wrong, I was wrong, you were wrong, but that's okay because I'd rather be "wrong" than "right" because "right" represented everything I was against. Punks aren't freedom fighters trying to incite a revolution; they are kids just like me and you trying to survive in an oppressive world that will not stop at anything until our culture has been diffused. I don't want change because every option we have been presented with is all the same; they all reek of neglect and disgust. I want something that has yet to be discussed. Something new. Something better. I want the freedom to be me, is all.

A Voice Wrapped in Static

I've got something to say. Something I need to say.

I'm getting older & my soul is rotting. I spent a century doing things that cracked my reflection in half, & I'll spend the following centuries mending the cuts that cut me deep & make me bleed oily vile that evaporates before it hits the floor. My world is melting & I can't hold on any longer. My vision is disintegrated & my perception is derelict & the world is shattered like the mirror after I took my skateboard & ran it through the glass. I'm back where I started, only the beginning is too far out of reach, and I'm running to catch up, I'm running but I throw up the last meal I devoured, my heavenly dumpster dinner that tasted like tainted flowers. How far can I fall before the train takes me out? How far can I throw before my arm breaks & the train takes me out? How loud can I yell before my voice catches in my throat & that dastardly train takes me out? I decide I might hitch a free ride, so I'm chasing after it but it only gets farther & then it's behind me & I stop running but the very thing I'm after explodes in a thunderous, blundering, humdrum cacophony of crass clapping bats that flap & scatter up & out, & now I just don't know anymore. I'm lost, & the TV is on.

The Greatest Joy in the World

Something cheerful
    something happy
        ——not so low——
I can do this, just let me think on it
        for a moment

Being onstage gives me shivers.
When I played in the band, standing onstage
was remarkable, I had never felt
a better joy in the world.
Which is why today I frequent open-mikes
to read my poetry.

Guess you could say
I get off on being the
center of attention.
Standing onstage and feeling

a thousand waiting, hopeful
eyes beaming at me—
nothing beats it.

Abuse or Be Abused

Everybody has a button to be pushed.
Everybody has been hurt by something or someone
at some point in their useless lives.
Me, I have a button too:
it's people who are intolerant of me
people who try to restrict me and keep me
neatly in line.
My button is people with buttons
who are cool with one thing
but not cool with another.
Who judge me solely on the fact
that one piece of art rubs them the wrong way
as opposed to taking me at full value——

This one's for you!

Everybody is damaged.
Everybody has a past jam-packed with abuse.
Me, I do too:
I've been picked on
ridiculed
and thrown into the gutter by those
who have buttons.

So You think you can stick your nose in the air
because somebody had hurt you;

you think you can act all high & mighty
because somebody had rubbed you the wrong way.
Well I was rubbed the wrong way too,
only it was people like you
who did it to me.

So next time you get upset with me because
you don't like something I produced,
just remember that it was people like you

who <u>ABUSED ME</u>.

An Old-School Punk Rock Number

I'm a saint but my skin is tainted, my teeth are crooked and disgusting, my mind is vile, but I'm a saint I'm an angel I'm a thief and I'm a crook and I'll do you in and I won't look back cuz I'm a saint and my brain is rotten and babe when the night begins with a rumble you bet I'll make you mine bring you home and together we might tumble cuz babe I'm a saint and my heart is on fire, girl I'm a saint and I might be a liar, but at the dead of the night when all is said and done, I'll walk you home and hold your hand and kiss you sweetly goodbye cuz I'm a saint and the world is mine///

Keep Your Hands Offa Me

The fucking faggot put his hands on me at the bar and started feeling me up. So I pushed him away. He goes, "Why'd you push me off you like that?" I go, "Because you were feeling me up. That's gross." He goes, "That's not cool." I ignore him. Then he says, "Do you know who I am?" I say, "No, and I don't care."

Jeremy Void

He goes, "You don't know who I am?" I say, "No, should I?" Let me back up for a minute. First he comes up to me, leans in close, and says, "Put your books down and talk to people." I say, "No." He goes, "This is a bar, so get up and talk to people." I say, "I'm enjoying myself right here," and he says finally, "Well I'm enjoying you." Then the above happened, and moments later I picked up my books and left.

on the outside looking in

       on the outside looking in   the crowd stands off to my right   in a solid drove   flanking the coolest one there   I dream of being   I wanna be flanked   I wanna be followed   be someone else   it makes no sense   why I'm me   and I'm sad   and lonely, lost in   stuck in a daydream   walking thru the brainstorm   as my head buzzes weighed down with   it sucks   the pressure is pushing me back forcing my back, my hand   holding me down!

       this daydream morphs into   it shifts   and changes   and the walls   the doors are jammed, locking me in   I bang the steel boards which   the walls are closing in   on me   I pace   in circles   I pace   back and forth, straight up and down!

       the crowd conjures   laughing at me   the laughter drills my ears, tears thu my head   the world   the walls   the locked doors   I'm twirling in place   scared   I'm searching   the crowd flanks me, the walls undulate   unfolding   the laughter   hands tear at me, claw me, my clothes ripping and   shedding beneath the commotion!

STOP!   this isn't   what I wanted   not quite what I expected what it meant to be   **coooooool**   I'm scared   the walls   the crowd   the taunting sneers   all peering thru me   like I'm made out of   my skin is translucent   and slimy   I backpedal   bump into the locked door stops me short   mutinous people   with hearts that throb   visible in their chests....

I CAN SEE THRU *THEM*

     treacherous   trickery   it hits me like a whip   the leather leaves a crisp, red welt across   my face stings   STOP!

     I'm   outside the bar   on the patio   sitting at a picnic table the crowd off to my right   I watch them thru the corner of my eye.......

Untitled

It's unhealthy to agree.

Reflection
from Chaos to a Void, and back again

I keep reflecting upon last night as if I had a miraculous revelation. I did, at least to me. In the past, I would fill my emptiness (void) with drugs and alcohol. I would alter my mind in any way possible. I also enjoyed the chaos revolving around round round drugs and alcohol. I was out of control. I was a mess. I didn't give a fuck. I did what I wanted when I wanted to, which is why I got the name Jeremy St. Chaos. Being clean and sober is boring to me. The chaos has dispersed. I am no longer Jeremy St. Chaos. I am empty again. My identity is gone. Without an identity (personality) I am nothing. I am a void. Jeremy Void....
But the chaos came back. I haven't touched a drug or picked up a bottle in 2 weeks. The quickest way to summarize last night is: After the bar had closed, I

told some guy I hadn't had a single drink tonight. He was in shock. I assumed the shock was because I appeared drunk with my natural slur or my care-free swagger. But he said it was because I was having a good time, I was out of control, I was fucking crazy. I didn't drink. I told him I'm just a crazy punk rocker. It was miraculous. I was Jeremy St. Chaos again, but sober. I'm back.... The void has not yet been filled but I'm working on it. At least I got my identity back, if even for just one night....

Through the Eyes of a Stranger
A Self-Portrait

I sit alone,
up all night
a lucid dream like a spider
spinning webs in my head.

How do I describe me?
Someone I admire more
than anyone I've ever met.
How do I describe this man

that goes everywhere I
go and doesn't leave me alone.
This man sits here, where I sit
and this man known me better

than I know myself.
I dread his company,
only I look forward to it
and how can I exist without him.

I come here today (tonight)

to tell you about this man.
Who is he? A void, maybe,
a lost soul bringing justice

to a world unjust.

Maybe if I think in terms
of describing a stranger
the words might come
easier and I can finally tell you

about me.

That Fuckin Drunk Retard

If that fuckin drunk retard laid one fuckin finger on me, I would have gone old-school on his ass. It's been forever since I'd been in a fight, and tonight I was itching for one. That guy was lucky.

> The guy gets in my face and goes, "What the hell you lookin' at?"
> _____
>
> And I go: "Nothing, dude."
> _____
>
> He goes, "I'll smack your half-Italian-looking face if you look at me again."
> _____
>
> And I go, "What the hell is so special about you that would make me wanna look at you anyway?" and then look away and go about my business.
> _____
>
> And the guy is still standing there like a fuckin retard trying to play tough.

Untitled

Tonight I'm gonna spray-paint my name on the moon.

You & I—Like Looking in the Mirror

THIS IS FOR ALL THE SCUMBAGS in the world.

I MASTURBATE
I CHECK OUT GIRLS TOO YOUNG FOR ME, you know the ones
I HATE EVERYTHING I DON'T UNDERSTAND
SOMETIMES I ENJOY WATCHING PEOPLE SUFFER
SOMETIMES I MAKE MYSELF SUFFER just so I don't have to feel normal anymore
I TAKE MONEY FROM THE GOVERNMENT AND USE IT TO KILL MYSELF SLOWLY
I DO EVERYTHING IN EXCESS
I LITTER   I STEAL   I CHEAT   I LIE
I TELL PEOPLE WHAT THEY WANT TO HEAR ALL THE TIME

shall I go on?

BUT HEY, DON'T HATE ME FOR IT
I'M NO DIFFERENT THAN YOU
KEEP PUTTING ON YOUR MASKS EVERY SINGLE MORNING
KEEP TELLING YOURSELF AND YOUR FAMILY AND YOUR COWORKERS
that you are better than this
KEEP LYING AND YOU WILL DIE with the truth buried deep inside
KEEP LYING AND VEERING YOUR EYES when you face yourself in the mirror each and every morning of your useless lives

because WE KNOW THE TRUTH
WE KNOW THE TRUTH
WE KNOW THE fucking TRUTH about you
because IN THE END IT'S NO USE

IT'S ALL A MATTER OF TIME!

Just Think About It

One man's garbage is another man's treasure. So is it possible that what's unhealthy for one person might be healthy for another?

Scum of the Earth

1. He tells me I only need to pay for the gas it would take to drive me to Burlington, but then when I get in his car he wants more—enough to pay part of his cable bill, he says.

2. He expects me to sign him up second-to-last at the open-mike and then he'll leave and come back in the nick of time to read, missing all the other performers.

3. He's basically upset that he wasn't successful in screwing me over.

people are morons

"You hate me and I hate you" is almost a universal concept. Why are people too thick to understand that? I can sort of sympathize with them if they can't pick-up on the cue right away that somebody dislikes them because, even though to share your dislike, disinterest, distaste, or indifference would be honest, it would be considered rude in this assbackwards society. Society doesn't value the truth; it values the spew of bullshit.

A Turkish Cherry Tree

1.

Life is shit
so let's go and frolic
in the putrid flames of existence.
Dance on
damaged clouds
inhale the toxic fumes
on top of
giant mutated mountains.

2.

I mean
life is really wonderful
when you're looking through
the telescope backwards.
Ain't this such a bashful existence?
I mean

Smash a Lightbulb: Poetry for Lowlifes

it never is what it is
when you truly think about it
reduce living to basic tactics
deduct a middle finger as
you fuck a Turkish cherry tree
through a crack in the serpent's forest.

3.

I search for a purpose
another pointless façade
a mask of one thousand faces
just something to pass the time with.

4.

Drift away honey—
go back to yesterday.
We'll scavenge the tainted factories
ramshackle the murderous enchantment of
one million ripe pirates torturing
the cross-eyed love child
of FBI's most wanted knight.

5.

A crash course in vigilante
is what we all really need.
Kill the malevolent leaders
Bring forth a thousand spineless followers
Then shoot the demonic breeders in their heads

and watch as the mutated drones bleed silvery pen ink
down the broken globe's golden spinal column

and

the dead

will

rise again.

It's happened once before
and it'll happened a million times more.

Untitled

I wish I could go inside a pop-up book, so that when someone opens it I can jump out and punch them in the Adam's apple....

One Can Hope, Right?
My girlfriend the valedictorian brings me to a party in their honor

I was planning on bringing books with me to NY, a lot of books, as many as twenty, if I can carry that much. The reason being, I assume there will be a lot of scholars at the party, people with significant occupations, who may be able to get me on my way to success. The plan is, while inside the party I will carry up to three books at a time and leave the rest in the car and I'll try to talk up some people and see if they might know people. I'll start with, "So, what do you do?"—a typical conversation starter. They'll tell me, we'll talk a bit, and then they'll ask, "And what do you do, my fine sir?" Typical of scholars to end a phrase with "My fine sir." It's how important people talk. So I'll say, "Funny that you ask." And then I'll spring my book on them like a magician picking a bunny out of a hat. Their eyes will surge open, saying, *Holy shit!!!* That's what their eyes will say. Keep in mind these are scholars I'm talking about. So their eyes will say, loud and clear, *Holy shit!!! You're a published author,* and wine will squirt from their mouths and splatter in my face. I'll take a napkin and wipe away the liquor, while simultaneously handing over my book. Part 1 of my plan complete. Now their eyes will bulge out of their sockets and they might even piss a little. Who knows? Ultimately they'll say—I mean say, like out loud for everyone to hear——they'll say, "Fucking A, you're a genius, a master of the arts, one of the most magnificent authors I've ever seen." With a wave of their hands, a friend will appear. "You might want to take a look at this," they'll say to their friend. He/she will reach in his/her pocket and pull out a monocle and fasten it around his/her eye, lower his/her head into the book, and then come up smiling, handing me a crisp one-million-dollar bill, and say, "You got yourself a deal." Mission accomplished. Ch-ching!

everything i touch

everything i touch turns to shit. and dont act like you can relate to this. if it was up to me, i would see to it that everybody on this fucking planet is sodomized and hacked up to pieces.

**FUCK EVERYONE!
GO TO HELL!**

TOP 5 THINGS
EVERYBODY DOES BUT NOBODY TALKS ABOUT

1. masturbate
2. poop
3. pee
4. vomit
      and
5. justify

Closure

Well, anyway, I've got things to do, images to distort, words to shape, and truths to manipulate.

A Drive to Be Antisocial

I have this theory that when people see my name associated with anything, they look away and simply ignore it. Which might just be my low self-esteem talking, I don't know. I've just kind of been feeling really depressed these past few days. I've been a nobody my entire life, and I'm just sick of being ignored all the time. When I was in Boston and using heavily, people couldn't ignore me because I was really aggressive and intense, and I pissed off so many people in the process, which is what I wanted to begin with. But I didn't want this. I've always dreamed of being infamous, because I had thought the only way to get a name for myself was by doing something bad, by <u>being</u> bad. But I've finally taken that aggression and turned it into something positive, and people probably just think, *Oh, that's just Jeremy, he's up to his same old tricks.* But I'm not angry all the time, that's the thing. I'm not breaking shit anymore, I'm not destroying myself or anyone else, I'm not stealing, lying, or cheating. I'm not doing anything I used to do, because I've started anew. But the thing is, I still have that drive to be anti-social, and I guess that's why my writing is so important to me; it gives me a positive means to be, as someone put it the other day, that "same angry nihilist Punk" I once was.

Yawn!

I. Am. So. Bored. Right now.

The End

Jeremy Void

478

Final proof

www.ingramcontent.com/pod-product-compliance
Lightning Source LLC
Chambersburg PA
CBHW031128160426
43193CB00008B/72